THE WIZARDS

Millionaire Magicians
of the
American Dream

MICHAEL CALDWELL

CREATIVE CLASSIC, INC.
CALIFORNIA

Publisher: Creative Classics, Inc.
                 P.O. Box 1790
                 Cathedral City, California
                 92235

Printer: Publishers Press, Salt Lake City, Utah

Editor: Mrs. Kathleen Caldwell
                 West Vancouver, Canada

Typography: Corrigan & Associates
                 Palm Desert, California

Photography: Angelo Giudice
                 Laguna Beach, California
                 (Chapters 1,2,3,4,6,9,12,
                 13,14,16,17,18,19)
                 Reed, Kaestner
                 (Chapter 8)

Research: Richard Sherer   Pam Leven
                 Karen St. George   Deborah Brown
                 Eve Belson   Kathy Doheny

ISBN 0- 9624479-0-0

CONTENTS

Mark Hughes
Herbalife International

-1-

HERBALIFE INTERNATIONAL

Thunderous applause, cheers and whistles join the rhythms of a popular, upbeat song as Mark Hughes makes his way to the front of the room, through the massive audience that packs the hotel's largest ballroom. He's stopped numerous times along the way for a handshake, a hug, or a pat on the back. On stage at last he motions for silence, but to no avail. The beat of the music and the roar of the crowd continue.

"Alright, gang!" he shouts as he dons his lavalier microphone, "Let's get started. I'm delighted to see all of you here, and I really appreciate the tremendous welcome, but we've got lots of work to do."

All eyes turn to the tall, slim, deeply-tanned young man who stands waiting for their attention as they settle down. He is the picture of health and prosperity in an expensively tailored black suit, diamonds glittering on wrists and fingers, luxuriant dark brown hair framing a handsome face from which shining dark eyes gaze at the crowd with warmth and affection.

The now silent members of the audience have come from around the world to this two-day workshop to learn about Herbalife International, and especially to listen to this man, Mark Hughes, founder and president of this phenomenal *company. They've come to hear how he took an idea and a dream, and in nine short years built a company that has already accomplished over $2 billion in sales and astounded the direct-sales industry with its success.*

Earlier, before his presentation, Hughes mingled with the crowd, with a warm handshake and an attentive smile for everyone. After the meeting he'll do the same, offering a bit of personal advice here, a compliment there, a word of encouragement over there. These Herbalife distributors will go back home and say, "I was talking to Mark Hughes last week in Los Angeles, and........"

Now they are listening to him, listening to his philosophy, his formula for success, his own story, and his vision for Herbalife's future — and theirs.

"First thing is to keep it simple. You need to keep it easy. And you need to keep it magical. Okay?....Stick to the easy, magical way of doing this business."

Life has not always been easy for Mark Hughes, but in the long run it definitely has been magical. From a childhood straight out of Charles Dickens, he has parlayed a natural persuasive ability and an inherent unfamiliarity with the concept of "shy" to create a multinational empire called "Herbalife International." His products are sold and his methods followed by distributors in Australia, Canada, Israel, Japan, Spain, New Zealand, Mexico, the United Kingdom, and the United States. In the coming years, Herbalife will stretch its reach to encompass South America, Europe, and additional Asian countries.

To attain this pinnacle, however, Hughes has needed all the magic at his command. He learned survival on the streets, was out earning a living when most boys were still worrying about acne. He was born in Lynwood, a suburb of Los Angeles, on New Year's Day, 1956. Hughes grew up in nearby La Mirada, one of the toughest areas in Los Angeles, the home turf of many drug users and dealers. His parents separated when he was born, and his mother and stepfather raised him until her medical problems became too much for the family structure to bear. Mark's mother and stepfather separated, and young Hughes went to live with his grandparents.

"My mom had a problem trying to lose weight. She wasn't really fat, around thirty pounds overweight. But she went to doctors who prescribed diet pills for her (amphetamines), and she got heavily addicted to them. The side effect was that she couldn't sleep, so they started prescribing sleeping pills. Then she started seeing five or six doctors, getting prescriptions from all of them......She died of an unintentional overdose when I was eighteen.

"During all these years my grandparents provided the only real stability in my life and taught me the meaning of honesty and integrity. For example, my Granddad was in charge of advertising for a large dairy for twenty-five years. He didn't make a lot of money, and sometimes media sales reps would offer him bribes to go with one radio station instead of another, and so forth, but he was never even tempted. From my Granddad I learned the importance of maintaining high principles in every aspect of your life."

Mark was more like a son to his grandparents, Larry and Hazel Hughes. During the troubled years of his mother's ailing condition, Mark often retreated to the haven of their home. Finding it difficult to concentrate on schooling, he quit at an early age, and went to work raising money for a drug rehabilitation center.

"We went door-to-door. I went to see the richest people, trying to get the biggest donation. I developed a lot of strategies to get past the secretary and into the president's office of the biggest corporations I could find.

"Every morning, early, I'd go into a building and I'd write down the names of all the companies. Then I'd go into the telephone booth, call each of them and ask, 'How do you spell the president's name?' Then, I'd walk up to the secretary's desk and say, 'Just tell Bruce (or whatever) that Mark's here.'"

For some individuals the fear of rejection, the humiliation of being turned down, make selling the hardest job in the world. For this sixteen-year-old boy in a snag-ridden pair of double-knit pants and a double-knit tie, nothing was too difficult.

"There was one guy, a stockbroker. His secretary said, 'You'd better not be selling anything.' I said, 'It's just kind of personal. I wanted to talk to him for a couple of minutes.' So she brings the guy out, and he says, 'You better not be selling anything.'

"On the one hand, we were selling something, and on the other hand we weren't really selling anything because we were asking for contributions. We had no product.

"I said, 'Look, it's just really personal and really private. I just need to speak to you for a couple of minutes.' Generally, if I could get a guy back in his office, we could wrassle around and I could do pretty well.

"I got back to this guy's office, opened the folder and had about three words out of my mouth when the guy literally picked me up by the shirt, threw me out of his office, and said, 'Don't ever come back here without an appointment!'

"So I went right downstairs, called him from a pay phone, and said, 'I'm calling to make an appointment.!' I went right back upstairs and got a $500 donation from him."

If you are not intimidated by the man who has just thrown you out of his office, how would you feel about the future President of the United States?

"One time I was in Pacific Palisades, and I got a donation

from someone right across the street from Ronald Reagan. He said, 'Why don't you go see Ronald Reagan? He's very interested in these kinds of projects.' Reagan had a guard station at his house; he was still governor at the time. So I left my brochures with the guard.

"Reagan's secretary called me and made an appointment for me to talk to the Governor over the telephone. I'll never forget that telephone conversation with him. It was on a Thursday at 2:00 p.m. After I explained the program to him over the phone, he said, 'I'll have it checked out,' and that was the end of that.

"We never got to talk to each other for another couple of years. One day in Westwood I got a $300 donation from a Ronald Ragen, an attorney, who said he got a lot of Ronald Reagan's mail mixed up with his because they were in the same building. He told me THE Ronald Reagan might be interested in contributing to CEDU and gave me the number of the public relations firm where his office was located, because there was no occupant listing in the lobby. So I went there, walked in and I said to the receptionist, 'Could you tell Ronnie that Mark's here from Cascade.'

"The secretary came out and said, 'Listen, we don't know who you are. You don't have a specific appointment; as far as we know, you could try to kill Mr. Reagan. Write us a letter.'

"So I went downstairs, wrote out a little letter reminding him of some of the details of our conversation, and at the end of it I wrote, 'I know you're a real busy guy, but if you don't like what I say in the first two minutes of our conversation, you can take your shoes off and beat me over the head with them. Give a trying kid a chance.'

"I went back upstairs and gave the letter to the secretary. A few minutes later she came back and said, 'He'll see you.' However, he couldn't do it right then, so she set up another appointment. The guy was spectacular. He spent forty-five minutes just talking to me, and he gave the foundation some money. And he talked about us on his radio show every day for about a month!"

Hughes left CEDU's employ when he was nineteen, but his commitment to helping drug-addicted and troubled youth continues. He makes regular contributions to the Cascade School, which evolved from the CEDU organization. Cascade has an excellent residency rehabilitation program, and Hughes has organized fund-raisers featuring top-name Hollywood talent on behalf of the school.

"We contribute heavily to the funding of that institution," he says with enthusiasm. "Once a year we put on a big party where we auction off prizes donated by some of the best known merchants in Beverly Hills. Last year we auctioned off a Mercedes Benz, some beautiful crystal, as well as beautiful art pieces and other items. At that party alone we raised about $300,000 for them."

When Hughes's mother died, he turned his attention to nutrition, and to weight-loss programs, in search of a product that would enable people to lose weight without harming their health. After he left CEDU, he worked as a salesman in a Beverly Hills menswear shop until he was introduced to direct sales.

"I became a distributor with a company selling weight-loss products," he recalls. "That company went bankrupt, owing me thousands of dollars. I never got my money, but while it was going I met some good people, including the guy who manufactures Herbalife products for us now.

"Then, at about twenty, I went with another direct sales weight-loss company. I did fairly well in both of those companies. When I say 'well,' I mean well for being a young man. I made a quarter of a million dollars in the second company, but right toward the end the owner, who was always switching marketing schemes, wanted us to buy franchises. So I bought Los Angeles, San Diego, New York City, and Chicago. Once my money was on deposit, the owner closed down the business and I never got a penny back.

"I didn't get a college education but I certainly got valuable business experience with those two companies. I learned a lot about nutritional products, and a lot about what makes a good marketing plan — one that's fair to both the distributors and the company. I learned what not to do in business."

"Here's what happened to Mark Hughes at the beginning of Herbalife. For the first six months in business I was simply an independent distributor, just like all of you.

I don't know how many of you have thought of this, but, you know, I never had a sponsor! I didn't have anyone to turn to for help when things got difficult. Before we even had the products packaged I got several of my best friends together and told them what was going to happen with this business. Do you know, not one of them believed me or joined me! You don't think that wasn't difficult to deal with? I had to repeatedly handle that kind of rejection completely alone until I finally sponsored my first distributors and started getting an organization together.

"That's why, when some of you tell me how difficult things are for you, I understand what you're saying. But I also know from first-hand experience that with persistence and consistence and hard work you can be as successful as you want to be! I want everyone to make the most of this opportunity, and that's why we're here to help you with training meetings, and with the Herbalife Journals, the television shows, and everything else the company does to help promote your business."

Mark resolved to create his own company to reach his goals. His two-fold purpose was to have a superior weight-loss program, with products that would promote good health, and to have a business structure that would enable people to earn good incomes simply and quickly.

"Because of my own bitter experiences," states Hughes, "I vowed that no one would ever lose money because of my, or my company's, action. That's very important to me."

Herbalife's beginnings were considerably more modest than those of many of its competitors.

"With a minimal amount of money I put my little company together in February of 1980," Hughes recalls. "My granny was my first customer. She lost twenty-five pounds the very first month, and helped me get twenty-five more customers. She's been the legend of the first weight loss in Herbalife. I was the second. I lost sixteen pounds in two-and-a-half weeks.

"The business was just me, and the first basic weight-loss products that I sold out of the trunk of my car. 'Headquarters' was a little office in Beverly Hills. It was a converted wig factory — about 800 square feet — and I did everything from packing distributor kits to sweeping the floors.

"I kind of miss that time of Herbalife," he says wistfully. "There weren't a lot of people to manage then. It was just me, and one person who helped fill orders and pack the distributor kits for the astronomical sum of fifty cents per kit. My only job was to find customers and sponsor distributors who wanted to find more customers."

Eventually, Hughes moved Herbalife International's worldwide headquarters to its current location, at the beginning of the final automobile approach to Los Angeles Airport. The corporate logo shines down on drivers leaving the San Diego Freeway and turning west on Century Boulevard. Hughes arranged for this prominent display by being the first tenant when the building was opened. In coming months, he expects to move his operations to a combined manufacturing and distribution facility in Los Angeles, that will accomodate the continued expansion of the Herbalife Empire.

Hughes adopted a sales strategy, known as *"multi-level marketing"*, in which people sign up as independent distributors. They sell products on a retail basis and recruit other salespeople, who work under them on their "team". When the second salesperson writes an order, the distributor who recruited that salesperson gets a percentage.

By developing a team composed of distributors at different levels, the original salesperson can realize a substantial income in addition to the profit earned by personal retail selling — if, of course, the team members are effective, and if the product they are selling is in demand. The Herbalife magic that brought about its phenomenal success is in the quality of its products and the attitude of management toward the distributors in the field.

Herbalife, like Amway Corporation and Mary Kay Cosmetics, has achieved its stature by using the multi-level structure effectively. Because the distributors are all self-employed individuals who buy their products from the company, the parent corporation can keep its own overhead to a minimum.

At the same time, the distributors reap the advantages of the advertising, marketing, and sales strategies developed and, in some measure, paid for by the parent corporation. In Herbalife's case, much of the advertising strategy has involved using national cable television, such as the USA Network, CBN, and Lifetime to reach large numbers of potential customers.

The ubiquitous bumper stickers and buttons and badges that say "Lose Weight Now/Ask Me How!" identify Herbalife distributors, many of whom use the same line in their listing in the telephone directory.

Herbalife has distributors who work at varying levels of activity, from the housewife who just sells part-time from her home to earn extra spending money to the highly motivated, professional individual who works from a business office as a full-time career.

While the distributors and supervisors and team members are all independent contractors, from Hughes's perspective, they are the most important part of Herbalife.

"The company's not here," he says, referring to Herbalife's home offices. "The company's out on the street, with all the distributors who are selling the products, helping people to lose weight, to feel better and look better, sponsoring new distributors, holding meetings three times a week, and teaching their people to do the same things. That's where our business is."

"The reason I chose a direct sales system to market Herbalife products is because of the person-to-person aspect of this way of doing business. When you put a product in retail stores, people just buy it and nobody calls to find out if they're using the product correctly and getting the results they want. With our system the customer gets the benefit of direct contact with someone who will follow up, because it's important to the distributor that his or her customers have good results. It's that personal attention, the individual involvement with the customer, that is the backbone of this business.

"Tonight you've seen and heard the stories of so many people whose lives have been changed because of Herbalife. We're videotaping many of these stories to use as commercials, and — can you imagine the strength of this? True stories on television — not simulated or acted, but

TRUE stories of REAL people that will be broadcast to millions of people! We want to get the word out there that we have a product and program that can help people look better and feel better and improve their lives."

Reinforcing the strength of his distributorship plan, Hughes continues to emphasize product development and quality in his long-range planning.

"I'm not interested in loading our product line with just any kind of product," he says. "We probably could come out with pencils tomorrow and make a couple of bucks on them, because a certain number of distributors would buy them for their in-house needs, but I don't want to have our company take on the appearance of a direct-sales supermarket. I want to keep our product line very, very selective."

Hughes freely admits to having no scientific background, but he always has been the prime mover behind Herbalife's product development.

"Here's how it works," he explains. "I get together with the medical people and say, 'This is what I want.' Then I'm involved in meetings on it as they make progress. Then we test the product to make sure it does what we want it to. My knowledge of what's in the product, and why it's in the product, comes from those meetings. I want to always be involved, so we make sure not just that it is good, but that everyone has stretched themselves to the utmost in order for it to be the BEST product. That's the most important part of our company, that we offer the highest quality of products.

"For instance," he says, "take our first product. I told the doctors I wanted a product that would help people lose weight, but at the same time I wanted one that would supply all the protein and vitamins and minerals the body needs. I wanted it to be health-oriented. I wanted herbs in it for their beneficial effects, and I wanted it to contain only the best-quality ingredients. I said, 'You construct the formula and I'll decide the packaging and how we're going to market it.' That's how we have developed and designed every product. If, after years of continuing research, we find anything we can do to improve a product, we'll do it. We've improved our first product three times so far."

Another example: by early 1989, Herbalife had increased its product line to twenty-six items with the introduction of the App-Attack Diet Disc, a formula to help control the appetite.

"I said, 'Let's put together a whole new diet concept again,'" Hughes recalls, discussing the genesis of the Diet Disc. "'I want something that's as different as our first products; something natural, something incredibly effective, something unusual that will control the appetite.'

"It was a rough challenge, because the only things on the market that would actually control the appetite were drugs. I didn't want anything like phenylpropanol, which is the active ingredient in most over-the-counter packages of diet pills, or addictive drugs like those my mom took.

"It took about a year to put the right combination of ingredients together, then another six months of designing a delivery system so you could get the product into your body without destroying the active ingredients.

"These are very sensitive ingredients, for which we developed a special disc that dissolves on the inside of your cheek. The ingredients are absorbed through the cheek membranes and passed into the blood stream. If you put it under your tongue, it would destroy the ingredients. If you swallowed it, your stomach would destroy the product, so the dissolving Diet Disc was the answer."

"Most of the people I first told about Herbalife didn't believe it would be the success it has become. They thought

I was just a wild-eyed, twenty-three-year-old kid with an impossible dream.

"But let me tell you, people have since learned that when I say I am going to do something — when I say something is going to happen in the company — it happens! I remember we had a President's Team meeting in January of 1981, and after that meeting I told everybody — and I looked them square in the eye and said, 'Mark my words, four years from now, this company's going to do $100 MILLION in sales.'

"That was a pretty gutsy statement when we'd only done $2 million in sales! I said, 'Mark it down in your President's Workshop manual.' We all wrote it down, and when we reproduced my manual for another President's Workshop, there it was to prove I had made that statement.

"However, I was wrong, because four years later, in the predicted time frame, we didn't do $100 million — we did $142 million!

"Another thing that I predicted in 1982 was that we would get hit with investigations, and I was right on that too, because it happens any time a company becomes so big and so successful so fast. In Herbalife's case there were two government agencies, the Food and Drug Administration and the Department of Justice, checking out the company's claims."

Hughes says the problem began with his expansion of the company's product line into targeted areas.

"I wasn't interested in coming out with just another multi-pack vitamin," he relates. "I really wanted nutrition-type products that could address certain problems — like osteoporosis, a brittle-bone condition. This condition leads to sudden fractures because of calcium deficiency, and is one of the leading causes of hospitalization for older women.

According to government reports, some 1,300,000 such fractures in the U.S. alone are attributed to this condition. I wanted a product we could market that could help this situation.

"I also wanted something nutritional that would help cardiovascular health. We were the first ones to put out a full-spectrum marine-lipid product, Herbalifeline. Before any of the drug companies were involved in similar products, we came out with this formula, and said in our advertisements and on nationwide television that this product would help lower cholesterol and triglycerides. That was the product, I believe, that really stirred up a lot of problems.

"Some drug companies were contacting the FDA and saying that we were making therapeutic claims for a vitamin supplement. The issue was whether the claims were drug claims or food claims. If they were drug claims, like saying 'this product cures a specific disease,' then you had to register the product as a drug, which has a different set of requirements than for registering a product as a food.

"We spent a year and a half opening up the product line, showing it to the FDA, testing the products, proving all our claims for the products, and in October of 1986 we came out of the investigations with the same claims we had been making — and for some of the products, better claims.

"We were the only nutrition company that went through such an intense investigation by the FDA, kept our products and claims, and came out of it with an excellent working relationship with them. They actually wrote a letter to all the FDA offices around the country, that stated Herbalife products were safe for human consumption, and the claims we were making for them were accurate."

In the midst of the FDA's investigation, the Justice Department challenged Herbalife's marketing plan. Rather than get into another protracted battle, Hughes agreed to settle the case for $850,000, which covered the costs incurred by the government during their investigation. The marketing plan emerged from this scrutiny intact, however, because nothing in the marketing plan had to be changed. "All that was needed was the addition of a policy requiring each supervisor to send in a form each month showing that he or she had sold products to ten retail customers." Hughes explains.

With the investigations behind him, Hughes was ready to move Herbalife in new directions. He started pushing for foreign expansion and took the company public to accelerate the program.

"By taking the company public," says Hughes, "the distributors are enabled to become shareholders and profit from these other ventures. Our company will always be a distributor-oriented business, because there is no way to substitute the personal attention customers receive through our marketing system."

By its very nature, a company like Herbalife requires intense, face-to-face effort to be successful. Hughes has spent the majority of his time travelling to meetings and rallies around the country and — now — around the world, recruiting, encouraging, and exhorting the troops.

In his personal life, however, he shuns crowds.

"I like to be alone with my wife, Suzan," he says. "We're very seclusive whenever we're not at a distributor event. We go out once in a while, but my idea of a great time is being alone together, preferably near the ocean."

Their meeting was in keeping with Hughes's personality as a salesman. "We met at a restaurant," he recalls. "I asked someone who that nice-looking girl was. Finally, I persuaded a mutual friend to invite her to come and sit at my table. We struck up a friendship and went out for about three years, until we finally tied the knot."

Suzan was operating her own court-reporting business at the time. Now, in addition to being Mrs. Hughes Suzan is an actress, and has appeared as a guest performer in a number of television shows.

The two divide their time between homes in Beverly Hills and Maui, Hawaii. They also like to relax on their yacht anchored off the California coast. Hughes's grandparents are frequent guests, as are his in-laws, and on holidays both families gather together for congenial celebrations. Several of Hughes's relatives work in Herbalife, and he and his natural father, whom he first met when he was twenty, have established a warm relationship. His father is a strong booster of the company and is regularly included in family functions.

"The whole Herbalife idea for me was trying to help people lose weight, to get a product that was going to be good and healthy that people could lose weight on naturally," he says. "And that's really been the concept of the whole company. The marketing end of it has been great, but we're a very product-oriented company."

"To this day, nothing gives me a greater thrill than to see someone get started on the weight-loss program and watch how their life blossoms as they start looking and feeling better. Every time I hear a new personal success story it makes all the work and the struggle we've been through worthwhile.

"I am now telling you that, as fast as we've grown before, you haven't seen anything yet! At the beginning it took us eight years to get into four countries. In the last ten months we've started up in five more. When I started Herbalife I made a statement that we were going to change the nutritional habits of the world, and that's exactly what we're doing. Country by country, language by language

we're taking Herbalife around the world.

"As many people as we've been able to help during our first nine years in business, there are still millions and millions of people who need to improve their nutrition and their health. There are millions and millions who want to look better, feel better and change their lives for the better.

"Taking Herbalife around the world is a monumental task, but **together** *we will be able to accomplish it. Your efforts will help Herbalife to reach its ultimate destiny — to have a positive impact on the nutritional habits of people around the world! Thank you, the best of health, good night and God bless."*

John Paul Jones DeJoria
John Paul Mitchell Systems

-2-

JOHN PAUL MITCHELL SYSTEMS

On a clear day, you can see forever. That is the feeling you have at John Paul's home, on top of the world, high on the highest hill in Beverly Hills, California. A gigantic Buddha watches over an expansive living room, which overlooks the pool, the redwood deck and beyond to the city of Los Angeles and the Pacific Ocean. There is a sense of calm, of timelessness. There is no sense of rushing, no pressure, none of the hustle and bustle of living in the fast lane.

What is the secret of John Paul's success? This man who has revolutionized the professional hair-care industry with his marketing philosophies, who went into business with a friend simply because he was a friend - how has a man like this become so successful? This man who was fired from several jobs because he did not fit the "corporate image", who didn't have enough money to go to college, who was told by one of his teachers that he would never succeed. How has he done it?

This remarkable man now has everything he wants; has three beautiful children, all the money he needs, good health, in his own words he "has it all". John Paul is also a warm and generous human being. Although he is now enjoying what he has, it is not in the selfish sense. He gives back a tremendous amount to other people; to people he admires, to his friends, his children, charities, and in fact, to people all over the world.

How did this man so young (still in his forties) reach these lofty heights, after years of working for others, of rather limited business success, an unglamorous existence much like those of us in the real world?

John Paul Jones DeJoria, known as J.P. to his friends, is first-generation American; his mother and father were immigrants to this country. Of Italian, Greek, and French descent, J.P. was born and raised in Los Angeles.

He recalls his early years. His first job was selling Christmas cards, at the tender age of nine years; from there he progressed to delivering newspapers in the morning before school. "After high school," he says, "I went into the U.S. Navy. The only other alternative was to become a gangster or something equally regrettable." After spending two years in the Navy in special communications and,later, dentistry, he returned home to face his future. With no money for college, J.P. went looking for a job. He regretted having to forego college but he claims that lack of a college education has never been detrimental to his success.

The first job he found was that of selling encyclopedias; it lasted about three years. He remembers, "I did rather well at that job. I was making about $20,000 a year, which was a whole lot of money back in the early sixties. I thought I was rich." Little did he realize at the time that this early successful sales experience would be one of the significant points in his life and would lay the groundwork for his professional future.

Growing tired of the life of door-to-door selling inherent in the encyclopedia trade, J.P. drifted into a series of different selling jobs. "I sold many different things over the next few years: dictating equipment, life insurance, medical towel and linen services," he recalls. "I once worked two full-time jobs at the same time. I'd check in on one, then the other, turning in some orders for each every day to keep them both going and collect two paychecks. That lasted maybe six months, then I got tired of trying to juggle two jobs.

"Then I decided it was time to get a real job, begin a career. I was about twenty-five years old at the time. I went to work for TIME, Inc. as Circulation Manager for the Southwestern United States. That job was a sophisticated way of selling magazines, a boiler-room operation, and I did rather well at it. Then one day I asked the person I worked with how to get ahead in the company. He said that not only would I have to be older, but I now would have to move to another location just to keep my current job. I didn't like that idea, so I resigned shortly thereafter. I was twenty-six years old then.

"This time I decided to get serious, and I consulted an employment agency to find out what good opportunities were available. There was a company called Redken in the professional hair-care industry that sold beauty products, and I decided to try that. They didn't want to hire me at first because I did not have any experience or know anything about hair dressing. So I agreed to work for them at their lowest salary — about $600. per month plus car allowance — but they told me I could move as fast as I wanted to. So they shipped me off to Texas to be their sales representative there. I later became district manager. After about eighteen months with Redken, I was promoted to home office. I was moving up rather quickly," J.P. recalls.

John Paul next became national manager of Chain Salons and Scientific Schools, staying with Redken from about 1971 through 1975. That was his introduction into the beauty industry, a good one, and he "had a great time." In 1975, however it became the opinion of the Redken general management that he had peaked, and that he really wasn't meant to be a manager. At that time, the management said with nice diplomacy, "You have gone as far as you can with us. We don't believe you're the manager type, and we don't want to put you back into sales, so it is best we let you go." J.P. remembers the experience as a good one, "They were very generous, they gave me an office for two weeks, with a secretary, and anything I needed to get another job. They were wonderful. They said, 'You should be selling big-ticket items; you're not cut out to be a manager.'" But J.P. was convinced he really was, and refused to let their opinion affect his own opinion of his capabilities.

After Redken, J.P. went to work for Syntex. Syntex is basically a pharmaceutical company, but was then entering the beauty industry. They bought a company called "Fermodyl," and hired John Paul to be the vice president of training and education. According to J.P., "When I joined Fermodyl they were doing approximately $9 million a year. When I left, a year later, they were doing over $12 million. The executives of the company said I 'didn't fit their corporate image, didn't hang out with them on weekends, didn't fit in, so they just had to let me go.' So I said 'okay, that's the way it goes!' That was their best year, by the way, they went downhill after that."

Then J.P. went to work for a company called the Institute of Tricology. The company was not an institute instrinsical-ly, it was a product company. He worked there about a year and a half, had a very good job, and thoroughly enjoyed it. Soon he was making more money than the owner of the company. J.P. recalls the way it was. "He didn't think I was putting forth enough effort for the money I was making. When I joined TRI, they were making about $400,000 per year, and when I left they were doing about $1.5 million per year. I approached the owner and said, 'Give me part of the business and we will really take off.' His reply was, 'No, I can't give you an equity position.' So *that* job was out of the way."

Next, John Paul tried his hand at starting his own business. He became a consultant to companies who wanted to enter the professional beauty industry, who wanted to sell their products to salons. He would counsel them on how to put their product together, how to organize their marketing strategies, and how to get distributors for their products. That business lasted only two years, never really getting off the ground. He never became financially sound, and most of the companies he worked with didn't have the necessary finances to do what was really needed. They were just stalling each other's future growth.

Then came the turning point. "In 1979 Paul Mitchell, a good friend of mine whom I had known for nine years in the industry, had this hair-care product line that he had been trying to introduce for about six months. Nothing was working, The products weren't packaged or priced properly." So as a favor to Paul Mitchell, J.P. decided to give him free consultation and help him launch his new company.

"The end result" he says, "was that we joined forces. The initial financing we were looking for was $500,000. At one time we had an investor interested, but he later pulled out. He said it was not a good investment at that time. Our embassy had just been taken hostage in Iran, and he didn't know what the future was going to hold for America. So we became rather desperate. Around February of 1980, we decided to give up twenty percent of our company if someone would invest $160,000. No one showed any interest. Then we decided to offer thirty-five percent for $140,000. Nobody would even talk to us.

"So we began anyway. We rounded up $700, which barely covered the artwork costs; the rest we got on credit. I owned an old Rolls Royce at the time. It was a 1960 Silver Cloud II — a beautiful car, in great shape for its age. I had a reputation as being a hot-shot sales person in the beauty industry.

"So I went to visit vendors dressed extremely well, driving my Rolls Royce, and told them about this company I wanted to build. I stated firmly that I wanted to do business with them. They gave me thirty-day credit. The deal with my partner, Paul Mitchell, was that I would handle the business end. Paul is a very creative hairdresser, so we were a good mix. He performed at all the hair shows and I covered the marketing and promotion."

When they started, Paul Mitchell was a well-known hairdresser. "Probably the best there was," according to J.P. "He started Super Hair Advanced Styling School, and was a fabulous human being who was well liked by fellow hairdressers. I knew the sales, marketing, and promotion areas of the business. I also knew how to get by with very little money. So we started our company, John Paul Mitchell Systems. With the first run, Paul went one way to do several shows and sell the product; I went the other way and created the marketing program to teach salesmen how to sell the product after the hair show, and also generate re-orders. At the same time I went knocking on beauty salon doors, to sell our products so the distributors would have customers to work with.

"It worked, thank God. We sold just enough in the first thirty days to pay the bills. John Paul Mitchell Systems was now in business. We have never borrowed a penny; it's all been financed on its own. In the first four months, the bank almost foreclosed on my home because I had no money to make a mortgage payment. For several weeks I slept in the back of my car. I took out the back seat, and we now had a company truck. We started the company with only one person doing everything, and a super hair stylist who did the beauty-show circuit."

And it worked well, very well. "In fact," J.P. remembers, "the first year, people thought we were a much larger operation than we actually were. We had an answering machine with a girl friend's voice that would answer the phone, and say "We will get right back to you." When I called back, I always said I had wanted to talk to them personally but was tied up."

"About six months later, the gentleman who was filling our bottles let us install a plain black phone in his office. When our phone rang, his secretary answered, 'Paul Mitchell Hair Care Products.' We seemed a lot bigger than we were. It was about fifteen months before we were able to hire our first employee. Three months after that, I hired my first salesperson to work with me out in the field."

So J.P. learned how to build a business with very little money, and how one person could do the job of ten. He notes, "The way it relates to our unbelievable success is that here we are, less than a decade from the day we started and we have about forty employees, and we are doing about $10 million per month in business. Our corporate profits exceed forty percent and we spend more money making our product than most of our competitors do. Our products are much more expensive to produce, but it costs us much less to run our business. Furthermore, our people are paid close to twice the industry standard."

J.P. recalls how he came to be known as 'John Paul Jones'. "When I was about twenty-three years old, I had divorced my first wife and had custody of my son. It was just the two of us. One of the many jobs I had was as an advertising manager for the *Southern California Clergyman*. It was a tabloid which went to all the clergy of every denomination in Southern California. We sold advertising to bible companies and religious artefact companies. The publisher made me advertising manager because he too had a one-man show, a very small company with just himself and his wife. The owner said, "No one is going to know the name DeJoria, why don't you call yourself something flamboyant.' Many years before people, in jest, had called me John Paul Jones. So I started leaving messages saying 'this is John Paul Jones, please call me.' They began to return my calls. It was an unusual and catchy name, and people were curious, so I continued to use it. In the last year, I have changed it to John Paul Jones DeJoria."

According to John Paul, their products, the Paul Mitchell Hair Care Line, are possibly the finest hair-care products ever made. He explains their uniqueness. "We were the ones who invented hair-sculpting lotion. It is a liquid, which when put on your hair, can make it do almost anything you want it to. The Paul Mitchell products are very innovative. If your hair is wavy, you can make it straight. If it is straight, you can make it wavy. If you want to change your hair style, you can simply re-activate it with water, and change your whole style without putting anything else on it. We have invented a lot of very novel products. We market strictly to beauty salons and to distributors who sell to beauty salons. There is such a demand for the product that some of our distributors and salons have been diverting it and selling it to drug stores and supermarkets at higher prices. We are totally against this practice; we don't think it is the way to do business. It is better to conduct business the honest way."

Paul Mitchell Hair Care Products are sold worldwide. Starting nationally, they moved into the international market when they were making about $20 to $25 million annually. Paul Mitchell products are now available in the United States, Canada, Japan, Israel, Hong Kong, Taiwan, Singapore, Thailand, and the United Kingdom (Scotland, Wales, and England), Finland and West Germany. Several European countries will be added soon. According to J.P., "We have strong distribution systems and the company continues to grow quite rapidly."

He continues, "At this time we are the second largest company in the professional hair care industry in the United States. We believe we are the highest-profit company in our industry. We achieve that by having fewer people doing more. That's the reason for our motto - 'fewer moving parts.'"

An experience John Paul recalls from his childhood made a deep and lasting impression. One time, just for fun, J.P., his brother, and his mother counted up all the cash they had. It totalled only twenty-eight cents. They laughed, and agreed that for the moment they didn't really need any more than that. There was food in the refrigerator and warmth in their home, so what did they need money for? This readiness to accept whatever was available, no matter how little, and to use it efficiently was to translate in later years into business success for John Paul Jones DeJoria.

In 1982 Paul Mitchell and John Paul bought a farm in Hawaii. They bought it because they did not know how long the business would continue growing at such a phenomenal rate. J.P. recalls their feelings at the time. "We had had no idea we would be this successful, although of course we had great hopes and dreams. With a friend of ours, Jonathan Tennyson, who knows how to build houses and live off the land, we decided to buy this land together. It started out being our hideout; even if everything went wrong, we would always have a place to live and be comfortable when the company stopped growing.

"Several years later, our hideaway became a solar-energy farm, where the entire farm was run off the sun. The sun even provided our transportation; we converted little golf-carts into solar-energy machines."

That venture took J.P. into sun power, and another success story was born. He recalls how it was. "Paul Mitchell and I financed the building of a solar-energy race car. That car was entered in a race that crossed Australia. It was so unique that it was written up in *Automobile Quarterly* as one of the best solar-energy cars. That particular issue of the book featured all the most unusual cars ever made in all the world. It told about the General Motors car that won the solar-energy race and our car, the Mona-La, which placed second in the speed trials.

"I got very excited about it, so in December of 1987 I looked into buying a solar-energy company. In January 1988 I bought a piece of Solec International, the third-largest solar-energy company in the United States. I now own fifty percent of the company. My partner is Ishaq Shahryar and this last year the company generated $3.5 million in sales.

"In the first ten months of 1989, we booked $7 million in sales. Ishaq, a genius of a man, was one of the three people who invented the solar cell. I had the marketing and sales experience and the finances, so I went into the business and bought new equipment so that we could expand, knowing full well that our business was going to grow."

J.P. has spent hundreds of thousands of dollars for new equipment. With the help of Ishaq Shahryar it was re-geared, so that now it too had "fewer moving parts." With his positive approach, knowing the business was going to prosper, John Paul had not hesitated to make this huge investment in equipment. He is now thankful that he trusted his instincts. "Thank God I did, because now we are able to fill some of these orders. At the rate we're growing, within two years we will probably be the second-largest solar-energy company in the Americas.

But J.P.'s phenomenal Midas touch didn't stop there. He tells of another recent venture. "My son's mother, Bella, has several gift shops in California — they're called 'Bella's' — where you can buy exotic gifts. She came up with the idea of having her own line of the kind of personal items you'd buy in a gift shop - potpourri, bubble bath, specialty soaps - that sort of thing.

"Bella wanted to go into competition with some of the giants. She had the expertise, knowing what really sold; I had the finances to start it. From my experience in the cosmetics industry, I knew how to build a company from the ground up. So in 1988, I became an equal partner in 'Bella's Secret Gardens.' The combination of Bella's designs and my business experience got it going. She is very creative in what she does and she knows the gift industry. Before we delivered our first shipment, we had more than $70,000 worth of orders on the books, and the company was only two months old."

What is the secret of his success? According to John Paul, "In the three businesses, I think the secret again is having fewer people doing more. Let creative persons be as creative as they can, and show them today's new ways of doing business, the new ways of management. Most of our competitors have anywhere from five to fifty times as many employees as we have, and our profit margins exceed theirs, yet our employees are paid much better than the industry norm."

John Paul explains how his company's employees are rewarded. "We have a warehouse man who has worked with us for about three years. Now a U.S. citizen, his income is approaching $50,000, just working in the warehouse. Our vice-presidents make considerably more, of course. Probably the lowest-paid person in our company is paid at least $15,000 just to sweep floors. We take very good care of our people."

But there must be more to this successful venture than paying employees a lot of money. J.P explains how he developed his style and business philosophy. He explains, "I knew that most of what I did when I worked for other people was related directly to what I was paid. If I wasn't paid very well I didn't do very well. But if I had ever been paid more than I was worth, which I never was, I would have put forth a great deal more effort. On this principle, our people are indirectly persuaded to put forth a great deal more. The result is that they tend to overachieve, and we are able to grow a lot quicker. When this happens, everybody wins."

How is it that one man can be so successful at running three totally different companies? J.P. responds, "With Bella's company it takes about five hours a month of my time. Solec takes only about seven hours a month. All the rest of my time is spent with John Paul Mitchell Systems — and enjoying life on my own. Now that I have the time and the money, I can relax and enjoy life a little more."

There are numerous proven formulas for achieving success; there are people who have "made it", and will teach others how to do it for a price. However, John Paul did not utilize any of these formulas. He created his own method by combining a unique style with an innate flair for business. He is comfortable with his current success, although he says, "I knew I would do quite well in life, but I had no idea it would be this well, no idea my income would approach $25 million per year. My dream was that if we could earn $1 million per year, we would be flying high, on top of the world.

"I spend very little money. I live well, but I spend much less than I make. Most of my money is invested long term — I cannot touch it for five to ten years. That has worked quite well, and even though I live very well, I live way below my means. But I do that purposely," he adds. "There is always that big nest-egg for the future."

John Paul shares his time and money with the community. He supports a camp for children with cancer, Camp Good Time, where children who are stricken with this illness can go to camp together. J.P comments, "You know, I feel that I have been really blessed and really lucky. I am earning a lot now and I would like to give some of that good fortune back."

He also gives money to feed the hungry every year, providing meals for five hundred to one thousand homeless people in Los Angeles at Thanksgiving and Christmas. He also supports children of wars, and a foundation called Quest, for children who eat themselves to death. J.P. is a big supporter of animal rights groups. All Paul Mitchell products carry a statement that they are not tested on animals. The products are tested on human beings by accredited hair stylists.

While education is important, it doesn't guarantee success in business. In high school, J.P. was just an average student. He took part in varsity gymnastics (side horse and rope climb), doing well and enjoying it. But in one teacher's opinion, he wasn't really going anywhere. He laughs as he tells a story of one experience. "In the eleventh grade, in Mr. Wax's business class, there was a skinny blonde-haired girl that sat behind me. She and I would pass notes back and forth, like 'see you at Winchell's' or 'what's happening with Darlene,' just innocent notes. One day Mr. Wax caught us and read the notes in front of the class. He said, 'These two people will never, ever succeed at anything in life.'"

"Well, Michele Phillips (Michele Gillian at the time) and I talked about this recently. Michele went on to become Michele Phillips of the Mommas and Poppas, and now Michele Phillips, the actress and movie star. We really had a good laugh and decided we should find Mr. Wax, send a limousine to pick him up and bring him over, and say 'Remember us? If you don't, let us remind you who we are and what we are now doing.'"

It is hard enough to raise children today, but those who have very rich parents sometimes take the affluent life for granted. J.P. is determined that his children will not grow up to be spoiled rich kids. His son, now twenty-three, was pushed out of the nest a few years ago with this message, "I will give you four months rent in your apartment. You need to learn how to work and support yourself. You can come back home after two years, and if you wish I'll help you start a business." Within four months, John Paul II had started his own business and was supporting himself. He has recently become a father and is beginning to be successful in his own right.

John Paul Jones DeJoria is a man of his word, even when it costs him dearly. Once he said casually, "If we ever get a single distributor who buys $1 million worth of products, I'll give him my Rolls Royce." True to his word, even though it hurt, J.P. kept the customer and lost the Rolls. He honored his word, which was more important to him than his cherished car.

John Paul Jones DeJoria is a happy man. He observes, "My general philosophy is 'Successful people do all the things that unsuccessful people don't want to do.' You should surround yourself with positive people. If the people around you are down all the time, get rid of them. If they are usually up but down occasionally, that's okay, but keep only the positive people around. My personal philosophy is to be happy and try to pay close attention to the vital few and ignore the trivial. Being alive and being able to feel is a blessing in its own right. I feel there is no other place in the world where people can succeed the way they can in the United States of America. It is a great country."

Now John Paul is in the process of building a new home. It is his "dream house", perched on a mountain top in Malibu. The house, about a mile from the ocean, will have a 360-degree view. It will be large, with a theater for his two daughters — who like to play-act — and all the amenities he could ever have imagined......... Another house, another goal achieved. One more step in the life of a man who is truly on top of the world.

Stephen Haselton

Sidney Syvertson

Re/Max of California

-3-

RE/MAX OF CALIFORNIA

The orchestra began to play. The lights faded to black. An anticipatory hush fell over the sixteen hundred diners. Suddenly, dazzling orange neon lights exploded into the darkness. Radiating from the stage in large capital letters was one word — RE/MAX.

The Hollywood-style fanfare signalled the beginning of the first of two lavish annual awards celebrations, for outstanding performances by real estate agents associated with RE/MAX of California, on consecutive Saturday nights. Sid Syvertson and Steve Haselton, co-owners of RE/MAX of California, made their appearance center stage in the main ballrooms of the Anaheim Hilton and the Santa Clara Marriott to present a staggering number of awards.

And truly there was much to celebrate. Before the festivities were over, more than five hundred RE/MAX agents had made their way up to the podium, to receive awards honoring each of them for earning more than $100,000 on commissions during the year. "One of our problems, now that we have so many people earning over $100,000, is how to present the awards to everybody without boring the audience," Haselton complains happily.

Other real estate companies wish they had that kind of problem. Barely five years old, RE/MAX of California agents have handled tens of thousands of transactions, totalling billions of dollars in sales. The phenomenal growth of RE/MAX, which had been virtually unknown in the Golden State as recently as 1983, by late 1987 had catapulted the firm past Coldwell Banker as the second-largest residential real estate brokerage company doing business in California. Syvertson and Haselton believe RE/MAX of California will dethrone the granddaddy of them all within two years.

RE/MAX of California has succeeded in a highly competitive, often cut-throat environment, by abandoning the established rules of real estate brokerage and applying the principles of a cooperative. The key difference, and indeed probably the definitive reason for the company's continued growth, is that RE/MAX agents keep one hundred percent of their commission.

This contrasts sharply with standard brokerage practices, where a sixty/forty split is commonplace, and where anything more is considered generous. Instead of splitting their commissions, RE/MAX agents pay a defined set of fees to the company. These include their pro rata share of monthly overhead, including telephone, rent, utilities, insurance and receptionist/secretary services; they also include a management fee to their broker, an independent RE/MAX franchisee, and a monthly advertising fee used for advertising at the regional level. The current RE/MAX of California advertising campaign includes billboards, radio spots on twenty-four stations, and television ads on eighteen stations throughout the state.

Any personal expenses, such as long-distance phone calls or individual advertising, are billed separately. Additionally, each agent pays monthly dues to RE/MAX.

Average total cost to the agent varies from $700 to $1,200 a month in RE/MAX offices throughout the state, although in individual cases it could be much higher. This may seem like a hefty nut to crack for the average real estate salesperson, but it's only ten to twelve percent of what the typical RE/MAX agent earns in commissions each year.

The "100 percent concept" has attracted the most seasoned, successful real estate professionals to RE/MAX. The typical RE/MAX agent has had more than eight years of experience selling real estate, a phenomenal statistic in a business where the annual drop-out rate among new entrants is a dismal eighty to ninety percent after only twelve months.

"Our agents are highly knowledgeable salespeople. More than fifty percent of them hold broker licences. They don't need training and they don't need pep talks. They have an established roster of clients, and any of them could open up their own real estate office tomorrow," stresses Syvertson. "They don't because they would rather avoid the hassle of dealing with a revolving door of salespeople that need on-going training. RE/MAX is the perfect solution — no hassle and more money!"

Agents are also attracted by the RE/MAX nationwide referral network, which efficiently enables RE/MAX agents to recommend one another across the country. "Unquestionably, we have the most successful real estate referral network in North America," asserts Syvertson. "One of the biggest endorsements of the effectiveness of the system has been the number of outside agents who choose to utilize it. And within RE/MAX there are top producers who rely solely on referral business for their income."

Referral networks of competing real estate companies use a central clearing house, where referrals are passed on to the owner of a local office who in turn passes it on to an agent. Thus, the referring agent is often three steps removed from the agent who will ultimately handle their client.

The RE/MAX referral network allows agents to deal

directly with one another, with no middlemen to muddle the transaction. "When an agent has a referral for White Plains, New York, how does he know that the person on the other end of the phone is a good, competent real estate person? He does if it's a RE/MAX agent, because only top people join RE/MAX," says Syvertson. He points out that RE/MAX is the most successful real estate company in the nation when it comes to closing referrals, with a closing ratio of twenty-seven percent, compared to an industry-wide average of around six percent.

RE/MAX International publishes a referral roster twice a year, which provides agents with a detailed list of pertinent information on each RE/MAX associate in the network: names, addresses, telephone numbers, numbers of years in real estate, professional designations, fields of real estate expertise, service areas and languages spoken.

Since 1983, thousands of top-producing real estate agents have seen fit to join RE/MAX offices throughout the state of California. Hundreds of RE/MAX franchises have been established during that same time period, and a new RE/MAX of California franchise opens its doors each week.

RE/MAX is not solely a California concept. Founded in 1973 in Denver, the idea first gained a foothold in Colorado and Canada. Today, RE/MAX International has offices in all major markets throughout the United States and Canada, with tens of thousands of sales agents on board. California is the largest RE/MAX region in the United States.

The strong presence of RE/MAX in California is directly attributable to the faith of Syvertson and Haselton in the potential of the cooperative system. Yet these men, as unalike as any two individuals could be in most respects, are not mavericks by nature. In fact, before they broke with tradition and put RE/MAX on the map in California each had quite a conventional existence.

Syvertson is the product of a midwest upbringing. He was born in 1930 in West Salem, a small town in Wisconsin where his father was a barber for the modest farm community of 1,100. The youngest of three sons, Syvertson was always affable, gregarious, and possessed by a strong desire to succeed.

After high school he joined the U.S. Navy, and following his discharge in 1951 he married and went to work putting his natural out-going talents to use in sales. He began by selling appliances — big-ticket items such as washers and dryers — for one of the largest mass merchandisers in Minneapolis, the biggest city close to his home in West Salem.

Within a year he was promoted to sales manager, and he ran the store for an additional two years before going into the real estate business. Why did he abandon a secure, decent-paying position for a commission-only job in a field he knew nothing about, particularly when he was now twenty-five, the father of three young children?

"Well, my bosses were also in the oil business. They bought and sold off the pipeline, and every day they would sit at their big desks with their feet up and read the Wall Street Journal. After they were through, they would put the newspaper in the waste basket. At the end of the day I'd fish it out and read it. One day I opened it up and one of the articles stated that the three top-paying jobs in 1953 were first, stocks and bonds; second, insurance; and third, real estate."

"I didn't know anybody with money, so stocks and bonds were out. I didn't know anything about insurance, and that left real estate. That I knew something about. I had already purchased some real estate, including some investment income property."

With only $43 to his name he joined the largest real estate

company in Minneapolis, and once more demonstrated an innate flair for sales; during his first year he emerged as the firm's top producer.

"But then I noticed something. A large number of my clients were moving to California. I thought about that for a while, and then asked myself: 'Why aren't I in California where they are going, instead of Minneapolis where they are leaving?'"

Syvertson's reaction was immediate. He bought an old used-furniture truck, loaded up the family and all of their belongings, and crossed the United States to the far west. "Actually it was a tractor trailer, a vehicle which I had never driven before in my entire life," says Syvertson, smiling at the memory. "When we arrived in Westchester, I found the only place large enough to park the truck, which just happened to be across the street from a real estate company called Marlow Burns."

Never one to hesitate, Syvertson went briskly over and introduced himself, and assured the owner that he would be the best salesman the owner had ever had if the latter would give him a job. As soon as he received his California real estate licence, he went to work there.

Over the next three years Syvertson sold real estate in and around Westchester, while at the same time acquiring properties for his own portfolio. In 1958 he relocated on the Palos Verdes Peninsula. "I moved to the Palos Verdes Peninsula because I wanted to live on a hill looking down on the lights, not up at them," he interjects.

Syvertson continued to sell real estate until 1962, when he decided to open his own real estate brokerage firm, called Spring Realty, in Palos Verdes. Repeating what was by now a well-established pattern in his life, his company did so much business that within thirteen months Spring Realty took over the number one position in residential real estate on the Palos Verdes Peninsula. In 1964 he opened his second office.

Right about that time Syvertson met Steve Haselton, then a twenty-six-year-old computer wizard working for Security Pacific National Bank. How this young, professorial-looking, conservative thinker blended so well with the gregarious Syvertson is a mystery to most observers, but not to Haselton. "Our personalities and our talents compliment each other," he says simply. "If we were alike, we'd probably be at loggerheads most of the time."

A California native, Haselton was born in 1942 in Pasadena, where his father was a printer of botanical books. A serious student, Haselton originally had set his sights on joining the Episcopal clergy. "No joke. I had been accepted into the Harvard School of Divinity, but I figured I should hedge my bet and first get a business background just in case," explains the ever-practical Haselton.

He applied to several good business schools, and ultimately entered Claremont Men's College in the fall of 1959, intent on getting his bachelor's degree in economics. "In the end, it turned out I didn't get a degree in economics, but in religion," laughs Haselton. "I backed into religion mainly because economics was so dry. But because I was at Claremont a lot of my course work was necessarily in business, accounting, and economics."

During the summer following his graduation in 1964, Haselton served as an aide at an elite business conference sponsored by *Fortune Magazine* at the Claremont Colleges. "I met some very powerful men who controlled fellowships that were given to various graduate schools around the country, and I was offered a Lincoln Fellowship to Claremont Graduate School in government," says Haselton. He took it. "It was a good deal. Room, board, tuition, and a stipend of $500 a month — and back then you could easily live on that. I figured the church could wait a little longer."

He completed his master's degree in one year, and was one of three students selected from around the entire country as an aide to Adlai E. Stevenson. "It was an interesting time, because of the Vietnam conflict," he says.

These experiences cast Haselton as the ideal candidate for yet another Lincoln Fellowship, this time for a Ph.D. in economics, again from Claremont Graduate School. "It was about a year into that when I realized I could no longer handle sitting around in a brown corduroy blazer with little leather patches at the elbows, stoking a pipe. I decided it was time to go to work," he asserts.

Haselton had an interview with Security Pacific Bank. "I told the personnel office that I considered their branch offices to be the Siberia of banking, and that I would prefer an exciting corporate position." The bank made him a site analyst. "I had to help find the best locations for new branches for the bank," he explains. "This had always been done using a sort of dartboard approach, but I knew there had to be a better way." He had finally found a use for what he considered his arcane micro-economics studies, calling upon them to develop an economic model. It soon became the standard for the bank in analyzing potential branch sites during its high-expansion periods.

"In the process I managed to alienate certain people in the marketing department who thought they should be the ones locating the branches," Haselton continues. "That's when I learned that the way you get rid of your competition is to promote them into your department! I was promoted to the marketing department and put in charge of a section called Feasibility and Evaluation. In reality, my job was to make the marketing department's wildest concepts seem credible for their presentations to top management."

While running that department, Haselton found himself in

a series of conflicts with the controller's department at the bank — "because every response we ever got from them said that financially we couldn't afford to do anything we proposed — to invest, even to be in business." He was soon promoted to the controller's office and put in charge of a division.

At twenty-four, he was the youngest division head in the history of the bank. His division, Cost and Profitability, did all of the bank's cost analysis. "I hired programmers and accountants, and I had one section staffed entirely by writers. They took all of the crazy ideas and numbers and manipulated them, trying to make them comprehensible, so that people could make sense of it all. My whole idea was to humanize banking and numbers, to take really complex ideas and make them simple and understandable."

During this time Haselton also taught himself a lot about computers. "I was dealing with a lot of computer technicians, and I learned how to use and program computers, basically out of a need to survive," he says. In addition to his job at the bank, he began teaching night courses at UCLA, worked sporadically on finishing up his Ph.D., and squeezed in occasional computer consulting work on the side.

It was at a seminar-cum-party on computers that Haselton first met Syvertson. "Sid was there to learn about computers, but I was there for the party," recalls Haselton. They chatted briefly, and three weeks later Syvertson contacted Haselton about helping him to automate Spring Realty.

"I started as a consultant, but after about a month I told Sid I couldn't manage what he wanted for Spring Realty — which was to make it a significant part of California real estate — on a part-time basis," Haselton says. Syvertson agreed, and proposed that Haselton join Spring Realty on a full-time basis. In short order, Haselton quit the bank, teaching, and part-time consulting, and even gave up pursuit of his Ph.D. He took a deep breath, and dove head-first into Spring Realty as senior vice president in 1968. He was then twenty-six years old.

While Haselton acknowledges Syvertson's formidable powers of persuasion, he believes he was more than ready to make the career switch. "Being on the fast track at the bank was not exactly my cup of tea," he says. "Clawing through the corporate maze is not my way at all, even though I understood how to do it. I also saw that no matter how high up you rise on the ladder, the pressures are the same. Here, the pressures are of our own making."

Over the next fifteen years Syvertson and Haselton built Spring Realty into one of the ten largest privately-held real estate companies in the United States. Haselton's expertise in computer technology made much of the expansion possible. At its height the brokerage company had thirty offices, stretching from Malibu to Long Beach, staffed with one thousand salespeople. The operation was supported by a licensing bureau and a full educational system and training center.

The dynamic duo also established an assortment of real estate-related enterprises, including an escrow department, a mortgage banking house, two title insurance companies, an insurance agency, and a construction and development company.

Despite the soaring success of Spring Realty along the Los Angeles County coast line, Syvertson and Haselton came to the realization that their goal of becoming a significant factor within organized real estate in California was virtually unattainable via the traditional route. "In many states Spring Realty by itself would have been a factor, but in a state as large as California with close to a million people moving in each year, we barely made a dent outside of Los Angeles County," says Syvertson.

"To become a significant factor we would have had to have in the neighborhood of more than one hundred offices, probably *well* over one hundred. We knew that to build them individually would be slow going, and would take more time than we had available," he adds.

They took a long look at the real estate market, and after travelling all over the country, talking with their peers, they made the decision in 1982 to become the master franchiser of RE/MAX in California. "We had seen some examples around the country, and the cooperative arrangement seemed to work. It looked like a good vehicle to propel us to the size of real estate entity we wanted in California," Syvertson says.

"We also had to look ahead ten years and ask ourselves what the real estate business was going to look like a decade from now," he continues. "We felt that the days of being independent were fast coming to a close. Clearly, the industry was being centralized by the powerful national and regional houses."

They became a part of RE/MAX rather than start a new enterprise based on the same concept because "RE/MAX already had the beginnings of a national network, a key factor in quickly opening up a large number of real estate offices statewide," explains Syvertson. "This was already becoming a land where the giants dominated the residential real estate market. We needed that national presence."

Indeed, RE/MAX International claims that many thousands of superior real estate agents have left other companies to join the RE/MAX network, and several hundred million dollars is spent each year on institutional advertising.

"Besides," Haselton adds, "Their system was a good one and we didn't need to reinvent the wheel."

At the time, California was divided into six RE/MAX

regions, and Syvertson and Haselton negotiated for five of them, all located in the southern half of the state. The northern California region was owned by someone else. "From the beginning we knew we wanted the whole state, because California is very much its own marketing area," says Syvertson. "We had some sophisticated computer resources, and we saw all sorts of networking advantages in viewing California as a whole." Two years later the opportunity to buy out the northern California region presented itself, and Haselton and Syvertson jumped at the chance to unite the state under one RE/MAX banner.

RE/MAX offices generally attract only experienced real estate agents, those who are able to clear comfortably the $700 to $1,200 monthly freight. Thus sales training, so vital in a traditional real estate office to maintain staffing levels, has no place in a RE/MAX enterprise. Acknowledging this, Haselton and Syvertson began to convert the Spring Realty offices. "As long as we were handling them and training new people those offices worked. Without new trainees, they wouldn't have survived. They would have made poor conversions," says Haselton.

This transition was not revealed to any of the Spring Realty agents. "The one thing we could not do was announce the conversion ahead of time. RE/MAX puts some competitors out of business, and we did not need bad rumors circulating on the street," Syvertson explains.

On 1 August, 1982, the managers of the offices were called into a meeting, utterly unaware of the monumental change that was about to occur. "It was a complete surprise. In one fell swoop we announced that from that day forward Spring Realty no longer existed and all of the offices were now RE/MAX offices," relates Haselton.

The anticipated trauma lasted about three weeks, with both men putting out fires at one location or another on a daily basis. "It wasn't one of our better periods," Haselton recalls wryly.

They then sold the offices to the former managers, helping to finance the purchases when necessary. "We lost very few agents during the conversion, because the majority were eight-to-ten-year veterans, for whom the RE/MAX system is ideal," says Syvertson. The conversions were completed by January of 1983.

All of the real estate-related companies that had been created along the way — the mortgage banking house, the title companies, the construction arm — were discontinued. "Each of us had to make a one hundred percent effort to bring home the RE/MAX concept," says Haselton.

Understandably, the reaction to the overnight conversion was utter amazement. Why would anyone abandon such a highly successful real estate operation as Spring Realty in exchange for an unproven commodity — at least in California — such as RE/MAX?

"Our friends thought we had gone crazy," says Syvertson. "Not only that, people in the real estate business thought we were insane. We got calls from all over the country asking us why were doing such a strange thing. It was silliness to them because cooperatives were not well known.

"Half the world had had us pegged as the model real estate agency. If such a model was changing over to a new concept they wondered why. They didn't see what we saw, and they didn't want to see it." However, there were others who thought the 100-percent concept was worse than mere silliness, that it would, in fact, destroy the real estate industry as they knew it, and they made their resentment known.

After converting the Spring Realty offices to RE/MAX, Haselton and Syvertson began what turned out to be a long and arduous process of bringing new franchisees into the fold. "It was tough," Syvertson allows. "Most people thought RE/MAX was a pill you took."

The almost total lack of awareness about RE/MAX within the real estate industry, not to mention the public, forced the pair to begin exhibiting at real estate trade conventions statewide. "That was a good shock for us," recalls Haselton. "Previously, we had always dealt from a strong power base. We weren't used to manning a convention booth ourselves and hawking a product. It was a melodramatic shift."

At first the two found they had to explain the entire RE/MAX story to anyone who stopped by their table. At the next convention there was still considerable confusion, but the majority had grasped the basic theory behind RE/MAX. By the third convention they could feel the excitement behind the questions, and the eagerness of many to become a part of their growing organization.

The multitude of conventions and months of hard work ultimately paid off. While they sold a grand total of only ten franchises during that first year, that number increased by fifty percent in 1984. Similar jumps were seen in the succeeding years, and today RE/MAX of California systematically opens more than fifty offices a year. "We attend grand openings on a weekly basis," nods Haselton.

With hundreds of franchises sold, Haselton and Syvertson have the RE/MAX success formula down to an exact science. They have set up a service bureau which handles all of the broker's needs, from the time the individual purchases the franchise all the way through to the grand opening ceremonies. RE/MAX of California provides training on how to recruit top salespeople, advertising formats, and advises on how to finance a franchise. They even offer a computerized service for laying out an office. "If they give us four walls and a door, we'll show them how to open an office," Syvertson says. "If a franchisee goes from point one to point sixty without making a two degree deviation, and if he follows exactly what is supposed to be done, he or she will make a success of a RE/MAX office."

Owners of RE/MAX of California franchises must have real estate experience, and Haselton and Syvertson have discovered that it is much easier to interest an individual in a start-up RE/MAX enterprise rather than to convert an existing real estate office. "It's hard for an established real estate office to let go of the new employees," Haselton says.

RE/MAX of California locates franchises within a certain geographic area based on the population and number of homes. No new RE/MAX office can be closer than a mile to another RE/MAX office. "We must approve all office names, and typically they will be called something like RE/MAX Professionals or RE/MAX Central," Syvertson says.

Almost without exception, RE/MAX offices are exceedingly luxurious. The franchisees generally have to provide elegant offices if they want to successfully recruit the high caliber and sophisticated sales force it takes to make a RE/MAX office work. "Other real estate offices have bullpens, where the desks are right next to each other, so the trainees can listen and learn from the more experienced salespeople," notes Syvertson. "In a RE/MAX office the salespeople just want to do business, and they prefer to do it in private."

The typical RE/MAX franchise has offices designed to accomodate about thirty agents, although many are significantly larger. There are even "super-mega offices," which are staffed by more than one hundred sales associates. The capital necessary to buy a RE/MAX franchise, to furnish the offices to the high expectations of the talent the franchise hopes to recruit, and to get up and running is a significant investment. "We've never had a problem persuading a bank to loan the money to a RE/MAX franchisee," observes

Syvertson. "They look at our track record and it's a done deal."

Many real estate brokers choose to buy a RE/MAX franchise because it provides a steady, consistent cash flow. Even the smallest RE/MAX franchisee in California can earn more than $100,000 a year in management fees, and if he or she is also acting as an agent, any commissions generated are additional income. "The real estate market is like a roller coaster — up and down, up and down. But a RE/MAX franchisee's income doesn't depend on the vagaries of the market. And it makes no difference if a top producer takes off for Tahiti for three months — management gets paid regardless of an agent's sales activity," says Haselton.

Several heavy hitters from major brokerage firms have bought RE/MAX franchises, and when one of the top managers from Coldwell Banker bought a southern California franchise, Syvertson was curious and asked him why. "He said that when any of his agents got an offer on a RE/MAX listing, they invariably asked him to come along and present it because they couldn't handle the RE/MAX salesperson's questions about the title report or the buyer's financial statements, or the like. He said, 'Hell! If I have to go with them each time I might as well join you people,'" says Syvertson.

RE/MAX fosters a cooperative spirit among agents through regional and national conventions, and encourages membership in special achievement clubs such as The 100 Percent, Executive and Presidents' Clubs. Even though most agents have years of experience behind them, advanced educational seminars are well attended at both the state and international levels, covering such diverse topics as team selling, personal-time management, condo conversions, and acquiring corporate and third party accounts.

RE/MAX in California has not limited itself to the

residential real estate market. "We've had a commercially-oriented franchise in Costa Mesa for a couple of years, and it's doing extremely well. But that's not a surprise because the average commercial real estate broker generally only makes a fifty percent commission," Syvertson says. Openings of additional commercial franchises are already planned for Long Beach, downtown Los Angeles and another in Orange County.

RE/MAX offices in California posted almost $10 billion in 1989 alone. Within the near future Syvertson and Haselton expect to have penetrated all of the major California markets, with a total of 550 offices staffed with between 12,000 to 14,000 agents. "We're right on track, and we're both very careful planners. When we reach our goal we will be the largest real estate company in California," predicts Haselton.

They have already fulfilled their original ambition — that of becoming a significant factor in organized real estate in California. Yet Haselton and Syvertson continue to work hard, to formulate long-range plans, and to set ever-escalating goals. Undoubtedly, both of them could retire to a beach anywhere in the free world and soak up the sunshine for the rest of their natural lives, but they choose to do otherwise. "I enjoy what we are doing and I don't like the alternative — retirement. It's unacceptable," says Syvertson emphatically.

Haselton echoes Syvertson's sentiment: "What we're doing is fun. It's a ticket that says, 'You've won.' It keeps you alive and excited about the future."

Mike Copley
Off-The-Wall-Products

-4-

OFF-THE-WALL PRODUCTS

"Off-the-wall" — a description of impulsive or unusual behavior — is rapidly becoming a household word. This is directly due to the efforts of one man, Michael C. Copley. Ask someone if they know of the clocks that you throw against the wall, and the usual response is, "As a matter of fact, I got one of those for a present this year."

Sometimes a bad mood can be good for the bottom line. As Michael Copley, the dashing, free-spirited president of OFF-THE-WALL Products, La Jolla, California, has learned, it can pay to start the day grumpy.

After waking up in such a mood one day about a decade ago, Copley was gloomily taking his morning shower when suddenly, the alarm he had forgotten about buzzed...and buzzed...and buzzed.

He stomped furiously out of the bathroom, dripping wet, picked up a nearby tennis ball and took dead aim. It knocked the alarm clock to the floor, effectively quieting it — and in the ensuing silence inspiration struck. "Then and there", Copley recalls, "I thought what a great idea it would be to have a clock you could throw against the wall."

The "action alarm clock" — appropriately called OFF-THE-WALL — sounds its alarm and then is thrown to turn it off. Five minutes later the snooze alarm sounds so the user must get up and go find it. (There is no truth to the story that Copley subsequently decided to integrate vertically by opening a wall repair business.)

In the past three years, over a million alarm clocks have been sold, and the company's product line now includes a variety of other novelty items. Not a bad achievement in the fickle, cut-throat world of novelty and gift marketing, where this year's hit is often next year's has-been.

To get the company started, Copley invested $100,000 of his own savings and secured another $150,000 in bank loans. He formed a joint venture with a partner, found a Hong Kong manufacturer, hired office staff and lined up sales representatives.

Distribution is now international in scope. As well as in the United States, his products are available in Europe, Canada, Japan, Australia, Puerto Rico, New Zealand, Scandinavia, Iceland, Israel, Turkey and Greece. In addition to the OFF-THE-WALL action alarm clock, which is designed to look like a baseball, golf ball, soccer ball, football, basketball, tennis ball or cricket ball, there are other zany products, many of them depicted in the company's eight-page, full-color catalogue.

All the products have a common theme: they appeal to the customers' desire to be different, to be a bit out of step with the rest of the world and proud of it. The current product line, for instance, depicts a musical grenade clock. The alarm sounds — what else? — reveille. OFF-THE-WALL also markets sports watches in the shape of soccer balls, basketballs, baseballs and footballs, that play "Take Me Out to the Ball Game" when tapped. Taking off on the same concept, Le Munch watches are only for the "taste-conscious." They're sold in the form of hot dogs, hamburgers and Oreo-like cookies. For cold-weather markets there is the hockey puck alarm clock called "Slapshot". There's a musical thumb, Tom's Green Thumb, that, when inserted into the soil of flower pots plays "How Dry I Am" when it's time to water. Sports wallets come in soccer ball, baseball, football or basketball style. Each is designed to look and feel just like the cover of a ball.

The next breaking product will be Zortz, avant-garde soft plastic characters that suction to refrigerators, wall and doors to hold notes, keys, pens and coupons, relying on the Zortz's big mouths to keep a grip on things. Zortz come in a dozen varieties, including Mona Groan (a nurse), I.B. Smart (a student), Jerome Blue (a jazz musician) and Mimi Memoranda (a secretary).

Not forgetting the sports-minded, there's also Jock O. Strap the football player, Jacque Croissant the chef, Spitball Walker the baseball player, Tex Tumbleweed the cowboy. Dick Fuzzinsky the policeman, Rip Rocker the Punk Rocker, R.X.Aminestein the doctor and Big Deal D Boss the boss. On the Zortz sales flyer, Copley runs an offbeat definition of Zortz, calling them a "family" of soft, squeezable characters having the likeness of several "humans" we all know.

It's hard to believe the president of such a fast-growing company is a man who was neither the class clown nor the class genius, but by his own account, the most reserved student around.

But make no mistake. Copley is also tenacious. And his good friend, Jonathan Brenner, an attorney in nearby Rancho Bernardo, loves to illustrate that tenacity by telling a story about his friend's former pet, a black and white pit bull named Diesel. "Diesel was quite a dog," Brenner says with a laugh. One day, he recalls, Copley left Diesel alone in his truck for a short while. Determined to get some attention, Diesel chewed through the steering wheel until he was finally rescued. "You know what they say about owners being like the dogs they choose?" Brenner says. Copley doesn't deny the story, nor the need for perseverance in his business.

Actually, Copley loves dogs. Before someone gave him a little, seven-week old pit bull puppy that subsequently grew to eighty-five lbs., Copley had a German Shepherd for sixteen years. "Gunnar died in my arms," Copley remembers. "I found him in the Colorado mountains when he was six weeks old. For sixteen years he was my best friend. He's still a part of me."

Some of the new products are Copley's brain children; others are someone else's idea, with the Copley "touch" added. For example: "The Zortz creator is a young man who lives in New York City and makes the characters in his apartment," Copley says. "He came to me with a great idea, so the company has taken on the manufacturing, marketing, and promotion."

Whatever their origin, products must be priced competitively enough in this business to attract large numbers of customers, Copley knows from experience; after introducing the action alarm clocks, he then designed lower-priced models and marketed them in discount stores. Secondly, the products must hold their own in the competitive gift industry. "The life of a novelty product is about a year," Copley says. "You're doing well if it lasts two years. And to have a novelty product last three years is exceptional."

Attracting attention seems to be one of Copley's strong suits. Since the company began, he has been the focus of much publicity. *Entrepreneur* magazine included him in a "40 under 40" feature last year. "Like everyone else," the piece began, "Michael Copley had mornings when he wanted to throw his alarm clock against the wall. Unlike everyone else, Copley did something about it." In a recent *Venture* magazine article, Copley's action alarm was one of one hundred "notable ideas," headlined, "Time Doesn't Fly, It Bounces."

Copley's ideas have drawn the attention of the popular press as well. Recently, *USA Today* gave him a lengthy and complimentary paragraph in its Money section, noting that "A hot gift item can go in - and out of - style in a flash." The article went on to note that OFF-THE-WALL "has done a good job of surviving this roller coaster...." Another newspaper's lifestyle section included Copley's clocks in a story on toys for grown-ups.

Further, Copley's alarm clocks made the front cover of *The Wall Street Journal*, were featured in the *Los Angeles Times* and even were covered by the BBC and other international networks. Numerous talk-show hosts have enjoyed throwing his clocks around - including those on Good Morning America, San Diego Magazine and the Regis Philbin Show, to name just a few. Due to his lively interview style, Copley has had calls from all over the world requesting radio interviews.

At first glance this may look like a case of effortless success. The son of late newspaper executive James S. Copley, Michael was raised in upper-middle-class surroundings. At forty, he's trim, athletic, and still prep-school handsome. He dresses in tailored trousers and shirts, sometimes topped by expensive-looking sweaters. He seems to make the time, friends say, to play a mean game of tennis and he surfs like a teenager. He loves convertibles, ocean views and other traditional Southern California amenities, and he lives in view of the Pacific, just minutes from the OFF-THE-WALL headquarters.

But when it comes to his company, nothing has been handed to him on a silver platter. And in fact, he is as surprised and pleased as anyone at what only appears to have been overnight success.

In truth, the company history suggests more of a "riches to rags to riches" story. In 1986 the company almost went under, Copley recently acknowledged in the conference room of his modest offices. He had trouble finding money to borrow. He searched for investors for months on end. He was logging long days. "And the start-up was even slower than it might appear," he concedes, because he didn't act on his idea right away. "I carried the idea around with me for about seven or eight years," he recalls. He would think about it — and then forget about it. Mull it over again — and decide, "No, maybe not." A radio deejay finally was responsible for converting Copley's inspiration into action. "One day in November 1985, I was in my car and heard a report on the radio about this person who had come out with a clock you could throw against the wall." Michael and his car came to a dead stop. "I said, 'He can't do that! That's my idea.'"

It was just the jolt Copley needed, and he decided to check into it immediately. "I asked an attorney to do a patent search. It turned out there were four or five patents on clocks you throw against the wall. But my idea involves putting it in a ball; the others didn't really entail the same concept."

In March 1986, Copley hired an engineer and then a sales manager. "We worked on one design, a clock you could put in a ball and throw against a wall." Key to the design, Copley explains, was a "deceleration" switch. "We spent months designing a switch that could respond to any jolt. When we were finished we found it was the same switch that Mercedes used for its air bags. Consequently, we had to redesign, but the principle is still the same."

Copley's team readied a prototype for the first public showing — the New York Stationery Show in May 1986. "It was crazy," Copley recalls with satisfaction. "Everybody loved it." The orders poured in. "Crazily, we took orders," Copley says with a laugh; they were not aware then of the production problems that loomed ahead. "In the next two months, we sold 200,000 clocks."

Orders came in from all over. From small, independent gift stores. From large department stores like Bloomingdale's, May Company, Macy's, Robinson's, and Bullock's.

Then the bubble almost burst. The Hong Kong manufacturers with whom Copley had signed an agreement reneged on the deal. It took time and considerable effort to find a new manufacturer. Worse yet, the idea was stolen by the same manufacturer that pulled out, and was copied before Copley could get into production. He filed a lawsuit and won, but the pirated clock is still being manufactured and sold. "We compete with "knock-offs" all over the world," Copley says. "In fact our product comes in several names, to gain market position — "OFF-THE-WALL," "TIME-FLYS," "TICKED-OFF" and "TIME-SHOCK." Now, in retrospect, Copley can look at the nightmare more philosophically. "Knock-offs are a big problem in the gift industry," he says resignedly. "If you have a product with any potential at all, there's always the danger of being copied."

Money problems added to Copley's knock-off woes. "I had already invested all my money," he explains. But that was not enough, so Copley searched for investors, day after day, for four months, running into one brick wall after another. Finally, he formed a joint-venture partnership with Roger Gimbel, the successful head of a giant leather-goods distributing firm, RGA Accessories, Inc. He has nothing but good things to say about his partner. Copley calls Gimbel "terrific, astute, a keen businessman." He says it's a good match, with his own best input being the creative strategy, while Gimbel contributes economic and strategic expertise.

But Copley's lack of formal business training doesn't seem to affect the bottom line. Before the first public showing of clocks, for instance, he had not bothered to analyze formally who would buy his product.

An even more startling fact is that, from conception through production, Copley had never considered the possibility of failure. "I just knew that people would want to buy them," he says now. "When I believe in something, 'failure' and 'can't do' are not part of my vocabulary."

The normal fears of failure didn't need to be ejected from his head, because they had never entered. "I just believed," he says. "Whether it was blind ambition or just a gut feeling, I just believed the product would be successful. I had an idea and went full steam ahead with it."

In the case of OFF-THE-WALL, a knowledge of human nature was perhaps just as important as, and maybe even more important than, familiarity with sophisticated market-analysis studies. "I had always heard people complaining about their alarm clocks," he says. And then he adds, with a combination of innocent candor and Harvard Business School acumen, "People have ALWAYS wanted to throw their alarm clocks against the wall."

His publicist picked up on this premise in a press release in the OFF-THE-WALL media kit, noting, "The wish to smash the object that destroys a million dreams is an impulse everyone has felt more than once in their lifetime. But for most people the urge to hurl their clocks across the bedroom has been nothing more than another dream."

Nowadays, Copley has a clearer profile of just who his typical customers are. "I think our best customers are adults, age about twenty-five to forty, equally divided between men and women." The attraction? It's an impulse buy, Copley believes, much like the pull of a pet rock. People feel they must have an OFF-THE-WALL alarm clock or one of his other novelty products. But that's not the whole story.

"As well as being a novelty the clock is tied into the major sports and it also has a function — it tells time. I think these three reasons underlie its success.

"The need for a bit of frivolity might also inspire purchase of the clocks," he says. "In these competitive and stressful times, we all need to lighten up. I have come in contact with so many hurried, competitive, on-edge industry executives that I thought these people could use a little fun and lightheartedness in their lives. When you're on edge, wouldn't you cheer up at the idea of throwing your grenade-replica clock at the wall? I want my product to bring a smile to people's faces...to add a little fun to their lives. At the very least, I want people to think it's OFF-THE-WALL!"

Ironically, Copley's own day doesn't begin by tossing his popular product against the wall. "I don't even use an alarm anymore," he says. "I just wake up - usually about 5:30 or 6:00 a.m." He's turned into a morning person, he admits. And once at the office, his day is divided into what he terms proactive and reactive time. The proactive time, he says, "includes doing productive things that I like to do; designing new products, composing new product lists, contacting manufacturers, dealing with selling and promotion." Reactive time, to Copley, is spent reacting to problems as they come up - hearing customers' complaints or dealing with stores that need to ship back products.

Copley also receives letters and phone calls every week from would-be inventors, people who claim they have next year's hit gift — "just in case Copley's interested." He answers every inquiry personally. "People deserve that respect," he says simply. And, who knows, the next letter might just describe next season's blockbuster.

The confidence that now seems to come easily for Copley wasn't always there, he says. "When I graduated from college, I was not a confident person," he insists. "It has developed. As I dealt with the failures, challenges and successes of my own firm, my confidence grew. We almost failed, we almost went under. We needed a Hong Kong connection so I went there. I'd never been to Hong Kong but I jumped right in . I was green, but I really wanted it to work, and I believed it *would* work."

At one time Copley doubted he would ever graduate from

college. His high school grades were not spectacular, he admits. And after high school graduation, he enrolled at the University of Colorado, Boulder, but dropped out after two years. Asked what he majored in, he quips, "skiing."

"I had no direction," he adds, "and my grades were poor." He returned to Southern California, going to work for the South Bay *Daily Breeze,* one of the newspapers in his father's empire. He was drafted into the army in 1971 and served two years. Just before he was due to be shipped out to Vietnam, his hand was severely crushed in the cargo hatch of a tank. " I was in the hospital for three months, and needed numerous operations to reconstruct my hand," he recalls with a grimace. "My hand is pretty functional now, but you can still see all the scars." In lieu of going to Vietnam, Copley was then assigned to work for the base newspaper at Fort Ord in Monterey, and eventually became its editor.

After being discharged, he returned to the *Breeze* for a year. Following the death of his father in 1974, however, he decided to go back to school — a brave decision, considering he had only 16 transferable units and about a 1.9 average from the University of Colorado.

He is not sure exactly why he decided to resume his education. "My father had always been big on education," says Copley, whose mother is also deceased. He enrolled in El Camino Junior College in Torrance, California and soon applied for entrance to Stanford University. Not surprisingly, he was turned down.

It might have been the rejection that finally lit a fire under him for good. Copley buckled down, determined to improve his scholastic record. A year later, he had won more awards in college journalism competitions than anyone in the state and was carrying a 4.0 grade average. When he reapplied to Stanford he was accepted.

"I remember that three separate times I drove the five hundred miles to Stanford just to meet with the Dean of Admissions. I had no appointment. And each of those three times I sat and waited, but never got in to see him. But I remembered two important things: If you believe in something, you can make it happen. And always be nice to the boss's secretary; it can work wonders. After I had been accepted and was enrolled I went by the admissions office and hugged the dean's secretary; to this day she probably doesn't know why." He calls his Stanford acceptance "one of the biggest events of my life."

He was older than most of his classmates, which he says didn't bother him. He was graduated with a 3.5 average and went to work at a now defunct newspaper in Menlo Park, California. Then it was back to San Diego in 1979, where he bought and sold real estate until 1981, but admits he had no real direction.

Indecision set in again. "At that point, I really didn't know what I wanted to do." he admits. Married, with a newborn baby, he decided he needed a future so enrolled at the University of San Diego Law School. He attended from 1981 through 1984. He was graduated in the top third of his class. "I took the Bar," he says, "but never practised. I guess law was just too focussed for me. I didn't enjoy spending all those hours in the library researching and researching. It was an excellent education though; and I think it's helped in my business."

Perhaps it was the law school discipline — or the 3.5 from Stanford — that helped Copley's confidence blossom. His close friend, Jonathan Brenner, who studied with Copley for the bar examination, paints his friend as a serious late bloomer. "I didn't go to law school with him," says Brenner, "but I heard he was a maniacal studier." For months, Brenner and Copley rode their bicycles from their homes to

Scripps Institute, near the water's edge, to find a quiet place to study.

Even though Copley took some time to turn serious, to gain a sense of direction, he suspects his creative bent has always been there. Inherent, too, seems his willingness to take risks, to shun the "gold watch" mindset. "I just don't need that nine-to-five routine, that twenty-year security at all," he says. "I'm not interested in a corporate ladder." From childhood, he adds, he has "always felt like an individual. Like I always wanted to do my own thing."

Those close to him concur that Copley definitely marches to the beat of a different drummer, but they also describe him as loyal, unpretentious, tenacious and fast-paced.

For Copley, the race to success itself seems to be a bigger reward than crossing the finish line. "I'm not generally the type of person who stops and pats himself on the back," he says. "The fact of getting there is the reward. Once I get there, sometimes I don't know quite what to do."

His publicist notes in one press release that Copley shies away from attention. At one Hollywood reception to kick off his action alarm clock, those attending couldn't wait to get a look at the mysterious inventor, but he was hard to find. It's not Copley's style to bask in the limelight.

The best rewards of his business success, to him, are rewards that others might consider minimal or even corny. Examples: "Walking down the street in New York City and seeing the product in a small store window for the first time — that felt good." Another day, he was sitting on an airplane and heard someone behind him talk about OFF-THE-WALL and how they'd like to meet the guy who invented it and how neat the products are. True to form, Copley didn't bother to stand up and take credit. Rather, he listened and smiled to himself.

His office manager, Cathy Schroeder, has worked for him

for over two years and respects him as a boss. "He demands initiative and results, but he is both understanding and supportive. It's easy for me to work for him because I have a similar drive to do the best job," admits Schroeder, a new mother who took very little maternity leave before resuming her forty-five-hour weeks. She explains, "In this fast-paced business you can miss a whole year in one day's work."

Besides admiring Copley's perseverance, Brenner marvels at his friend's ability to take an idea and see it through to marketing. "Most people get stuck in the idea phase," he says. "They think of innovations and never follow through. Michael's quite a guy. Growing up around wealth usually changes a person, yet he's the most unpretentious person I know. He lives modestly. He drives a VW bug." (Copley admits he also has a beautifully restored 1971 Mercedes 280 SE 3.5 convertible hidden in a nearby garage.)

James W. Badie, a New York attorney who has worked for Copley, calls him "a very honest person and very fair with everyone." Badie says he developed an instant rapport with Michael. "He is driven, to the point where he *has* to be successful in creating and promoting products that will be popular items," says Badie.

Driven he may be, but Copley insists he tries not to be a workaholic. When he started his company, he admits, he worked twelve-to-fourteen hour days. He has learned, since then, that balance is the key both to business success and personal happiness. He surfs when he can. He doesn't drink or smoke, preferring to keep his mind clear for business decisions. He exercises regularly and watches his diet, but isn't a health food fanatic. A McDonald's hamburger now and then won't hurt, he reasons. Divorced, Copley also dedicates time to be with his two boys, eight-year-old Michael and five-year-old Christopher, who live nearby with their mother. His fiancee, Elizabeth Cairncross, is a big part of his life. "She helps me remember there must be time to enjoy life, instead of just work, work, work."

He sometimes depends on the kids for feedback. He may give them a new product to play with and just observe their reaction or may ask for more formal feedback. "Usually I just let them play with it and see what they think," he says. "They love the alarm clock, although they play with it more than they use it to tell time."

Although Copley would definitely fit a doctor's definition of a fast-paced, Type A personality, he says he doesn't have to be busy every minute to be happy. On his frequent plane trips to Hong Kong, for instance, he might catch up with paperwork, but he might also just sit back and enjoy the peace and quiet. "Some of my most relaxing times are on the plane to Hong Kong," he says, "because for fifteen hours, no one can reach me by fax, phone or letter."

"Vacations are a rare part of my life," he admits. He tries to squeeze in some days off, pleasure trips, and enjoyable weekends whenever possible. Reading is another leisure passion for Copley, who prefers mysteries and espionage tales and counts Robert Ludlum and John D. MacDonald as his favorite authors.

The biggest business stress he faces now, Copley believes, is the necessity of constantly coming up with new ideas. He knows that in the novelty business you are only as good as your last big seller. And fear of recession is a real one to novelty manufacturers, who know their products will be among the first to suffer. But Copley has found a way to temper the pressure. He obtains ideas from observing society, he says, and from letters and phone calls. "Two guys had an idea for making the food watches," he says, "but not the money to manufacture and market them; so they called me, and we developed a joint venture. One of them, Joe Robinson is now my sales manager." Some products, like the grenade and sports watches, are what Copley calls "logical follow-ups."

Experts in the gift and novelty industry say that Copley's OFF-THE-WALL idea started a whole generation of similar novelty ideas. For example, sports ball banks, sports ball gym-locker locks, stress balls that when thrown sound like breaking glass, "Freud" balls that when shaken scream. Does Copley take this as a compliment? "Yes, in one way I do, but many of these products are using the deceleration switch I designed. I have to admit these other ideas are great spin-offs. I wish I had thought of them."

These days, Copley is busy formulating a business plan that will help him decide the best direction for his company. "I am expanding my company," he says. "Not everyone would agree that's the smartest move. Some say if you get a hot idea, sell it for the best price and get out. Then start over. But right now my goal is to build upon a solid reputation that is well-known in the industry. And at that point I may be ready to sell it."

Does he see his company going public, perhaps with a spot on the New York Stock Exchange some day? "I don't think so," he says. "I have to be realistic."

The future offers many opportunities for Michael Copley. He has always wanted to be in movies. He has had an offer to do a TV show on entrepreneurship, but he lacks the time right now. He has also been approached to syndicate a column for inventors.

Currently he is attempting to obtain the movie rights to one of his favorite novels. "I'd like to produce and perhaps star in a movie of this literary character. I know it seems impossible, but so did OFF-THE-WALL several years ago," he says.

The last few years haven't merely instilled confidence in Copley; they have taught him that goals don't always become reality as quickly as one hopes. "My goal when I developed OFF-THE-WALL was to come out with a great product and to make a lot of money, and I learned that it's not so easy. Coming out with a product for the first time is a learning experience. You make a lot of mistakes."

But in the process, Copley also learned the true definition of an entrepreneur. "Being an entrepreneur," he says, with the voice of authority, "is like being a salmon swimming upstream; you can't stop swimming for one second, because if you do, you're all washed up."

Luckily for Copley, he's a strong swimmer.

Ralph Mann
Glen Ivy Financial Group, Inc.

-5-

GLEN IVY FINANCIAL GROUP, INC.

Timeshare ain't what it used to be. The industry's old image of fly-by-night operators is being replaced by a new mantle of respectability, to such an extent that prestigious names like Marriott and Hilton are now happy to be linked with it, and even squeaky-clean Disney is testing the timeshare waters.

One of the men given credit for the double finesse of cleaning up timeshare's tarnished reputation in financial circles while at the same time raising the industry's credibility in the public's esteem, is Ralph Mann. He is president and CEO of the Corona-based Glen Ivy Financial Group in California, the man who created a timeshare empire by developing a $325,000 investment in an RV park in 1975 into a behemoth corporation that saw $90 million worth of business in fiscal 1989. But business shrewdness was only part of it; you can't re-establish an industry's credibility with a strong fiscal performance alone. In an industry notoriously devoid of integrity in its early years, it was Ralph Mann's concern for doing the right thing that paid off in spades.

It is hard to believe, therefore, that the man dubbed by one colleague as "the consummate boy scout - trustworthy, loyal, honest" is the same man who arrived in California in 1971 leaving a trail of hard drinking and hard playing not far

behind him. If any man was ready for an epiphany, Ralph
Mann was he.

A six-foot three, 210-pound bear of a man with arms like
Popeye's and fists like hams, when Ralph Mann tells you he
was the best bricklayer in Milwaukee, Wisconsin, you believe
him. What you don't expect is the modesty with which he
recounts his subsequent achievements. "We", not "I", is the
word he favors most; he knots and unknots his massive
fingers self-consciously as he discusses his emotional
catharsis; he dismisses his genius for business as simply an
instinct, a gift.

"I owe a lot of my success to my belief that, in order to be
successful, I must surround myself with talented people," he
says. "It's this entire group of talent that has led us to the
success we have had."

Long-time associate, corporate attorney Maurice Hart,
shakes his head at such modesty. "He is probably as close
to a business genius as you can get," he says. "Without any
formal training, he can look at a balance sheet and a
profit-and-loss statement and analyze them faster than any
financial analyst I've ever seen."

Many successful men chart their climb to the top in terms
of seizing opportunities, applying street-savvy, out-thinking
the opposition, taking risks. Ralph Mann likes to add one
more of his own — learning tough business lessons in what
he refers to as the School of Hard Knocks. And for him,
some of the hardest lessons of all came early in life.

The eldest of ten children, Mann began working for his
father's small construction business at the age of ten, picking
up sticks and two-by-fours at building sites after school and
during summer vacation. By the time he was twelve, he was
paying twenty dollars a week for room and board to help
bring money into the family. Because it was illegal to join a
union before the age of sixteen, his co-workers kept an eye

out for inspectors so he could hide until they were gone.

He was already a strapping six-footer at the age of fourteen, and, egged on by a father who expected him to work harder than the other employees, he took up bricklaying. By the age of sixteen, while still in high school, he became a labor foreman, supervising workers much older than himself. How did a mere kid earn their respect? "Know your job, work hard, treat people fairly," says Mann. "In construction in particular it's important that you know what you're talking about. People will follow if you lead well." He laughs, adding, "My size didn't hurt, either."

Young Ralph Mann knew very early that construction was going to be his life...but that laying bricks wasn't. He wanted to establish himself in the business side of construction, and that took money. So he squirrelled away his hefty bricklayer's wages, worked extra jobs on the weekends, and lived meagrely until, at sixteen, he had saved enough money to buy a select plot of land on which he planned to build a house and then sell it for a profit. He paid the $1,500 in cash to avoid any complications in going through the loan process as a minor.

By the time he was ready to graduate from high school, he had managed to save the $7,000 he needed to build his house. But his father's business had begun to founder, and Ralph Mann, Sr. came to his son to borrow the money to help shore up the business. The day before Ralph was to graduate, the business went bankrupt and the $7,000 was lost.

"My Dad gave me the greatest lesson he could have ever given me," says Ralph Mann. "You have to be a dreamer to take the risk and gamble of starting a business. If you were realistic, you would probably never start a business anyway, but you should always fully understand the downside risk. That day taught me what risk is all about."

Ralph Mann also learned a lot about his own talent for business. With his family facing the spectre of losing their home, young Ralph took it upon himself to cobble together a settlement to offer the finance company. "I set up a situation where the few assets my Dad had left would be protected, and I went in and bluffed this hot-shot guy," he remembers. "I was seventeen at the time. And I bluffed him and won." To this day, Mann has no idea how the ability to do this came to him. "All the ideas I get just pop into my head. I don't know where they come from. It's a gift."

Today, a mellower and wiser Ralph Mann can look back on the incident with indulgent hindsight, but at the time it tore his life apart. He harbored great bitterness toward his father, and even though he believes now that his father had every intention of repaying the loan at the time, Ralph Mann was unable to bring himself to speak about this for the next fifteen years. The loss gnawed at him; within six months he had dropped from 205 pounds to 165 pounds. He threw himself into his work, working around the clock, barely stopping to eat.

According to Mann, the gruelling work set his mind free to contemplate his future. Because commercial construction required too much start-up capital, he decided he would have a better chance for success if he went into residential construction. He had no experience in that field, however, so at nineteen he took a severe cut in pay in order to join a residential construction company as an assistant expeditor, the equivalent of a construction co-ordinator.

Within two weeks he was promoted to the position of expeditor when his supervisor quit. The fact that his boss did not raise his salary with the promotion, and in fact never increased his salary over the two years he worked for him, has stayed with Ralph Mann for thirty years. "Again, it was a good lesson for me," he says. "You need to recognize good people and give them raises without their having to ask. If a man is good at his job and really puts out, he expects to be recognized for it."

No one could accuse Ralph Mann of not putting out. He worked from five in the morning till nine or ten at night. Young, aggressive, and with a real knack for the job, within a year he was virtually running the whole business. He endured the low pay and long hours until he felt he had learned enough about the business to move on. His employer offered him half the business to stay, but, although Ralph Mann says he was tempted, he stuck to his plan. He wanted to be his own boss.

Living and working out of the house he had managed to build for himself on weekends, he went into overdrive. Funded by a modest $10,000 loan from his widowed grandmother, he purchased a second lot and began to build a model home, from which he hoped to sell future homes. In order to support himself, he took an additional job supervising the construction of an apartment complex, and by the end of that year, 1961, he had twenty houses under construction, was working full-time, and was also tending a brand new marriage.

Ralph Mann laughs. "When you're young, you can go twenty hours a day. Even so, I would sometimes just go into one of the rooms that was under construction and sleep for an hour during the day." His efforts paid off. His fledgling company, Crestline Homes, saw $100,000 in profits that first year. The figure doubled the next year.

"I wanted a competitive edge," he explains, "and my competitive edge was my design capability. I wanted to beat my competition by giving the most house for the dollar." His unorthodox design ideas met with strong resistance, and it took considerable coaxing to convince his draughtsmen and his architects to give them a try. His triumph was sweet; not only did his houses sell like the proverbial hotcakes, but he won a series of design awards from the Homebuilders' Association. Most satisfying of all, perhaps, was that his ideas were adopted by many of the naysayers of the time, his competitors.

"Yet I never had an original idea in my life," he grins. "I would spend Sundays driving around, studying what my competition was doing, sketching ideas on a scrap of paper. Sometimes I would take ideas from five different houses and incorporate them into one. Other times I would just take an existing idea and improve on it a little. Like adding an extra door to make a bathroom accessible from the bedroom and the hallway, thus eliminating one bathroom while still getting dual usage."

That innovation was a first in Milwaukee. So was his idea of replacing stone fireplaces with metal ones. "They still had stone fronts," he points out, "so although the fireplaces looked the same, we saved $1,200 on the cost of the house. I knew what people wanted in a house was what they could see, so I would cut corners in the things they couldn't see — and I'd still build a good house. It was important to me to be able to get a competitive edge, make a profit, and still come up with a good product."

His "good houses" give Ralph Mann enormous satisfaction, even twenty-five years later. "It's a ritual for me, when I go back to Milwaukee, to drive around and look at my houses. I am always proud of how good they still look, some even look better." Today, many of the areas he selected for low-priced housing back in the early sixties have grown into high-income neighborhoods and his houses have proved to have been excellent investments for the original buyers.

The year his company did $10 million worth of business, 1965, was also the year Ralph Mann made his first million, and he was ready for a change. With a friend, a plumbing contractor named Ron Schroeder, he formed a partnership for the purpose of building rental apartments as a security investment. "I liked the idea of security," he says, noting how his father's business failure always haunted him. "I wanted something to fall back on. I would take enormous risks throughout my life, but I always made sure I had a fallback. I never wanted to go to zero the way my Dad did, because if you're at zero you'll never have the capital you need to make money, and you're not going to get it from anyone else, either."

Suddenly, with the business doing well, Ralph Mann found he didn't need to keep up the feverish pace he was accustomed to. By seven o'clock at night he would find himself with nothing to do...and yet not quite ready to go home. He admits that his marriage had hit a rocky patch. He began to spend his evenings out on the town, drinking with the guys. "I was sowing my wild oats late in life," he says. "I was living the childhood I never had." He enjoyed his money and spent it freely.

Even a young son, Mark, could not stop Ralph Mann from straining against the bonds of his life. By 1971 he had had enough. He sold his business to three senior employees for a cool $1.5 million; he and Schroeder liquidated their apartment holdings for another $20 million, and with every intention of retiring young and enjoying his $10 million personal wealth, he took off for Atlanta, Georgia.

Ralph Mann leans back and laughs heartily at the naivete of his plans. "I was tired and wrung out from a lot of hard work and a lot of hard play over the years, and I thought I wanted to retire. I thought I knew myself, but I didn't," he says. The man who was weaned on twenty-four hour workdays could not deal with the long, empty days in Atlanta. He began drinking heavily and would have continued to do so had he not received a call several months later from his old friend, Ron Schroeder, who was in Las Vegas getting a divorce.

"I've got an opportunity to build some condos out in Palm Springs," Schroeder told him. "Why don't you come out and take a look?" Mann didn't need to be asked twice, and his plans for an early retirement were quickly shelved. "That whole episode was a good lesson for me," he says. "I'd never be tempted to do the same thing again."

Although Mann finally decided to turn down the condo project, feeling that it was located in the wrong area of Palm Springs, he did fall in love with California, and by September he had moved to Los Angeles, where he and Schroeder bought fifty percent of a struggling advertising-specialty business. "It was interesting, it was totally different, it was a good business to learn," says Mann, adding, "I especially learned that I didn't like it." He would eventually sell his share of the business to Ron Schroeder, but in the meantime Schroeder and Mann bought out the original partners and the business prospered.

While he was living in Los Angeles, Ralph Mann travelled back to Wisconsin regularly to visit his son, whom he missed deeply. He decided at last to patch up his difficulties with his wife and bring his family to California. He bought a beautiful home in the elegant gated community of Canyon Lake, mid-way between Los Angeles and Palm Springs, and his family arrived on the fourth of July 1972. Barely three months later, Ralph Mann would receive the news that would turn his life around—six-year-old Mark was dying of leukemia.

Mann was devastated. Although he continued to go to work, he has no recollection of doing so. The business continued to prosper, but for Ralph Mann Mark came first and business second. "For the first time in my life, work was not important," he says quietly. "Life with my family was all-important."

For the next six years Mark was treated at the City of Hope, the renowned Los Angeles cancer-research center. Mann credits that facility with helping him learn to deal with his son's illness. "As a parent you feel so helpless," he explains. "At the City of Hope they let you become involved, so you feel you are really doing something." Thanks to their dual microscopes, he became a "blood expert", learning to identify platelets and polymorphs, and distinguishing the healthy blood cells from the leukemia cells. During Mark's hospital stays, Mann stayed at the special hotel provided for parents right on the hospital grounds.

Once a month, Mark had to submit to a painful spinal tap. Although it was the nurse's job to hold him in position, Ralph Mann took over the job himself. The day after the ordeal would always bring a special reward for Mark — usually a trip to Disneyland. "I've probably been to Disneyland one hundred times," muses Mann.

Three years after Mark's diagnosis, the Mann's second son, Brian, began to show alarmingly familiar symptoms. Against astronomical odds, Mark's brother had also developed leukemia. The blow broke Mann's spirit. "The day after I took them for their treatments I would get so drunk that I would have to be driven home. I never realized at the time I was doing this intentionally, but looking back I now understand it was the only way I had of releasing the emotions inside. It was a defense mechanism against breaking down completely."

Mann also admits he was not always the perfect husband during this time. He eventually divorced his wife and married his second wife, whom he would later divorce as well. Throughout these upheavals, his sons were the sole focus of his life.

As Mark's condition worsened, Ralph Mann became

increasingly desperate for a miracle, and he flew his son to Houston for Interferon treatment. But Mark continued to weaken, and it was clear that he was dying. "Emotionally, he was my whole life," says Mann. "I felt that when he died I wouldn't have anything to live for."

Mann brought his son home, and watched helplessly as the boy was administered morphine every two hours to ease the severity of his pain. He describes Mark's last hours. "I knew it wasn't going to be long so I said, 'Let's hold hands and pray.' Then suddenly Mark said, 'Dad, the pain's going away!' For the last ten hours that he lived he didn't need any morphine. He became happy, joyous. Suddenly, I knew there was a heaven, and that there was life after death."

Ralph Mann becomes pensive. "I had been raised a Catholic, but I had grown completely away from the church. But that night was the single biggest joy of my life. I missed Mark terribly, but now I knew there was a reason for living. That night changed me dramatically as a person, and it changed me for the better."

The final step in Ralph Mann's personal odyssey came in 1982, when he married his present wife, Eva, shortly after Brian died at the age of six. He credits Eva, a former model, with being the person who really put his life together. "I don't run around anymore," he says, "and I very rarely have a drink." Although he doesn't wear his religion on his sleeve, he considers himself a deeply spiritual man, and today his wife and three young daughters, and twenty-three-year-old son from a previous marriage, are the focus of his life.

Like a personal metaphor, the growth of Ralph Mann's timeshare empire paralleled his decade of self-discovery. After three years of commuting to Los Angeles, he decided he wanted his work base to be closer to his family, so he sold his share of the advertising business to Ron Schroeder in 1975 and purchased the Glen Ivy RV Park, named for the famous natural hot springs nearby. In a pattern he would later repeat with almost every property he acquired, Ralph Man closed the deal at a bargain $325,000. When he eventually timeshared it (one of the few times an RV park has ever been fully deeded), it sold off for $5 million.

In the meanwhile, however, he set about upgrading and expanding the park's facilities. He enjoyed going back to his construction roots, and in the face of his sons' illnesses he found tremendous therapy in doing much of the work himself. By 1978 he had built up rental revenues from $50,000 per year to $500,000 per year. For Ralph Mann, however, the numbers just didn't add up. "It was not making money for return on investment," he says simply. He had an appraisal done with every intention of selling the property. The appraiser, however, had a suggestion.

"Instead of selling it," he told Mann, "why don't you turn it into a timeshare?" Mann had never heard the term before, and on the appraiser's recommendation he flew to Sacramento to talk over the idea with industry consultants Jim Vellema and Ken Gromacki, who had converted an RV park on California's central coast to timeshare.

He liked what he heard, and he threw himself into learning about the business, attending timeshare conventions, crunching numbers. Pre-paying for the right to use the campground for the rest of their lives struck Mann as a good product for the consumer, and in spite of high sales and marketing costs it had potential for generating a healthy profit margin.

The RV park sold off quickly. The first 700 ownerships were snapped up within five months by the park's longtime regular clientele; by 1979, all 1,575 available ownerships were gone, and Mann was sitting on $5 million.

"Even then I didn't really know the business," says Mann. "I thought I could sell the ownerships and that would be it."

Instead, he financed the receivables himself and the Glen Ivy
RV Park became the Glen Ivy Financial Group. "I realized
then we were really a finance company," he says. "Even
today our major asset is our receivables."

With the 1979 gas shortage seriously inhibiting RV sales,
it became clear that the RV timeshare business would be a
limited one, so Ralph Mann turned his attention to
hotel-condominium timeshare and bought a small motel in
the heart of Palm Springs. He remodelled the twenty units,
installed modern kitchens, and in August of 1981 — when
temperatures in Palm Springs soar past the 100° F mark —
he opened The Villas for sale.

"Only Ralph Mann would try to get people to come to
Palm Springs in August to buy a timeshare!" laughs attorney
Maurice Hart. "But he did it. They sold out. But from that
experience he developed the concept of off-site selling,
which is what *really* revolutionized the business."

"We certainly had to work harder to get them there in the
summer," concedes Mann, "But we also recognized that if
they lived in Southern California they would probably be
driving down in an air-conditioned car. We reasoned that if
we had them in a nice setting alongside a pool and a golf
course and got them into a nice air-conditioned room, they
would not object to the heat so much.

"The big lesson we learned was that we couldn't leave our
marketing to outside companies, that we had to bring
everything in-house and do it ourselves. They were selling
wrong, selling in order to get a sale, not selling the product.
Sure, there's tricks you can use to get people to buy, but the
problem is if they aren't happy with their purchase they
don't continue to make their payments." Indeed, Glen Ivy's
customer-rescission rate has consistently been one of the
lowest in the industry, while the percentage of owners who
complete purchase agreements is one of the highest.

In 1984 Ralph Mann and Bob Radez, his senior vice-president in charge of sales and marketing, re-wrote the book on timeshare marketing when they introduced the concept of off-site selling for their Park Plaza timeshare in Park City, Utah. "You can't sell people when they are on vacation as easily as you can sell them when they are at home," Mann explains. "When they are on vacation they are busy vacationing — they don't want to sit down to a presentation." A skier himself, Mann knew that this was particularly true in ski areas, where few people would be inclined to attend a sales presentation at the end of a hard day of skiing.

The concept of off-site selling was not new, but it had never worked before with any measure of success. Ralph Mann knew why. "The facilities they were using were all wrong for what was being sold," he notes. "They would invariably bring people into a small office and show them pictures, perhaps even a film. I felt that if we could put in a facility that was in keeping with the feel of the resort we were selling it would work better. We created a full-size model which the people could walk through and touch and thus get a feel for the units, something no one had ever done before."

The first off-site sales center in San Diego was such a success (sales doubled immediately) that four such centers now operate under the aegis of his Glen Ivy Properties subsidiary. The latest, a 15,000-square-foot facility, opened in chic Newport Beach in February 1989. "The industry is always trying to copy what we do," he laughs, "but they don't quite get it. We are still the only ones selling successfully off-site."

The creation of Glen Ivy Properties is typical of most of the subsidiaries that make up Ralph Mann's empire, which includes Glen Ivy Resorts (for acquisition and development of resort properties), Glen Ivy Timeshare Mortgage Corporation (the issuer of financing bonds), Glen Ivy Management (resort operations, member services and reservations), Glen Ivy Construction (construction and renovation of resort properties) and Glen Ivy Travel.

Although profitability was the driving force behind Ralph Mann's business decisions, getting the job done right was what ultimately created his business legacy. He created Glen Ivy Construction because his experience in the building industry told him he was paying too much for remodelling work without getting the quality he knew owners would want. The creation of Glen Ivy Management was a similar story. "We couldn't find anyone else to manage our properties to the standards that we wanted." He shrugs. "There's a saying that if you want a job done well you have to do it yourself."

He credits the success of his business to the company's attitude to customer service. "That's true for all businesses," he says, "but you can't just *say* you care about your customer — you have to work at it. And we simply couldn't find any management company that managed the way we expected them to." Today, the company's policy is that it will only sell properties it can manage during and after sellout. Ralph Mann believes this kind of commitment to after-sales service was pivotal in separating the Glen Ivy operations from the rest of the industry.

His biggest coup in customer service was the creation of Glen Ivy Travel in 1987, which began with an enviable client base of 23,000 families. Surprisingly, no one before him had ever thought of taking advantage of the fact that these vacation owners had to make travel arrangements to get to their timeshare destinations each year. "I was thinking of ways to synergize with that enormous owner base, to come up with ways we could offer more services and make a profit at the same time."

Within its first year, the operation became the largest travel agency in the county, with a sales volume of $3.5 million. With its current owner base of 30,000 families increasing by about 600 per month, volume is expected to top $11 million in 1989. In-house reservationists can now arrange a family's entire vacation — including booking the timeshare — during one phone call. The travel agency's clout inevitably caught the eye of several airlines, who were eager to cut deals with Glen Ivy Travel and offer discounted air travel to its timeshare owners.

Ralph Mann likes to look back on that first little twenty-unit timeshare in Palm Springs. "I was looking for a destination resort, but I wanted to start small," he explains. "I strongly believe that in business you have to crawl first and then walk before you can run. You learn the business, put the pieces together, do it right. If you jump right in, you never really run the business. You may make some money over a short period, but not over the long run."

This, according to Ralph Mann, was at the heart of timeshare's bad public relations in the beginning. "First the marketing companies got into it, and they had no conception of how to run a timeshare after it was sold. Nor did they care. They were in it to make a quick buck and get out. Then the real estate developers got into it and underestimated their selling costs. They had no idea how to mass market." According to Mann, their failure was inevitable.

"But we became the experts at coming in and taking over those failed projects," he adds, "which was one of the reasons we were so successful. We became work-out specialists — almost every project we have resulted from either a developer or a lender in trouble. We were able to buy below cost and sell at a fair market price."

Financial solvency, however, is not enough to resurrect an

industry's reputation completely. Even today Mann admits that winning back the public's confidence is still timeshare's biggest challenge. Fortunately, an inevitable shakedown eliminated many of the "suede shoe" types who were responsible for the industry's earlier problems. "I don't believe there is a disreputable timeshare company left in Southern California," says Ralph Mann. "Here in California the laws protect the consumer very well, so anyone who is trying to rip off the public doesn't last long."

Even so, Ralph Mann likes to keep a close eye on his company's marketing and sales department, with its hundreds of active salespeople, to ensure nothing is being misrepresented to the public, even accidentally. "We spend a lot of time policing our own efforts," he says. During solicitation phone calls, for example, prospects are told immediately that they are being invited to a timeshare presentation, and the odds of their winning any prizes being offered are fully explained. Over ninety percent of survey exit cards from the 80,000 people who attended sales presentations in 1988 gave the company a positive rating. "There is no deception," explains Mann, who proudly points to his company's record of never having had a single consumer lawsuit.

"The man's integrity is amazing for an industry that never had any," says Maurice Hart. "Any problem is inevitably resolved immediately in the consumer's favor, no matter what. I've seen him give a television to someone who thought they were promised one for sure. He would have given it to him even if he came on the wrong day. Even if the invitation was for the guy's *neighbor* he'd still give him the television set! He just doesn't want to have anybody believe he isn't doing the right thing. Even if it ends up costing him."

In 1988 Ralph Mann capitalized on his company's reputation and solid financial position to achieve a first in the timeshare industry — a $29 million, AAA-rated bond issue, the first timeshare receivables-backed offering ever made on Wall Street. Checking off his company's "firsts" is something Ralph Mann enjoys enormously. "We were the first to push auto-drafts," he says, "where we draft the account instead of sending a bill every month. With sixty-one percent of our accounts currently on auto-draft, our receivables perform much better than those of our competitors."

With help from Peter Giummo, his senior vice-president in charge of finance, Ralph Mann was also the first to introduce the idea of 'assumptions', or assumable timeshare loans, so rather than having a loan go bad on them when an owner no longer wanted to continue with his ownership, they could simply let a new owner come in and assume it. "Somebody once compared us to Drexel Burnham Lambert, because we were the first ones to create an after-market in timeshare paper," he laughs.

What Ralph Mann doesn't reveal so readily is that all these ideas were his.

Mann's commitment to the well-being of the communities where his resorts are located has also helped boost the public image of timeshare in general. "When you go into a small community," he says, "they have the feeling that you are coming in to rape and pillage and then leave. We let them know that we are there for the long haul because we will also be managing the property, which makes us a permanent part of the community."

Ralph Mann is a fervent believer in "putting something back" into each community, and to that end the company has a policy of becoming actively involved in local charities by donating money, or donating vacations to help raise money, as well as encouraging resort employees to donate their time to worthy causes. "If you are doing well and making money from a community, then it is your obligation to share a portion of your success with that host community," he says simply. "I sincerely believe that what goes around, comes around again."

These days Ralph and Eva Mann devote themselves to charitable activities. "When Mark died, I made a promise to myself that I was going to support the City of Hope, and then little by little I got into other children's charities as well. I also made a company commitment to support charitable organizations in general." Each year, the Mann Family Foundation distributes over $200,000 to such organizations as the City of Hope, the Cystic Fibrosis Foundation and the Muscular Dystrophy Association, while the company donates close to $300,000, as well as $200,000 worth of vacations to help raise money. In addition, the money that would normally be spent on employee Christmas gifts each year is instead donated in each employee's name to a charity of his or her choice.

"There's no question," says Mann, "that helping others gives you a good feeling. In a way, Mark's death was a gift from God. I have personally been able to help so many people who have lost loved ones because I know the feeling so well. I simply feel I have an obligation to help others."

Ralph Mann takes a rare moment to lean back and contemplate his accomplishments. His timeshare empire now spans nine locations from Texas to Palm Springs and from Utah to Hawaii. Two new timeshare resorts (one on California's central coast and one on Maui) are currently under development. He looks around the room, a spacious but modestly-decorated suite in his sprawling offices in Corona. Why has he kept the headquarters of his megalithic corporation here, in this sleepy little desert town half-way between Los Angeles and Palm Springs? "We're here because I live only twenty-five minutes away," he answers.

He doesn't even own the building he works in. As Ralph Mann sees it, the rental market is so good he finds it just makes more financial sense to rent space rather than put up his own building, even with his background in construction. Although pleasant, the commercial park that houses the Glen Ivy Financial Group is a far cry from the marble-and-brass opulence favored by most captains of industry. "I don't want to build a monument to myself," he laughs. "I think profits are the greatest monuments you can have!" In fact, the only luxury he has permitted himself is a Lear 35 company jet, but only because it saves the company time — there are very few airlines that fly directly to his resorts.

By the beginning of 1989, Ralph Mann was at the top of his game. His well-oiled corporation was running smoothly, he was heaped with accolades for changing the face of timeshare, his company was the largest in the nation. And in May 1989, he sold the entire operation to Miami-based General Development Corporation, a giant land development and home-building concern, for a whopping $89 million.

At a glance, the move may seem out of character, but perhaps those who know Ralph Mann well do not see it in that light. "I wanted financial security for my family," he says simply. "I've been a risk-taker all my life. When you have a private company, you are really at risk for everything because you have to guarantee enormous amounts of money. If something happens, even if it is beyond your control..." His eyes fall on a photo of Eva with their three daughters. "My company was very successful and I wanted to get rid of some of that risk. That's all."

As part of the package, Ralph Mann will stay on as president and CEO for five years. He has not thought about what he will do beyond that. Retirement, however, is out of the question — he learned his lesson early. "I still love the

Hannes Tulving
Hannes Tulving Rare Coin Investments

-6-

HANNES TULVING RARE COIN INVESTMENTS

Most people look at coins and see only their face value. A precious few look and see a work of art, and a possible investment. Hannes Tulving, on the other hand, looks and sees long-term growth, short-term performance, net profits and buy-sell spreads.

Of course, Tulving is not looking at pocket change, but at serious coins, collectible coins. And there are many coin people who look at coins and weigh their present value against their possible future value. But Tulving's perspective is truly unique. He sees more than a simple investment in an aesthetic object; he envisions a profitable investment strategy based on many of the same tactics investors have been using successfully for years in real estate, stocks, bonds, and precious metals. Tulving was one of the first people to consistently apply established investment strategy to the rare-coin market.

Today, Hannes Tulving Rare Coin Investments stands as the leading rare-coin investment firm in the country, with sales revenue that will top $30 million in 1989..."a long way from the kid with a penny collection," he says. And he is proud to claim that no customer has ever lost money on an investment managed by his firm. "In fact, no client has made less than ten percent; our average has been over twenty percent since we started."

An early obsession with collecting things ultimately developed in Tulving an appreciation for the investment value of some of the collections cluttering his boyhood room in the family's modest suburban home east of Los Angeles. "I collected a thousand oddball things, like glass insulators, and some pretty standard things, like baseball cards," says the young entrepreneur, "more for their perceived value than for their actual value. But coins became something special."

His father and namesake, Hannes, Sr., owned and operated a service station, after emigrating from his native Estonia. On Saturdays and after school, the younger Tulving could be found sorting through the cash drawer at the station, looking for the pennies and nickels he needed to fill his collection books. "There was a childhood fascination with watching the empty slots fill with coins," he admits. "It wasn't really a conscious effort to find a particularly valuable coin; I was just into it for the fun of collecting."

While sorting through a batch of coins one Saturday, Tulving noted a rather odd quarter, like nothing he'd seen before. He shoved the coin into his pocket and at the next opportunity, he walked it down to a coin shop near his home. "The dealer offered me twenty dollars for it," he recalls. "That just amazed me, twenty dollars for a quarter I found digging through my dad's change. Well, that little event made me take another look at my hobby."

Not yet consumed by his interest but definitely piqued, young Tulving continued to pursue coin collecting, stealing quiet moments from his other developing passion, basketball. The coins provided a good balance for him, a way to satisfy his interest in numbers and figures as against the more physical pursuit of basketball. Off to college on a basketball scholarship, Tulving earned pocket money by continuing to trade in coins with local dealers.

"Laddie Rich, a local 'vest-pocket' dealer with whom I traded helped me refine my coin senses," says Tulving. "He took me under his wing, showed me what to look for and how to trade in coins. And he did one other thing for me, he loaned me my first portfolio, about $500 worth of coins. I was in the coin business."

Although coin trading had been only a hobby to this point, Tulving toyed with the idea of making it his life's pursuit. Weekends found him with a booth at a local swap meet, buying and selling collectible coins, mostly with vest-pocket dealers like himself. "I knew I'd made it when, after three months, my net profit amounted to just over twenty-five dollars for a day's work," says the affable trader, "about three bucks an hour. While it wasn't money for nothing, I felt it was easy work and I got a big charge from dealing with people. It was fun money."

After leaving college, Tulving moved from odd job to odd job, filling in the idle hours with basketball and learning the coin trade from Rich. "He introduced me to the silver dollar which was and still is, an extremely exciting side of the coin trading business," says Tulving. "I was pumping gas, and I was working as a bouncer for extra money, I was just floating around looking for some sort of career move. Coins fulfilled my passion for numbers and statistics and I became more involved with the business working with Laddie, at first to repay him the original loan and then to learn more about something I liked."

Tulving's period of experimentation as a young man showed him many sides to life, inside and outside the world of coins. "Almost from the minute Laddie began showing me silver dollars, I was really excited about coins, not so much aesthetically, as for the fun and excitement in trading them."

Under Laddie Rich's tutelage, Tulving learned quickly just

how profitable silver dollars could be. He did well, picking the coin game up quickly from his mentor. It wasn't long before Rich introduced Tulving to his long-time friend and fellow numismatist, John Love.

"John is a giant in the business, a legend, a god," says Tulving. "He's probably the most respected authority on silver dollars in the world, and a master numismatist. For whatever reason, Love took a liking to me. I graduated from Laddie's school of vest-pocket trading to John's school of international trading."

Love tutored his student carefully, recognizing in Tulving an extraordinary talent for selecting coins with investment potential. They worked together frequently, buying and selling silver dollars and other investment-grade coins through Love's coin business.

Love, an authority on silver dollars, worked with Tulving to refine his grading expertise. He showed the young dealer the nuances behind the art and science of coin grading. He nurtured Tulving's interest, curiosity, and zeal for coin trading and showed him the ropes behind the deals. He also vested Tulving with $10,000 worth of coins, "...not because he liked me so much, but because he thought he might make some money on my trading," laughs Tulving, "and he did."

He adds, reflectively, "But Love showed me more than just the trading side of coins, he led me through the business of coins. In his shadow I learned the hands-on buying and selling of coins, the true market experience of dealing with the coin community. The coin world is a relatively small clique and one with exceptionally high principles. Ethics really mean something in this business, one never sacrifices integrity for the short-term return. And Love taught me to be a straight shooter."

Even at the highest level, coin trading is often conducted on just a handshake. Multi-million dollar deals go down on verbal agreements. "To this day, a man like Love or myself can walk into a coin show, draft a check for $1 million and walk away with his purchase, no questions asked," says Tulving. "People still trust each other. They know you and know you well, based on your reputation. People who can't pass muster never crack the top because the market just won't allow it. When someone says the check's in the mail, they mean it."

Tulving was not only an eager student, he proved to be a shrewd one as well. His original "deal" with Love was repaid within months and Tulving, with some help from Love and a certain sagacity of his own, was making a decent living from coin trading. "I learned to pay attention to the details, to analyze coins the way some people analyze stocks, and I did pretty well projecting winners," says Tulving. "John Love calls it instinct, some have called it blind luck. I call it good business."

Which is just how young Tulving regarded coins and their trading—as a business. Travelling from show to show, buying and selling, Tulving started charting his trading portfolio of coins. "With John's training in grading and assessing coins and my 'instinct' for good purchases, I was consistently profiting. Sitting down and plotting my coin deals, I began to wake up to the potential in coin trading. I could see, on analysis, that coins were a proven investment vehicle. Their short-term and long-term growth, their relative safety, and their aesthetic appeal all made for an incredibly stable performance record."

In 1976 Hannes Tulving started Hannes Tulving Rare Coin Investments (HTRCI) with a small stable of investors, mostly family and friends. "My parents were my first investors." recalls Tulving, "and I felt personally responsible for their investment. And to this day I won't sell any rare coins that I wouldn't recommend to my folks." He managed his modest portfolios from his apartment in Covina, California, spending nearly half his time on the road at coin shows, looking for the rare coins to back the claims he had made to his small, initial investor group.

By the end of 1979, his third year in the coin business as a dealer, Tulving had earned himself a position among the top twenty silver-dollar experts in America. He was regularly producing a good income from his travelling and trading, and he became convinced, not unreasonably, that he could do as well for investors as he was doing for himself.

Tulving had no problem backing his claims. "The market for coins in the mid-seventies was very strong. Some of my clients earned thirty to forty percent in one year on the coins that were purchased for their portfolios. It was an exciting time to be in the coin business." Tulving's early success is summed up best, perhaps, by a striking example: "I have a client who started with me back in 1976 with a $126 initial investment; he was a school teacher and didn't have a lot of extra capital to invest. I think he initially invested with me because he wanted to help me out.

"Now his original investment is worth $6300. Later investments in similar amounts have earned him over $100,000 in the interim. Not a bad profit at all. Some of the coins he purchased have become his retirement income, coins originally worth $5 and $10 are now worth $500. Very few investments can return that kind of growth that quickly and that safely."

Tulving's client base continued to grow steadily through customer referrals. Within the year, he had opened an office, and was managing over $100,000 in rare coins for clients. "Word of mouth provided an increasing amount of business. I had an occasional enquiry at coin shows, but most of my business came from people outside the coin community."

As Tulving sharpened his buying skills and attracted new

clients, and began working on an investment-management scheme that would eventually revolutionize the rare coin business. Tulving was multiplying his wholesale coin investments with outstanding performance, consistently earning twenty percent or more annually for his clients. "The majority of my clients at that time could not afford to speculate with the money they had saved so scrupulously, many for their retirement. I worked very hard to protect that investment, and that generally helped me form my conservative approach to rare-coin investing. The formula was, and is, quite simple. I always put the security of the investment first and I stay with proven large-market-based areas of the coin market that are affordable. I avoid esoteric and expensive coins."

In 1979, Tulving moved HTRCI from the San Gabriel Valley to Newport Beach. "I figured the time was right to make my move," says Tulving, "and employ some of the strategies I had been working on and testing with my small base of home-grown clients." Tulving had been preparing a plan whereby rare-coin investors, like other types of investors, could earn a higher and more consistent profit, the plan being based on the same sort of strategies that were used successfully with other types of investments.

The strategy, at first, was simple and straightforward: to provide a safe, steady growth-investment opportunity. Tulving's expertise in the coin market put him in the unique position of being able to ferret out secure yet profitable coin investments, much as he had done for himself over the years. Business grew, and he began to see the full potential in the rare-coin market. Based on their short-term and long-term return, he felt assured of a sound service. His friends and family, that initial group of investors, also recognized the potential.

As his reputation in investment circles spread, so did his

growing image in the coin community. "If John taught me about coins and the coin business, my father taught me about work," says Tulving. "He worked hard his whole life, struggling at times to make his business grow. But he almost never complained about it. Through the hard times and the lean times, he always adapted. He got up every morning ready to tackle the day and its challenges. Not that he didn't have his share of problems and crises, but he always maintained a positive attitude.

"And he overcame many problems by simply working to solve them. Problems were challenging and he enjoyed the pressure. I think in many ways the same ethic drives me. I haven't taken a vacation in ten years - and I don't even miss it. I enjoy being here, in my business. I enjoy coming to work and meeting the challenges that investing brings. I really *like* what I do! Yes, I make money at it, but I think I do well because I enjoy what I do. The financial reward comes when money is not the central, driving force in your life but the process of earning it is. I'd probably feel the same way if it were basketball, real estate, law, or medicine."

There is much of the curious little boy left in Tulving. He gets excited by what he's doing and by the challenge of mastering the next step; yet he still marvels at the beauty of a rare-issue silver dollar, much as a child might behold a new toy in wonderment. This, he claims, is what keeps him vital. "This business is still fun. When it stops being fun, I'll probably leave it behind."

Tulving's client list blossomed in his new office in Newport Beach. While referrals continued at a steady pace, he saw a much bigger picture on the horizon. "I started advertising in magazines and newspapers, with startling results. Within a year I was getting calls from all over the country. Maintaining portfolios by doing virtually everything myself, including all the buying, became quite tedious in fact. I was also watching the coin business change."

Actually, Tulving himself was as much a reason for the changes in the rare-coin business as he was a spectator. Through the mid-seventies, that business had been largely a voyeurs' market. Traders and investors were "coin" people who participated largely because of their interest in the coins themselves. "It was a collectors' market, filled with people who collected coins for their aesthetic and intrinsic value as much as for their investment value," says Tulving. "Few collectors seriously managed a coin investment portfolio."

However, the younger collectors like Tulving altered the picture of the trader to a considerable extent. "We made it an investor's market, rather than a collectors'. In the seventies, people like my parents didn't know anything at all about coins. Now they, like my clients today, see coins as a way of realizing their financial dreams. They trust traders like me, who know something about the market, to make sound investments for them in coin portfolios that will appreciate. They don't collect coins because they're beautiful or possess some rare quality, but because they will earn them money."

Despite his reputation in the coin world as one of the world's authorities on coins, Tulving maintains he is not a coin dealer. "My firm is an investment firm. I don't go looking for ultra-rarities, one-of-a-kind coins that are very expensive and appreciate very slowly. I hunt for sound investments, coins with investment potential, with excellent track records for growth and market availability. You can't manage $125 million in coins any other way."

Tulving has also decided at this time not to collect coins himself. "It would be a direct conflict of interest," a principle simply stated, strictly adhered to.

HTRCI carefully carved a niche for itself in the market-place, dealing almost exclusively in uncirculated numismatics, usually United States coins. "There are Greek and Roman coins, for example, that are also very rare, but so is their audience. People, especially investors, want something they can feel safe with, something familiar. U.S. coins fill the bill. Our investors are able to take physical possession of their coins, and we feel it's very important for them to be as close to their investment as possible. They're like blue-chip stocks in a sense, they have resilience, even in hard times, and tremendous collector and investor appeal," he explains.

Having defined his market niche, largely by instinct, Tulving started putting together bigger and bigger coin deals. "My reputation as a straight shooter in the market helped me buy, at an excellent value, coins with great potential and then resell the coins to clients so they could take advantage of the upcoming price moves. I use my inside knowledge for the benefit of my clients, make them money, while enhancing my reputation. I've always taken the secure road, and one of my very first commitments in managing other people's investments was never to lose money."

That commitment has cost him business at times. Early in HTRCI's history, a client approached Tulving with $300,000, with the directive to buy coins, each of which must be valued at over $10,000. "No HTRCI investor has ever lost money. It's my honest commitment to them. I told the prospective client I doubted he could make money with that strategy. He walked to a competitor, who sold him what he wanted. He lost a lot of money, because he invested in the wrong coins at the wrong time. I restrict my investment activities to coins with the potential to make money, typically those specimens that cost from the tens of dollars to several hundred dollars. These are the coins that show the greatest growth potential."

As his client list grew, Tulving's ability to manage all aspects of his business diminished accordingly. "Buying coins is a physical process. You can't do it over the phone with an investor sheet in one hand and a check in the other. You need to hit the coin shows, examine and analyze the products. So at this point I hired one of the more respected buyers in the business to help me collect the portfolios on the road." Greg Roberts now attends over one hundred and fifty coin shows a year for HTRCI, bringing back the coins HTRCI wants to sell to investors.

This move, along with a few other key personnel moves, allowed Tulving to concentrate on the side of the business he maintains is his heart and soul, "My initial interest in coins was born of my interest in statistics. I grew to love numismatics as an art, but I've always measured my true interest in collectibles against my fascination for numbers and how they add up."

Keeping track of the market was fairly simple. "It's a simple market to understand, supply and demand drive it. Managing investments in the market is a good deal more complex." As his client base was growing, Tulving found the computer the key to managing his client's investments effectively, "But an ordinary spreadsheet program was not what we needed." So, with some help, he designed a computer software program that could keep track of his clients' accounts and provide an instant window on activity. "If a client has expressed an interest in maximizing his profit and liquidating a portion of his portfolio, we can instantly evaluate his position and make a recommendation."

In other situations Tulving can be just as exact in his analysis. "This kind of innovation makes otherwise laborious tasks simple and easy to perform, helping us to manage our client's investments better. We can act very quickly in their behalf."

This is just one of the dozens of innovative programs Tulving has introduced to the rare-coin market. "With the kind of help I've been able to attract to the company - some very good people - I've been free to develop my ideas on diversifying the coin investment market," explains Tulving. "Most of these ideas have been around in one form or another in other investment markets for awhile, we've just molded them to fit the numismatic market. Some are brand new."

Few have approached the business of investing in rare coins with the enthusiasm, skill, and understanding of HTRCI; fewer still offer the diversity and results that have become the hallmark of the industry. "Each investor presents a unique profile at any given time. We are in the business to service the client. Most of the time that means maximizing profit, but sometimes it can mean minimizing a tax liability. We can, and have, in the client's best interests, sold coins that have performed slowly on a percentage basis to minimize tax exposure at the client's request."

Tulving's real innovation has been the marketing of rare-coin investments. HTRCI has no sales force, maintains a limit on the number of clients it accepts, and deals only with portfolios of a minimum of $5000. "It may appear at first that we're snobbish or elitist," says Tulving, "but it's actually just the opposite. By keeping the client list small we can offer maximum service. If I don't know every investor personally, I know each and every portfolio inside and out. We're not in this business for the short-term windfall but for long-term security. We stay away from shotgun approaches and historically volatile areas. In that way we can guarantee our clients' portfolios. My intention is to be here for twenty-five, fifty, one hundred years and that kind of longevity demands performance."

HTRCI was the first firm in the industry to guarantee it would buy back on demand any coin it had ever sold, at the same grade it was purchased and at a minimum of wholesale bid. The firm has repurchased over $23 million in coins from clients in its tenure, netting them over $9 million. Total collective profits will exceed $50 million in 1989, on a total managed amount of $125 million.

HTRCI also offers the client a managed liquidation sales program that locks in a return of twelve percent above the prevailing wholesale. And any purchase made through the firm can be returned in sixty days for a full refund. "We can offer these service guarantees because we are confident our clients will be pleased with their investment results. Sure, we've had people take us up on them and we've delivered. But, more important, our guarantees provide a measure of security the investor cannot match with any other kind of tangible investment," explains Tulving.

"When was the last time you had a real estate investment firm or stock broker consistently deliver such performance? I believe this kind of stability has made coins one of the more solid investment opportunities in the marketplace."

Within the last ten years, as a result of investment firms such as Tulving, many pension funds and other group-investment vehicles have adopted rare coins as part of their investment strategies. "A lot of this has made numismatics a legitimate investment which has attracted a lot of interest in coin investing from outside the small community of coin people. Most of my clients don't know rare coins, but they do know good investment potential." Indeed, many leading investment advisors, newsletters, and others recommend that a percentage of a total portfolio be kept in coins. "It adds a dimension of diversity and performance other types of investments can't," says Tulving.

Interest in rare coins from outside the coin community has stimulated Tulving's creative instincts. "Clients were looking for vehicles for their investments that met certain ends, like income-producing portfolios, retirement-savings vehicles, college funds and other 'dream' securities," Tulving explains, "and some wanted to leverage their acquisitions against future purchases. We worked to provide as many vehicles as we could to cater to investor needs."

The staff, now over thirty strong, including his brother Alan and several other key administrative and management personnel, went to work designing the various programs investors could use to enter or expand their rare coin investments. "Basically, it was a matter of finding my clients' comfort zones, defining them, and catering to their needs. All of HTRCI's programs have been developed in answer to consumer demand. We can even convert existing holdings, like bullion and certain coin portfolios we don't recommend, into better, safer, more profitable holdings."

Short-term portfolios, called Limited Term Portfolio Accounts, systematic income accounts and other custom-designed programs are all HTRCI innovations that have reshaped the industry. A well known investment counsellor claimed that Tulving was the Thomas Edison of numismatics. "No other individual" he wrote, "has had such a profound impact on the rare-coin investment market as Tulving has had. He's a rare individual in a rare market place."

Unassuming and modest about his accomplishments, Tulving claims he's been "lucky." The big man likens his approach in business to sports, "Half the game is knowing the rules and the game plan, the other half is reaction, gut instinct. What happened yesterday isn't important, it's what you'll do today and tomorrow that counts. Yesterday's record is only as good as your next game."

Despite Tulving's intense and focussed approach to numismatics, he still finds time for an occasional game of basketball, and he contributes both his time and his money to several philanthropic organizations. "I have to admit, though, I do love this business. It continually challenges me. HTRCI will never be the largest but it will always be the most competitive."

Tulving's competitive nature has lured him into investing in other markets. "Horse-racing," he laughs. "I've been in the horse-racing business since 1984 with my friend and mentor John Love. John has spent twenty years in the business and has applied himself to horses as he has to coins. We employ great trainers and spend an enormous amount of time in research. And we make money every year. Nothing is fun if you lose: whether it's profiting for ourselves or earning excellent returns for our clients, winning is everything. I hate to lose."

The horse-racing keeps him sharp. It has proven to be productive. His horse-racing experience has inspired a translation to the coin business. This year he has started a speculative rare-coin fund. "It is a limited partnership," he divulges, "with me as the general managing partner. This fund is speculative by nature, but allows me to expand my scope by buying and selling non-conservative coins to clients. There's slightly more risk, with more potential gain. The fund is unique - no legal fees, no management fees, no transaction fees are charged to the limited partners, and total cash-out in a maximum of two years.

"The first twenty-four percent annual profit goes directly to the limited partners. All profits over the twenty-four percent are split fifty/fifty with the partners. Obviously, I feel I can return substantially more than the twenty-four percent annualized profit. That is the only way that I, as the general partner, can recoup my expenses and make some money. I didn't do this to work for free. This private placement was sent to our best clients and sold out in less than two weeks! We raised over $2.4 million.

"This is a totally *new* approach to investing, but one I can now see has tremendous potential.

"It worked in horse-racing," he beams, "with a few modifications, it will work for coins."

Twyla Martin and Sandra Kravitz
San Martin International Bridals

-7-

SAN MARTIN INTERNATIONAL BRIDALS

The bejewelled bride poses on the finely-manicured lawns of the elegant Beverly Hills Hotel. The cathedral train of the deeply embroidered, shimmering white gown is arranged in a perfect semi-circle, revealing the intricate hand-made lace. The photographer coaxes a delicate smile from his celebrity subject and... click!

Cut...to a quiet, nondescript street lined with a hodge-podge of dull industrial buildings in the vastness of Los Angeles. Behind one of a series of chain-link fences is a small glass door covered with an iron grill. An irritating buzz lets the visitor into the cramped reception area, graced only by a chair and a lone tree struggling bravely for light.

Welcome to the working worlds of San Martin International Bridals, one of the largest manufacturers of wedding dresses in the United States. Revenues have doubled each year since the firm's inception five years ago, and 1989 appears to be right on track for another double-header.

The young company was propelled to the front line of the $2 billion bridal business through the sheer energies and talents of its two founders and co-owners, Twyla Martin and Sandy Kravitz. Their initial decision to break with the industry's traditional marketing and manufacturing practices was the key to San Martin's almost overnight success in a trade steeped in tradition.

Both women were already entrenched in the bridal business when they met for an introductory lunch in New York in the spring of 1984. Sandy had just left an executive post with a leading bridal manufacturer in Philadelphia, and Twyla was busily staging bonanza bridal shows in Southern California.

"I was looking for a business to go into, and I was considering doing bridal shows. There was nothing like that on the east coast at the time," recalls Sandy. "Twyla happened to be in New York, and a mutual contact at *Modern Bride* magazine suggested we get together while she was there."

Twyla, on the other hand, was somewhat reluctant about the hastily-arranged rendezvous. "I had dealt previously with Sandy over the telephone when I tried to get the company she was working for to give away dresses at my bridal shows. She hadn't been too enthusiastic. Honestly, if there had been anything else to do when she called I wouldn't have met her for lunch. But my husband was going to be busy that whole day, so I thought why not?"

The luncheon, which began as a polite encounter to chat about business, soon developed into a serious discussion about the possibility of the pair working together. Over two bottles of wine, Twyla convinced Sandy that the bridal-show business was a lot of hard work for relatively little reward.

"Besides, I had this other plan, a merchandising plan that I had always wanted to do," says Twyla. "The idea was to go to the bridal-gown manufacturers and get them to give us certain dresses on an exclusive basis. We would charge the manufacturers a fee to market their gowns, and also collect a fee from the retailers selling the dresses because we were including their store name in the advertisements."

The plan meshed well with Sandy's background, and

would not require her to relocate; she could sell by phone from her home in Philadelphia, and Twyla could do the same from Los Angeles. By the end of the meal, the two had agreed to go into the merchandising business. Or had they?

"Well, quite frankly after I left New York I didn't know if I'd ever see her again," Twyla says. "We'd had a nice lunch and we had talked, but who knew if anything would happen? But Sandy was very aggressive. She called me two days later and said, 'I've thought of a name for our company — San Martin.' I loved it." The name ingeniously combines part of Sandy's first name with Twyla's last name.

Within two weeks of that serendipitous lunch, three manufacturers had signed contracts empowering San Martin to market their dresses exclusively.

With the business now firmly in hand, the first priority was to develop advertisements that would sizzle off the page and sell the merchandise. Brides-to-be scan the bridal magazines looking for dresses, and when they are ready they go to the bridal stores and ask to try on the gowns they've seen in the advertisements.

The bridal stores generally carry samples of several different dresses. When a bride selects a gown, she doesn't take home the store sample but orders a custom-tailored dress to fit her particular measurements. The store, in turn, then places the order directly with the manufacturer, which is the reason wedding gowns usually are ordered several months ahead of the wedding date.

Twyla and Sandy knew well that the focal point of any marketing campaign in the bridal business was the advertising — the luxurious, four-color, picture-perfect ads that grace the pages of the various bridal magazines. And this is where the pair's ingenuity and intuition came into play.

"We began using starlets and celebrities to model our gowns. This was simply not done at that time in the industry," Sandy recalls. "Everybody tried to dissuade us from using celebrities. They'd say, 'It won't work. It looks bad. Models are better...' Well, it did work. The ads were very successful."

Unfortunately, however, the manufacturers didn't hold to their end of the bargain. "Even though we had contracts signed by every manufacturer that they would not sell their dresses to anyone else, and even though we followed these up by phone, none of them kept their word. They sold to everybody!" Twyla states.

After two seasons the duo had lost their credibility with the stores. "The owners were refusing to pay us because the dresses weren't exclusive, and we had no control over the manufacturers. That's when we first started talking about manufacturing the dresses ourselves," says Sandy.

Setting up a manufacturing facility in the United States was totally out of the question. The women simply didn't have the financial wherewithal to purchase heavy machinery, bulk fabric and laces, let alone pay salaries for staff or commit funds to a major building lease.

"But I had heard that manufacturing might be possible in the Orient, so I suggested we each put up some money and take an exploratory trip," recalls Sandy. Both women were ready to gamble $5,000 apiece to see what was there. "The bridal industry is a very controlled one. After all, you're not selling sweat shirts. Your dresses have to arrive when you say they will arrive. They are all individually ordered, and they all have due dates," Sandy explains.

The pair arrived in Taiwan with little more than a few bridal-gown sketches worked up by Sandy during the flight over. Through sheer perseverance they unearthed two factories that claimed they could make wedding gowns to Sandy's specifications, and with nothing to lose Sandy and Twyla placed an order for several sample dresses.

Sandy's sketches reflected the metamorphosis she had observed in the bridal industry. "The taste of girls was changing," she says. "The average bride had become older, more independent. She had a better body because she went to the gym and worked out. She wanted to look sexy, not like a vestal virgin. My sketches were glamorous, designed to make the bride look good."

"But the factories were very primitive, with people cutting while squatting on the floor. I really wondered if we would ever get the dresses," admits Twyla. She and Sandy flew back to the United States and waited... they needn't have worried. The samples arrived on time in February 1985, and were shipped to the stores by the third week in March.

Now that they had the dresses, the rush was on to prepare an ad for the bridal magazines. "We went with quality all the way," stresses Sandy. Top-fashion photographer Harry Langdon was hired, along with the best hair and make-up artists, and, of course, a celebrity was used to model the gowns.

"You know, a lot of companies can create dresses, but there aren't too many that can create excitement. With our celebrity models we bring excitement to the store owners and the brides," Twyla says.

However, allocating top dollars for the production of the ad left bottom dollars to buy the advertising space. As a consequence, the decision was made to run pictures of three different dresses on a single-page ad. "Back then it was unheard of to put more than one or two pictures on a page of advertising, yet we built a multi-million dollar business on three pictures to a page!" laughs Sandy.

From the outset, San Martin's target audience was middle America. "We hit middle America with our $400 to $700 dresses, not the chosen few who can afford to spend $2,000 or $3,000 on a dress they will wear once," says Twyla. The average price of a wedding gown at that time in the United States was $600.

The response from middle America was electrifying. The orders poured in, with no let-up in sight. And the rush was on again — this time to secure financing to pay for the dresses they would ship to the stores.

"At first we were really excited. We prepared a detailed, five-year business plan with figures and projections, and we went to ten different banks and showed them our orders. They all said no," Twyla recalls with disgust. "Even the SBA turned us down."

When a friend connected them with yet another lender — Santa Monica Bank — the frustrated partners took along to the meeting every sample dress they had. "We brought twenty-five dresses, and pulled them out one at a time," says Twyla. The overwhelming enthusiasm of the women employees for the dresses in the impromptu fashion show impressed Mike Walling, the bank's vice-president. "We were told we'd get a decision within a week," says Twyla.

The decision, when it came, was positive and in June of 1985 San Martin was given its first credit line of $200,000, exactly the line it maintained until the fall of 1988. How did they increase sales to $15 million on a $200,000 credit line?

"We worked hand in hand with our overseas manufacturers," Sandy responds. "The owners of those factories are women. They were small-time, trying to be big-time, and so were we."

The Taiwanese owners were more than mere business acquaintances. Mutual trust and strong friendships had been cemented during the summer of 1985, when Sandy lived there for two months. "I wanted to get to know them, and how they did their business," says Sandy of her extended visit.

So deep was the friendship that Twyla and Sandy became

godparents to one Taiwanese owner's child. Not surprisingly, the two factories that the partners initially selected to
manufacture their dresses still work with San Martin today.

During that first year Sandy and Twyla consistently
worked twelve hours a day, seven days a week. "We did
literally everything," says Twyla. "We packed the dresses,
sold the dresses, did the accounting, and answered the
phones." The hard work paid off. Sales for the first year
were $750,000, which was phenomenal for a start-up
operation. "We even had a profit of $47,000," Twyla adds.

Sales jumped to $4.7 million in 1986, by which time there
were eleven employees on board to ease the long hours. The
first 800-square-foot closetlike quarters were abandoned for
1,300-square-foot offices, which the firm again quickly
outgrew. As volume increased, the company incrementally
increased the size of the offices.

Just as they were beginning to see success, they were
courted by a major manufacturer of formal wear. "They
wanted to buy the company, and offered us million-dollar-
plus management contracts," says Twyla. While the offer
was tempting, it wasn't strong enough to persuade Sandy
and Twyla to give up the satisfaction they enjoyed in
building and owning their own company.

Contributing to the fast-paced growth of the company was
a major design coup. The manager of one of San Martin's
bridal salons asked Sandy to design the "ultimate" wedding
dress. He wanted one with everything on it — all the lace,
buttons, beads, and ruffles she could put together. Sandy
obliged, and the dress was an immediate hit. "Girls would
walk into the store and say 'I want that dress!' says Sandy.

When it came time to order the gowns from Taiwan, just
for fun Sandy decided to ask to have a couple of them made
up in pink. What she didn't realize was that in Taiwan the
standard color "pink" is not the soft, muted, pastel baby pink

you would expect to see in the United States. Rather, it's a very, very bright baby pink.

"When the bright pink dresses arrived I showed one of them to a couple of our local salesmen, and they hated the color on sight. Right then I knew it would be a success," laughs Sandy.

"Actually, the dress was breathtaking. It probably wasn't appropriate for a Beverly Hills debutante, but for the rest of America I didn't think it could miss."

Sandy was so confident it would be a hit that she urged the fashion editors at *Modern Bride* to feature the pink gown on their cover. The editors agreed with her suggestion, and for the first time in the publication's history a pink wedding gown appeared on the cover of the October/November 1987 issue of *Modern Bride*.

The public's reaction to the pink wedding gown cover? "It was the most requested dress in the market. We couldn't keep up with the orders," Twyla responds. "We were right on target. Our pink sold everywhere!"

"It set a complete new trend for the industry," Sandy adds. "A pink wedding dress became socially acceptable."

One unusual marketing concept that boosted the company's sales early on has been San Martin's participation as a major advertiser in the *Woman's Day* special-interest magazine for brides. For the past three years San Martin had paid handsomely to be the only bridal gown manufacturer appearing in this semi-annual publication.

"It's a big financial commitment. It costs us $250,000 for the two issues, but it has 500,000 circulation," notes Twyla. "It's unlike other bridal magazines because it stays on the newsstands until it's sold. With other publications, they're removed after two months to make room for the next issue. It's been very good for us." The stiff advertising dollars give San Martin not only several pages of exclusive bridal-gown advertising, but also the cover gown twice a year.

San Martin's consistent design and marketing victories helped push company revenues to $7.4 million for 1987, and to $15 million in 1988. Bursting at the seams, in July of 1987 San Martin moved into a 16,000-square-foot facility, and by the spring of 1989 had committed to 7,000 square feet of additional space.

Even though San Martin was ranked among the top five bridal manufacturers in the United States within five short years, it must be remembered that Sandy and Twyla together brought almost forty years of marketing and manufacturing expertise to the partnership.

Sandy was born into a fashion family. Her father was a clothing manufacturer, and in the later years of his life he served as a vice-president of Christian Dior in New York. Her mother ran a fine retail specialty store for women. "I literally grew up on Seventh Avenue," says Sandy of her childhood.

But her penchant was for design. "I've been drawing since I was five years old," she says. "I never sewed, because my parents always had sewing done for me."

She honed her design skills at The Pratt Institute and the famed Parsons School of Design in New York, and soon was putting her talents to work designing a wedding dress — her own. "It was an incredible dress. It was very special. But even that dress my parents had made up for me."

She then went to work for a women's lingerie manufacturer. "Those were the days when people wore fancy lingerie, hostess gowns, and bed jackets," Sandy recalls. "That's where I learned about using fine laces and where I finally learned how to sew."

Soon after that, Sandy decided to fulfill one of her lifelong dreams, and moved to Europe, the mecca of the fashion world. She found work as a management consultant to manufacturers in both Finland and Denmark. "This was during the Cuban Missile Crisis, and I saw students marching on the American Embassy. It was the first time in my life I had seen any anti-American sentiment. It was also the beginning of my political education."

Her consulting work took her to Holland, where she met an American who was studying medicine there. They married, and their first daughter, Suzanne, was born in Amsterdam. In the late sixties, the trio moved back to the United States so Sandy's husband could complete an internship in New Jersey, and here a second daughter, Cathy, was born. Later the foursome moved to Philadelphia, where her husband did a psychiatric residency.

Sandy's political passions were now reawakened as she involved herself in the peace movement. "I even have pictures of my girls distributing leaflets for the cause," she says. While her daughters were attending Montessori, she herself returned to school part time, ultimately getting a liberal arts degree from Antioch College.

Her studies and political involvement reached a new high when she began working at the University of Pennsylvania for R. Buckminster Fuller, the renowned futurist, who believed political change came through technological advancement.

One casualty during this full and varied period was Sandy's second marriage. When it became clear that it was over, the petite blonde looked around for a way to support herself and her daughters. "I'm probably the only princess in America who didn't take a dime from her ex-husband, the doctor," she says.

Fashion was in her blood, and when she scanned the "help wanted" newspaper ads she naturally gravitated toward the garment industry. There wasn't too much to choose from in Philadelphia, so when she saw an ad for an administrative position at Alfred Angelo, one of the leading manufacturers of wedding dresses in the country, she applied. "Going in I knew very little about the bridal business, but in the nine years I worked there, believe me, I earned my Ph.D. in it," asserts Sandy. While she hadn't been hired as a designer, she did everything else, including public relations, advertising, marketing, and formulating the *Woman's Day* special-interest concept in concert with After Six, makers of formal wear.

When the company brought in new management, Sandy decided it was time for her to leave. "I was part of the old guard, and I wouldn't have been happy there. Anyway, I was ready for a change," she says. "That's when I began to think about staging bridal shows on the east coast, and that's what eventually led me to Twyla."

Twyla was born in Flat Rock, Illinois, population 500. "Now it's 499, because I'm gone," jokes the vibrant, six-footer with eyes to match her auburn hair.

While Sandy drew pictures throughout her childhood, Twyla simply recalls being an ambitious youngster. "I was possessed by ambition as far back as I can remember. Whenever there was anything to sell, I always sold the most. In first grade in the midwest there were magazine sales to raise money for the Red Cross, and I sold the most. I always sold the most magazines. Or the most cookies. The most whatever. It wasn't difficult for me; it was very natural."

Raised by her grandparents on a farm, Twyla joined her mother, Amanda, in Chicago when she was fourteen. "My mother told me if I came to live with her in the city I could go to modelling school," says Twyla, and the inducement brought young Twyla to Chicago, where she immediately enrolled in a modelling school. Her ambition to "be the best" quickly surfaced, and soon she was doing catalogue modelling and run-way modelling — a little bit of everything.

She was so successful that the school asked her to teach modelling, and then they asked her to sell their modelling courses. "I was only fifteen, but I looked thirty," she says. "When they found out how young I was they fired me until I could get a work permit. I ended up selling those modelling courses for them for a long time, and that's really where I learned how to sell."

Like Sandy, Twyla also suffered through two ill-fated marriages. Shortly after her second divorce she met her present husband, Ernest Martin. "He's a successful Broadway producer, and he's the one who has really allowed me to stretch and grow. He's had so much success of his own that he's never been threatened by mine." Indeed, her husband is the other half of the Broadway team of Feuer and Martin, which staged such well-known hits as "Guys and Dolls," "Silk Stockings," "Can Can," among many others. They also produced the movie versions of "Cabaret" and "A Chorus Line."

For the first five years the couple travelled around the world, and Twyla thoroughly enjoyed her introduction to theatrical life. "It was exciting. I was backstage every night, meeting celebrities and entertaining them, living a lifestyle that most people only dream about. But after a while I became bored. I wanted to do something, but I didn't know what. Everyday we would run around the track at UCLA and we'd talk about what I could do."

At the time her husband was the managing director of the Los Angeles Civic Light Opera at the Music Center, and he suggested she volunteer her sales abilities in public relations to spread the word about the Music Center. "I sold a lot of tickets and I enjoyed it," says Twyla. When her husband's contract was up at the Music Center, she decided to organize fashion shows and fund-raising events for many of those organizations she had worked with.

"I put on fashion shows for the senior citizens, who were thrilled because no one had ever done this for them before. I used senior models and featured comfortable clothing. That was indirectly how I became involved in bridal fashions," says Twyla.

A women from Santa Monica Women's Bank asked her to do the commentary at a bridal show sponsored by the Santa Monica Chamber of Commerce. "I told her I didn't know one lace from another, but that I would give it a try," she relates.

"Well, that show was not too successful; certainly it wasn't anything I wanted to be associated with. But I began thinking that perhaps I could stage a bridal show on a bigger scale." She investigated a couple of other bridal shows, and concluded they, too, were "rinky-dink."

Convinced hers was the idea whose time had come, Twyla produced her first show, a one-day affair at the Anaheim Convention Center in 1982. She filled 125 booths, staged five fashion shows, and pulled off the biggest extravaganza the bridal industry had ever seen. "I had revolving turn-tables and outer-space scenes — all the things I had been exposed to through Ernie," says Twyla.

"I'm really the dean of bridal shows. People from all over the United States came to my shows. Not only brides-to-be and their mothers, but people who wanted to go into the bridal-show business. And of course, that's how I met Sandy."

The women ultimately made the bridal shows a part of the San Martin company. "They give us an opportunity to actually work and interact directly with the brides," adds Twyla.

Twyla also keeps in touch with brides across the country through the thirty or so trunk shows she does a year. "Trunk show" is an old phrase, used in the fashion trade to describe a designer who packs all of his or her dress designs in a trunk and then travels from one store to another to show them off.

"I go out into the stores, and I become a salesperson for a day or two," Twyla explains. "I ship my entire line there, work with brides and sell them dresses. The reason I started doing this is that Sandy and I have a strong grass roots background and attitude as far as selling is concerned. We believe that if we are friends with the stores — and most of the owners are women — they will sell our dresses better.

"When a bride doesn't know what she's looking for, I want the owner to think, 'Oh, it's really easy to sell those San Martin dresses. I'm going to bring out that dress that Twyla told me about.'"

In 1987 San Martin diversified into a small couture line that sells very well in the very un-middle-America price range of $2,000 to $4,000. "We wanted to reach more stores, but there were many high-end bridal salons that would not even look at our dresses because we didn't have a couture line," says Sandy. Once San Martin introduced its hand-embroidered "wearable art" couture gowns, several of those salons became die-hard customers.

It was inevitable that San Martin would expand beyond wedding dresses, and for the past couple of years the company has also produced an "After Five" line of evening dresses and a series of prom dresses.

In the spring of 1989 San Martin unveiled its first collection of bridesmaids' dresses, and the partners are hopeful that fall sales will be good. Helping lift the new line off the ground will be the company's year-round push for sales.

"Unlike most bridal companies, we sell twelve months a year. Most of the others just have the two markets — in the spring and fall. They're not aggressive in their advertising or their selling other than for those two markets. We push,

push, push and sell dresses every day," says Twyla. Evidence of the push is San Martin's advertising budget, which topped $2 million for 1989.

Twyla and Sandy place top priority on customer service. "We bend over backwards to keep our people happy," says Sandy. "For instance, if for some reason we deliver a dress that is wrong, we'll do everything we can to satisfy the store and the bride. We'll do rush alterations, or ship a new dress — whatever it takes. You have to invest in your customers."

"You know, we've gone from no customers to a 5,000-customer base in four years," Twyla says. "There are only 10,000 customers in the country, so we've got a pretty good percentage. Most of our accounts are active, buying from us all the time." San Martin also is truly an "international" bridal company, with strong sales in England, Australia, Canada and Europe.

Today the company counts eighty-nine full-time employees on the payroll, including cutters, fitters, designers, order fillers, order takers, bookkeepers, accountants, sales representatives, and a rash of finger-tappers to run their banks of computers. The company operates a showroom in New York, staffed by Sandy's mother, Jean, and her eldest daughter, Suzie. "My daughter graduated from Philadelphia Textile College, and she's done some merchandising and marketing. We like to keep everything in the family," says Sandy.

Despite their success, Twyla and Sandy have not changed their style of management. You won't find them secluded behind closed doors in plushly-carpeted or expensively-furnished private offices. Rather, they share an office cluttered with phones, sketches, racks of dresses, and piles of bridal magazines. One wall is filled with small posters printed in Chinese characters, another has blow-ups of press clippings about San Martin from *Fortune* and *Venture* magazines.

The duo seem to thrive within their own environment of organized chaos. One minute Sandy will be checking a design on a fitting model, and Twyla will be solving a billing problem. The next minute, they may both be looking at negatives from the latest photography shoot, while simultaneously studying new beaded fabrics.

No one knocks before coming into their office. Problems are dealt with quickly and openly. The partners know exactly what's going on in their shop at all times, and they like it that way. "Because there are two of us it's easier to maintain tight control. My weaknesses are Twyla's strengths, and vice versa," Sandy says.

"This in an exciting business and one we both like. We like the dresses, we like the girls, we like the travel — we like the business. That makes a difference," says Twyla.

They also like each other—and in the end that's what really makes the difference.

Michael Stansbury

Thomas Gay

National Decision Systems

-8-

NATIONAL DECISION SYSTEMS

Years before the landmark book *In Search of Excellence* was published, the marketing-research firm of National Decision Systems had identified and taken a very similar path to excellence. Comprehensive customer service and true teamwork were the watchwords for partners H. Michael Stansbury and Thomas R. Gay.

The two are quick to say in no uncertain terms that the success of National Decision Systems has depended upon a strong team. Jim Shaffer, executive vice-president of systems, and George Moore, executive vice-president of sales and marketing, are among the major decision makers; with Stansbury and Gay they form a leadership team that comprises each of the four standard personality types. "There is no single 'right' way to manage a company," Gay says, "Just different ways." And by having such a variety of personalities involved in the decision process, the firm benefits from several perspectives and styles and, interestingly, from the conflict that is so often the source of creativity.

National Decision Systems was formed in 1979 as a spinoff of Marketing Information Systems, Inc. (MIS), the first company founded by Stansbury. By 1986 National Decision Systems had achieved a net profit of $1 million, and this grew steadily to a net profit of $4.5 million in 1988. Now one of the largest marketing-information firms in the world, National Decision Systems will open offices throughout Europe in the 1990's, in preparation for the removal of trade barriers within that continent in 1992.

During the past two and one-half years, the firm has hired an average of one person per week, bringing the total number of employees to well over two hundred and fifty. They are based in sales offices in New York, Chicago, and Vienna, Virginia (near Washington, D.C.), and at headquarters in Encinitas, near San Diego, California.

Top management visits these offices every few weeks to provide support, stay in touch with the team, and to accompany sales representatives on calls. "It's an opportunity to pass on the culture and insure focus on the mission," Stansbury says. "This is a major way to build a business," he adds.

National Decision Systems was a pioneer in supplying computerized marketing data in compact laser disk form. "At the time," Stansbury says, "we thought, 'if we can be ahead of our industry with applications and information, why can't we do it with delivery systems for information?' We first looked at the mainframe time-sharing information business, but line charges were high and it was somewhat archaic. Out of that came the development of the Infomark work station CD-ROM (compact disk — read only memory). Now, marketers can put a personal computer and a compact reader on their desks and access all the marketing information they need when they need it. The introduction of CD-ROM was the end to demographic time-sharing services."

With Infomark IV, as with other National Decision System services or products, customers can also define their own market boundaries. Through *Business Facts*, a national address-specific database that lists 7.8 million businesses, customers can assess and comprehend their target markets and, therefore, their own business potentials. Reports from National Decision Systems can be delivered via hard copy, magnetic tape, on-line downloading, on-line electronic mail, floppy disks, graphic maps, and the Infomark Laser PC System.

Enhancing its service further, National Decision Systems was acquired by Equifax in 1988. According to Gay, "They had a wealth of data and didn't have the target marketing experience to know what to do with it. However with annual sales of more than $700 million, they had sufficient capital to fuel continued growth of our company."

Equifax has a consumer marketing database that contains information on more than one hundred million individuals, and is updated as often as fifteen million times per day, according to Equifax literature. Part of this database is being integrated into National Decision Systems' already extensive databases. By means of the acquisition, Equifax gained access to ten thousand new business clients and a company with an effective target-marketing strategy.

"The two firms engaged in some joint ventures," says Stansbury, "for about two years prior to the acquisition, so I am very comfortable with Equifax's style, and they appreciate the unique entrepreneurial aspects of our company. There is no pressure to change us; their plan is to use our resources."

Due to the dynamic nature of the marketing information business, National Decision Systems has no traditional long-range plan. Instead, it has a strategic plan, with the goal of redefining the way business is done in its industry every two to three years. This means expanding the customer base, increasing the number of products and services, and updating the technology. "The velocity of change in technology and the information industry is so great that five-year plans are fantasies. If you measure the dynamics of the industry, and plan two to three years into the future, you can remain a vital force in the industry," Gay maintains. "We are very clearly on a realistic path and our people are clearly focussed," Stansbury adds.

"Our real objective," Gay says, "is to make our current position of leadership obsolete by controlling those dynamics. We are the largest company of *our type* in the world and, recognizing that the technology is changing and the competition is changing, we know that if we simply commit to replicating what we've done in the past we will soon become out-dated by the changing world around us. So we are going to make ourselves obsolete by moving the frontier out further than where we are today. In order to do that, we're going to change the technology again. We're going to improve the information sets, improve the applications software to make things easier and better, and improve the distribution vehicles in order to put our information in the hands of the people more conveniently."

National Decision Systems's annual gross sales are expected to be between $80 and $100 million by 1994. Gross sales for 1988 were $20.3 million. "We could be twice our size again in one year merely by becoming more efficient and circulating the story of our services, not because of some technical advance or some sudden spike in demand. The demand is there. We have the products ready to fuel that growth," Stansbury says, without revealing what any of those products might be, "and we have the organizational structure to permit that growth."

The National Decision Systems team plans to achieve that growth by continuing to be ahead of the power curve and focussing on product development and competition. "Look at our track record and competition," Stansbury says. "It reads, 'first, first, first...' in what we're doing with our new-product applications. In 1982 we were a demographics firm, selling demographic reports. That year we predicted the information explosion. That was before *Megatrends* was published. We knew this information explosion was going to force somebody, either ourselves or our competition, to sell other types of information to solve clients' problems. We needed to put other kinds of databases together. We started that process three years ahead of our competition."

Even today, according to Stansbury, "This is a supply-driven market. It just keeps getting bigger; it's nowhere near saturation. We're in an environment in which we are not battling for market share as much as we are battling the universe, n terms of knowledge of the value of these tools and how to use them. Our goal is to make marketing information tools more useable and more valuable to prospects and, therefore, to create demand for our services." Gay adds, "They're hungry for information and for the ability to use that information to solve their particular problems.

"So our challenge is to make our information and applications technology more useable, more understandable and, by extension, more valuable to the prospect. The more we stay dedicated to that, the more our growth is fuelled. Achieving success here means maintaining continued growth. Each sale we make is a success."

The firm's commitment to its customers is its hallmark. "People want ¼ inch holes, not ¼ inch drills," Stansbury explains. In other words, give the customers what they need. "The relationship lasts longer than the deal you just closed," he elaborates. "We're effective because we do a better job than our competitors at solving problems" Gay says, and "We solve problems, rather than just sell information." Stansbury reiterates, "Keep in mind, that is a key ingredient here. We're not just an information company selling numbers. If you recall our consulting background and consider the information explosion, something we do better than all other companies is put the two together — with the application of that information — to solve the customer's problem."

As Gay explains, "There are some very large companies out there that have enormous databases. But we're constantly gaining market share because of our commitment to building customer value. Some firms are more concerned with selling an element of data than with selling an element of valuable decision-focussed information. We sell information by making it valuable to the customer.

"We are extremely competitive, but we will not cut price. Therefore we over-deliver on what our competitor does not — service. Whatever our customers want, we give it to them. Whatever it takes to get the job done...we win five out of every six competitive bids even though we're often priced fifty percent higher than our competition." Despite the pricing, National Decision Systems only rarely loses a customer to the competition. "Our loss of customers is almost one hundred percent attributable to corporate changes — leveraged buyouts, mergers, acquisitions, and bankruptcies. Almost no attrition is due to migration," Stansbury says. Their customer base of ten thousand clients includes a strong representation of such Fortune 500 companies as Amoco, Mobil Oil, Citicorp, Merrill Lynch, McDonald's, Sears and Aetna.

As anyone with the company will tell you, their success is also the direct result of taking care of their employees as well as they take care of their customers. "We have an organizational style that gets the job done," Stansbury says. "There are channels of communication, leadership and management that you typically find in other organizations, but it's how they are implemented — how they're administered down through the organization and back up through the organization — that makes National Decision Systems successful and different from most companies." According to Gay, "There is no pecking order. There is an organizational system but there is no rigid structure that prevents communication. It's not a democracy either. There is a decision-making protocol that works, but people on one level are not held hostage or threatened by people at another level because of rank."

"'Team' is an overused word," Stansbury says, "But it is teamwork, taking care of each employee and bringing employees together, that is responsible for our success. There are no one-man shows," he emphasizes; and Gay adds, "National Decision Systems is a reflection of Mike and myself, but it is not *us*. It's two hundred individuals who collectively make it what it is."

"People need the room to roam...the freedom to create...and we reward them in many different ways as part of this team," Stansbury says. This is where the business-unit concept is applied. Managers are given the opportunity to manage their own unit, and to develop their ideas and sell them into the marketplace. If an idea is successful, its originator can be catapulted into the position of 'head of a company,' a business unit of National Decision Systems, without having to invest any of his or her own money. "As their business grows, they are rewarded accordingly," Gay says. "The overall driving force in this company is that as we expand, with more business units to fit more markets, each business unit could grow to the point where we could incorporate it and make it a subsidiary of National Decision Systems. The result of this creative freedom, is that our company has the brightest marketing and technical team of any group in the information industry.

"Eventually, we expect to see ten to twenty different

business units," he says. Currently, National Decision Systems has seven such units. "It's not difficult to identify a target market in which to position a business unit. If you look at fifteen business units, each doing a $5 million business, you have a $75 million corporation. Certain of those business units will be $10 to $15 million opportunities," Gay explains, "yet we have a commitment not to grow too fast, in order to maintain our current level of customer service. You mustn't spread yourself too thin. As a market proves it has potential, then another business unit can be established with another owner. That builds entrepreneurial management, the *esprit de corps* that is also a key to our continued growth."

National Decision Systems develops its software products in-house, but, surprisingly, what the managers of this marketing/technical firm claim is that normally they do not hire computer specialists, because of their tendency to focus on technical aspects rather than on problem-solving. Instead, the head of the technical department, Jim Shaffer, has a B.S. in chemistry and an M.B.A., and his second in command is a physicist. Dozens of other employees have degrees in mathematics or economics. National Decision Systems has a reputation for occasionally hiring people who have just been graduated from high school, and teaching them about technology. "We have a great capacity for producing technical people," Gay says. "We let them have access to our four VAX systems (powerful mini-computers) and we let them create. Out of that come both the products that solve problems and the brilliant employees who permeate the organization. Some of the sixteen-year-olds the firm has hired in the past have since obtained university degrees and will soon be senior executives here, and they are still in their twenties. The key to being hired is a person's ability to understand and structure problems." The firm recruits problem-solvers, with the idea that if a problem can be identified and a strategy formulated for its solution, National Decision Systems will be able to provide staff with the business acumen and technical ability to put the strategy into practice.

"There is a mutuality in terms of commitment to exellence and to each individual's growth and financial success. We are one hundred percent dedicated to the needs of each individual, so team members have the opportunity to become everything they can be and want to be. We have people working to help each other succeed," according to Stansbury. "You establish that philosophy by example," Gay adds. "It starts at the top and works its way down throughout the organization. You show by doing. As a result, we have complete dedication. It's an everyday thing, a lifestyle. The consequence is that people are accountable, and they want to be, and they stay. In the ten years we've lost two people to competitors. It's very difficult for competitors to create an atmosphere and attitude that will attract our employees to their firms.

"Each department is both customer and supplier to another department and each person is both customer and supplier to another at National Decision Systems," he explains. To emphasize this, and the importance of servicing each customer, annual 'Do What It Takes' awards are presented to the staff members who do what it takes to get the job done, to meet the needs of the customer.

"I started with the idea, when the firm was formed, that you have to take care of employees," Stansbury says. So, for a light touch, the firm has had flowers delivered to every female employee each Monday since the company was founded. Men who request them get flowers too. "It shows a style, a philosophy of how we care." Stansbury adds. A few years ago, Gay started the Presidents' Club, an incentive for outstanding achievers. About fourteen percent of the staff have achieved membership. The reward is an expense-paid trip for two to some exotic location; for the fiscal year 1989, the destination will be Hawaii. It is estimated that over forty employees will make the trip.

In the firm's early days, Stansbury was noted for walking through the office throwing dollars on the desks. It was a light, corny touch that did help keep morale up, but also caused conflict between Gay and himself. It was difficult for Gay to adjust to Stansbury's freewheeling style after the traditional, corporate atmosphere at Sherwin-Williams. "Tom and I originally worked together in a client/consultant relationship, " Stansbury explains. "One day, while still at Sherwin-Williams, Tom called and said he was going to change jobs and wanted my opinion on whether he should be looking at a large company or a small company. Since I had had some experience, primarily with small companies, and he had always worked with large companies, he felt there was valuable insight to be gained from me. I said, 'If you're looking at small companies, would you consider the possibility of our working together?'"

Gay adds, "We talked about it a number of months, and then got together in September 1975. I moved to San Diego from Cleveland, with the hope of getting into the marketing/location research business and developing something that I'd find more fulfilling." It was, in fact, the same type of work he had done for Sherwin-Williams. "I had enjoyed the work there but not the large-company politics," he says. "I was too much of a driver to be constrained by the protocol of a large company, so I unshackled that harness to do something that was more aligned with my own style."

"It was quite a commitment on our part to bring somebody out to our company," Stansbury says. "Gay had had some security in his previous position, and yet he decided to join a firm in which you are only as good as your last job. I had never seen anybody as good as Tom, in terms of what he could do for the company...from the basic consulting work to the expertise in the retail field, to selling, to taking care of the client. It's a compliment to the company that he wanted to join us. He was crazy..."

"The company" at the time was the four-year-old MIS, which specialized in retail-company consulting and site selection. It was small and freewheeling, with about ten employees and no financial foundation. "At that point we weren't smart enough to know how to raise capital; today it's a non-issue. What we earned in those days was consumed instantly," Gay says. "It was a materials-tight business in which you were only paid for the hours you put in. There is a finite amount of time and because of that constraint, it was not likely we could achieve our goals — only twenty-four hours in a day. It was feast or famine. That was the starting point for National Decision Systems." The two realized that with a tangible product, as opposed to consulting, income would not be limited by hours worked or by the cyclical variations that affect retail-store developments, their primary source of revenue. It took them until 1979 to decide exactly how to address that issue.

"We had different styles, that complemented each other," Stansbury says. "Even so," Gay adds, "we went through a two-year period of conflict trying to define our respective roles. It was a growing process for both of us. The difficulty was unexpected, and revolved around the 'mantle of authority' and environment and, as much as I was trying to get away from it, I don't think I understood what not being in that kind of environment would be like," Gay says. Stansbury, on the other hand, was "180 degrees in the other direction," the latter admits. "I couldn't understand a more formal organized environment. I was a very loose manager.

What we had was two persons, each with some great ideas and creativity, who were at either end of the spectrum — which actually made it a very good working relationship. While this creates conflict, it also creates ideas, growth, and success."

The conflict it generated however was resolved only after Gay left National Decision Systems in 1976. "I went back to Cleveland with my wife, who didn't like California. Mike and I had not been able to agree on the direction of the company. It had to be bigger, more focussed and organized or I would not be a part of it...Eight months later we negotiated a partnership to make it bigger and better.

"It was a long, drawn-out process of sitting down and discussing frankly what we liked and didn't like about working with each other," according to Gay. They now compare the process to resolution of conflict in a marriage. It meant a lot of compromise by both parties. For Gay, among other things, it also meant returning to California without his wife, who could not accept the risks of the entrepreneurial lifestyle. Stansbury adds, "If we hadn't liked each other as much as we did, and liked our partnership, we would have split. The fact that we were able to resolve those issues to a great extent allowed us to create the environment that has helped us to do as well as we have since."

As it was, Gay became a partner with the title of President and Chief Operating Officer. Stansbury became Chief Executive Officer and Chairman of the Board. Their management styles are still different. "I'm a quiet force," Gay says, "I don't need or want any more limelight. Mike is more expansive. He has been our public face."

Stansbury is well-known in the community, and is chairman of the board and president of the "65 Roses Sports Club" - San Diego Chapter of Cystic Fibrosis Foundation; and is on the board of the Cystic Fibrosis Foundation. He sits on the board of the American Marketing Association; he is a member of the National Association of Corporate Real Estate Executives and the American Association of Individual Investors, and he is an active elder of the Presbyterian Church. In contrast, Gay maintains a comparatively low profile and doesn't divulge his personal commitments. His focus is the business.

Management at National Decision Systems may have different philosophies, but their goals are one and the same, to provide their clients with the ultimate in quality and service. "We have an organizational style that gets the job done," Stansbury says. Judging by their customer-and employee-retention rate, they are succeeding.

"Looking back," Gay says, "there were several keys to National Decision Systems' success. The first element was getting acceptance in 1983 from senior management that the company had to focus on longer term strategy and technology changes or become obsolete by 1988. Jim Shaffer's skills, as executive vice-president of Systems, in being able to translate new technologies into business products gave us a tremendous leap ahead of competition. The hiring of Executive Vice-President George Moore in 1984 resulted in the joining of the best and brightest in the industry in terms of marketing and business-targeting systems."

Finally, Gay says, "the 'success-focussed' entrepreneurial teams' commitment to action and to winning in the marketplace and serving the customers' needs overcame the lack of capital and the much larger, better-financed competitors in the mid-1980's." All of this then coalesced in 1985 when National Decision Systems introduced Infomark CD-ROM laser technology and rewrote history in the distribution of data in the information industry.

Interestingly enough, the blackest moment came during

the early days of MIS. The year was 1973. The company was busy completing contracts and negotiating new proposals. Then suddenly—there was no new business! In the face of this disaster Stansbury retained his staff. "I told them, 'Knit, wash windows, whatever it takes, but be here. I'll support you. I don't want to lose you. We'll get the business.'" He, in the meantime, was frenetically priming the pump for more business, and was generating his payroll for eleven people by playing poker. "I played poker for almost a year in Las Vegas — in card rooms, in private games, anywhere I could. Pressure is calling a $5,000 bet and knowing that your ability to meet your payroll depends upon the outcome." he says.

The need for those intense poker games is long past. With the addition of Gay the company gradually became more structured, but an informal atmosphere still remains. A walk through the offices reveals a group of people — most of them in slacks and knit shirts — who aren't nervous about the boss walking in; also evident are top executives who know all the members of their teams by name. "They said all this would disappear as the company grew," Stansbury boasts, "but we have about 150 people working in this building now and still maintain a small-firm familiarity." "There is structure, but enough informality to keep it fun," Gay says.

"I preach balance," he adds. "You have to service all aspects of your life. Without balance, you will find yourself eventually failing in an area you're good at." As a result, the team works hard from 8:00 a.m. to about 6:30 p.m. and then goes home. He believes weekends and evenings are times for being with the family and doing enjoyable things. Gay does admit to taking some work home, but only work that doesn't interfere with his family life. "We work smart," Stansbury smiles.

Both Stansbury and Gay live near the office in prestigious Rancho Sante Fe. "It is more like the east than any neighborhood in San Diego," Gay says. Stansbury, at age fifty, is a newlywed. His bride is the firm's director of market planning who overcame the stigma of dating the boss and has proven herself at the company for nine years. "We see very little of each other at work," he says. His first marriage, of twenty years, fell victim to the demands of building a company and raising a family. There was very little communication.

Stansbury and his bride have just purchased a new 6,000-square-foot home. "We have a very informal lifestyle. I'm happy just walking with my wife on the beach. Don't stifle me with formality; we are very low-key," he says. Yet, paradoxically, the reason for buying this particular house was its ability to handle thirty-five to forty people from church or charity meetings, again showing his involvement in the community.

"I'm just a kid in a fifty-year-old body," Stansbury says, and he still enjoys poker, water-skiing, golf, running, and the restoration of a 1937 Buick Special. He also performs magic shows for children's hospitals and for birthday parties. Most of his time, however, is devoted to business and to community support. A typical day begins with prayer, exercise, work, and then proceeds to committee meetings for the various organizations he helps support. He has spent the past year establishing an all-denominational database to help churches develop congregational programs that suit their market. This, he says, is a "labor of love."

He also occasionally teaches marketing, principles of retailing, and advertising classes at San Diego State University (SDSU). "I have no teaching degree, but the experience factor is what they like to convey to their students. I have almost twenty-five years of case studies in business." His objective he says, is "to give back at least a part of what I've received. I'd like to see more of my people involved in community support," he adds parenthetically.

Stansbury says he hopes to be respected "just as much for my work outside the company as well as in it, and for the corporate culture I founded." He says he sees himself as a supporter rather than as an expert. "Knowing a little something about several things allows me to contribute in several areas instead of being restricted to only one or two." Stansbury was reared in Kansas City, Missouri and moved to San Diego in 1952. He earned a B.S. in marketing from SDSU in 1966. Until 1970, he was a vice-president of a forty-person consulting firm. "I learned to take care of clients there. The company was acquired by a large real estate firm," and Stansbury was eventually fired because of his philosophical difference — wanting to take care of the customers versus top management not wanting to, he says. He then founded MIS.

Gay, the more corporate of the two, is also, unpredictably, the more casually dressed, clad in slacks and a purple cotton sweater. He says he dresses this way "even when Equifax visits. It's part of our commitment to our staff that we won't change the way we do business."

Before his experience heading the corporate market research and store-planning departments for Sherwin-Williams, Gay earned a B.S. in marketing from Northeastern University in Boston. His entrepreneurial spirit, however, developed naturally. He was working when he was ten years old and was earning enough to cover most of his personal expenses by the age of twelve. His father, a machinist for twenty years in Boston, eventually started his own firm in the mid-fifties. "I hold him as role model for doing what is right. He had very high ethical standards," Gay says.

In the late seventies, after maintaining for some time a

long-distance relationship with a lady he had met back East, Gay remarried. Like Stansbury, he and his wife — an interior designer — also have a new 6,000-square-foot home in Rancho Sante Fe. "We designed and built it ourselves, after tearing down the old home that was on the lot," he says.

Gay keeps a 37-foot Tartan sloop — a superb cruising vessel — in San Diego Harbor, as well as a small racing sailboat. At home he has a standard poodle, and about twenty fish in a marine aquarium. He enjoys hunting and fishing at his second home, in the mountains of Idaho. Gay says he has a passion for cars, but admits he is fickle. He drives a Jeep Laredo regularly, but also keeps a BMW 735i and an antique Mercedes sports car.

His true passion seems to be travelling. "I can't travel enough. I'm on the road about two weeks each month for business." But he also travels frequently to Hawaii, Europe, Mexico, and anywhere else his imagination draws him. "I haven't put down roots," he says.

Gay describes himself as a fast thinker and a problem-solver. "I'm good with people, and I've managed all the 'people' issues since I've been with this company." Professionally, he says, he is perceived as being very fair, and focussed on employees' needs straight down the middle. He has high standards, and high expectations of his staff, and his team delivers.

He usually starts his day by 6:30 a.m., when he prepares breakfast for his young daughter, and starts reading. "I stand and read and talk during breakfast," he says. He is a voracious reader, subscribing to about thirty magazines and ten newspapers, which explore all fields of interest. His familiarity with the classic is evident, and his conversation is sprinkled with literary references. He says he particularly enjoys reading women's magazines, because most consumer goods are purchased by women and those magazines are an

Milan Panic
ICN Pharmaceuticals, Inc.

148

-9-

ICN PHARMACEUTICALS, INC.

No one, unless he is incredibly naive or optimistic, expects to get to the top in life without encountering a few obstacles. But Milan Panic has had to overcome more obstacles than most. His most difficult has been to rebuild his entire company from scratch after accounting rules turned international profits into disastrous losses.

Panic (pronounced pan-ish), who fled the communist tyranny of Yugoslavia to come to America, heads ICN Pharmaceuticals, Inc., a research-based health-care company on the cutting edge of medical science, with sales in the $200 million range.

Despite the difficulties he has had to cope with, he remains philosophical. "For me," he says, "a problem is just another challenge to be met."

At ease now in his Costa Mesa, California office, Panic reminisces quietly about his life and his battles, sipping from an unending supply of diet colas delivered at almost clockwork intervals by a secretary from the outer office. Occasionally his voice rises with emotion; he is a man who feels deeply, and cannot always hide his feelings.

He appears younger than his sixty years, and is still trim as an athlete. Only a slight trace of an accent suggests his lineage. With characteristic good humor he jokes about the accent, once described by *Fortune* magazine as that of a benign Bela Lugosi combined with the spirit of a world-class salesman. "When I was at the University of Southern California, I passed all the written tests. But I wasn't required to take courses in speaking English. That has proved to be my biggest problem — I never learned." He pauses for effect.

"I speak correctly phonetically, but I just do it my own way. As long as you understand me, that's what counts. I have made many speeches since that time, to lots and lots of people, and they all listened, to my astonishment. One of the listeners claimed he only listened because I had that heavy accent, and he had to concentrate to understand what I was saying."

Panic takes an active role in civic and community affairs, supporting political candidates and art museums, and helping the next generation of scientific researchers through fellowships at Harvard and the Massachusetts Institute of Technology. In 1986 he was awarded the Congressionally-sponsored Ellis Island Medal of Honor in recognition of his "distinguished service in preserving the American way of life."

Solving problems began early for Panic. His father died when he was only three, and as a youngster he raised vegetables to support his mother and two sisters. He remembers, "I used to wake up in the dark and sit on the steps outside my house. My mother would come out and ask 'What are you doing?' I would tell her that I was waiting for the sun to come up so I could go to work." It was a difficult time in eastern Europe; Hitler's armies overran Yugoslavia in 1941, and three years later, at the age of fourteen, Panic joined the Partisan resistance movement led by Marshall Tito. For a youngster, it was a dangerous decision.

"You didn't get taken prisoner if you were in the resistance," he recalls. "You got killed. We were not regular army, so the Germans — who never had any ethics in war — weren't obliged to keep us prisoners." Backed by Great Britain and the Soviet Union, Tito's guerrillas — and Acting-Lieutenant Panic — drove the Nazis out of the country in 1945.

When the war ended Panic entered the University of Belgrade. He began competing as a bicycle-racer and skier, and was soon named to the national team in bicycling, competing throughout Europe. But despite the honors he found life under the communists oppressive, and began looking for a way out.

"In a communist country," he says, "the number one people are the diplomats, and second are the athletes, because they represent the country. So they do everything for you if you are an athlete. They will bend over backwards — as long as you don't represent a political threat.

"Therefore, you could not talk freely. It is very difficult to explain what this means. If you took a train trip of two hundred miles, somebody would ask for your identification five times. Under those conditions, it is very easy to suppress people even as talkative as myself. You don't talk, because they are all over you all of the time!

"It's funny now, looking back on it thirty years later. If you are on a train, travelling only two hundred miles, you're checked repeatedly by the police. You go abroad and the secret police call you to ask who you talked with on the corner of some street. Well, then it happens. You start thinking three times before you open your mouth, because you can go to jail! In an instant! For nothing!"

However, despite his status as an alternate on Yugoslavia's Olympic bicycling team and a national champion racer, Panic's independent nature continued to assert itself. In

Luxembourg he defied an order to refuse a prize, and was disqualified for three months......he began to plan his escape.

"It was very well organized. I did not run over the border because at that time they were killing people at the borders. With machine guns. With dogs. I was an athlete. I told the guys, 'Sometime I'm not going to go back.' They didn't believe me! I had some scary moments, because I thought of myself as being a much bigger fish than I was. Some of the people they would kidnap back; you've seen those old movies. But it looks like I was not that big of a fish!"

On the way to an international meet in the Netherlands in 1955, Milan Panic left the team in Vienna. His wife, in the meantime, had procured a visa for Italy, and they met in West Germany. Their infant son remained in Yugoslavia; it would be two years before they would succeed in getting him out of the country as well.

In Germany Panic found his troubles were not over. Defectors were viewed with suspicion, and if they could not prove their political status, they were confronted with the prospect of being returned to their homelands. Panic underwent an agonizingly long ordeal before the Germans finally granted him asylum.

"I went to Nuremburg. I was given a hearing in the same buildings where the Nazis were tried — it was not a very nice experience — by German judges! If you were an economic refugee, they could send you back, so it was essential that I get political asylum. And I did. I received a letter from the German authorities saying, 'Welcome to Germany. You have all the rights of a German citizen, except that you cannot vote.'"

While waiting for his application to be approved, Panic spent three semesters at the University of Heidelberg, and also worked for a moving company. "I became boss in about three months: Germans were lifting and I was ordering and organizing."

West German approval was only one step in the plan Panic had laid out for himself. His next goal was the United States, where he hoped to enroll in a university. But McCarthy-era fears of communist infiltrators kept the borders closed, and Panic and his wife had to endure even more scrutiny before getting their clearances to cross the Atlantic.

The log-jam was broken by then Vice-President Richard M. Nixon, who was touring Europe on behalf of President Dwight D. Eisenhower to study the refugee problem. "Mr. Nixon came to Europe to review charges that there was some possible unfairness in treating people like myself — students and young guys with their own reasonably good ideas about leaving communism — and he organized a program called 'Presidential Escapee Program,' P.E.P., and they selected people to come to America, and I was one of them."

Remembering Nixon's help, when Milan Panic became a naturalized citizen he registered as a Republican. Although he switched parties later, he still has a fondness for the former president.

Arriving in America was a dream come true. For Panic, the most concrete symbol of his freedom was his anonymity. "In New York, I was so impressed with so many people and streets and no policemen on every corner, and nobody to ask you questions about anything. Nobody cared about me! That made it a great place. Really! That was the first thing I said: 'Finally, nobody is looking at me and asking who I am!"

The Panics arrived in New York on 1 August, 1956 with two suitcases and $20. But Milan had not been idle during his stay in Germany; he had his future mapped out. In two days, he and his family set out by train for Los Angeles, where Panic obtained a scholarship at the University of Southern California, a job on campus, and a teaching assistantship in the chemistry department — and then encountered his next problem.

Panic's specialty was chemistry, but most of the major employers in that field were Fortune 500 firms with big defense contracts. Panic learned that his Yugoslavian origins would block any attempt to obtain security clearance, making him, in effect, unemployable in his chosen profession.

The solution to this particular problem was simple: Milan changed his focus to biochemistry, and began working at a small firm called California Corporation for Biomedical Research. Within a few months he started his own company, International Chemical and Nuclear, on a $200 shoestring. Reflecting on his early years in war-ravaged Europe and his ambition to help humanity through new and better medicines, he adopted a company motto which to this day adorns the entrance to ICN headquarters: "He who has health has hope, and he who has hope has everything."

Among those involved in the early years of the company were Max Dunn, dean of the Graduate School at the University of California, Los Angeles; Dan Campbell, chairman of the Department of Immunochemistry at CalTech; Weldon Jolley, Loma Linda University professor; Roberts A. Smith, UCLA professor of Biochemistry; and the extraordinary medicinal chemist Roland K. Robins (later to be named 1988 Alfred Burger award winner by the American Chemical Society).

"The idea was to develop medicines in areas where there were no existing drugs and no knowledge. I was working with DNA and RNA, so the drugs would be developed from modified DNA parts and RNA parts," Panic remembers.

This was 1959, the dawn of the biological revolution. Watson and Crick had only a few years earlier discovered the double helical structure of deoxyribonucleic acid — DNA. RNA and DNA were barely recognized by the scientific community, let alone viewed as sources of new therapeutic drugs. "That was way out. Nobody spoke about it. They would laugh at you."

To get financing, Panic and his colleague Smith approached a group of physicians in the affluent Los Angeles community of Glendale. "I thought they would understand what we wanted to do," Panic says, adding that, to his surprise, the doctors had no idea what he was talking about. Still, they were impressed with the revolutionary view of the medical future, and with the glib immigrant who made genetic research sound almost easy. At the end of his presentation, they invested $100,000 for a piece of that future.

Medical research — then as now — was capital-intensive and time-consuming. A capitalization of $100,000 would not go far in providing the means to explore the medical uses of genes and proteins.

To provide the cash flow necessary to start the laboratory, Panic and Smith started manufacturing and selling basic chemicals for use by other researchers. From salmon sperm, the company extracted DNA, then radioactively tagged its building blocks, nucleosides and nulceotides, and made them available to scientists throughout the world for research studies — thereby helping the new era of molecular biology to unfold. As a result of this, the company became a leading world supplier of biotechnology research chemicals. This business still operates today, and it also manufactures diagnostic equipment that enables physicians to diagnose disease states faster and more accurately.

In retrospect, it was a sound strategy, but Panic credits it as much to luck as to foresight. It also brought dividends far beyond the cash flow that he was able to convert to practical purposes: "One, we would make money; and two, we would learn about where research was going. Our theoretical thoughts, where we should go, would be checked practically by what other people were thinking about. It was a very good thermometer."

As the company grew, it became evident that Panic could not be both an effective administrator and a laboratory researcher. Lester Korn, founder of Korn Ferry International, advised Panic to move out of the lab and into the boardroom for good.

"I didn't like it for a while, because it's tough not to see what people are doing," Panic says. "But now, I think I have made the transition. I can control things through financial reporting, as well as through conventional management styles and skills and having other people do certain things. The art of delegation is important. I think I have done reasonably well in that."

By 1963, the year Panic became a naturalized American citizen, the young company had enough cash to start its first research program. Panic persuaded friends and colleagues from the leading universities around Los Angeles to serve as unpaid scientific advisers. It was this group that had earlier suggested ICN focus on DNA. It was this same group that now proposed that the first line of enquiry should focus on antiviral drugs.

Medical science had made enormous strides toward control of bacterial diseases, beginning in the 1940's with the introduction of antibiotics. But viruses presented a different set of problems. Scientists had only a vague notion of how they functioned, let alone how to treat viral diseases. A handful of virus-caused illnesses — most notably, polio — could be prevented, but there were no effective antiviral drugs when Panic and his associates began tinkering with basic genetic structures.

The heart of a virus, its nucleus, is surrounded by a thick wall of protein. Before you can destroy the nucleus, you must penetrate that wall, or find some other way of disabling the cell. While science had been looking at bacteria since the 1600's, it was barely able to describe a virus, let alone figure out how to destroy it. Viral diseases ranging from herpes to the common cold and many other ailments escaped treatment because no one knew enough about viruses to even start on a cure.

"They would laugh when you told them you were going to work on the common cold," says Panic of the mainstream scientific community in the early 1960's. But not long after that the laughter turned to amazement as ICN received FDA approval for the first antiviral drug in history.

In the overall scheme of medical practice, ICN's first antiviral drug was of minor consequence — a specialized treatment for herpes of the eye. ICN didn't patent it, but instead registered it in the FDA's master file and began wholesaling the compound to major pharmaceutical houses, which in turn marketed it to the public.

But the significance of ICN's achievement was not lost on the world. In a stock market already feverishly seeking technology companies, ICN became a name on everyone's lips and in everyone's portfolio. Other antiviral drugs followed the first one, and the company's fortunes soared with its share price. ICN doubled its earnings five consecutive years, one of the few New York Stock Exchange-listed companies to achieve that feat.

It looked as if Milan Panic's problem-solving skills would lead to a comfortable retirement, but the initial success was followed by a thudding crash — and a new set of challenges.

Panic reasoned that an 'International' Chemical and Nuclear Company should expand its markets beyond the borders of the United States. Faced with the task of setting up new distribution channels for the rest of the world, he chose the easy way out; he bought existing companies in his target countries. The companies he bought were profit generators, and could insert ICN's products into their lines without disturbing anything.

Panic bought well; his newly-acquired companies continued to report profits. But when the dollar turned weak against foreign currencies in the early 1970's, Panic suddenly found he had purchased a paper disaster and a nightmare for himself and his shareholders. Overnight a bookkeeping rule enforced by the Financial Accounting Standards Board turned profitable companies into losers, even as they continued to generate profits.

The rule in question stipulated that companies must record foreign debts at the exchange rate prevailing on the closing date of the balance sheet, while foreign assets were reported at the exchange rate in effect at the time they were purchased.

As a result, an asset purchased with a $100 million loan would stay on the books at the purchase price, but assuming the dollar had declined by fifty percent the loan would increase to $150 million on the books! With no real cash in or out, the company would suddenly have "lost" $50 million through a "foreign currency translation."

To Panic, and to many in the financial community, the rule seemed to penalize aggressive foreign expansion unfairly. *Forbes* magazine reported on ICN's woes in a 1975 article entitled "Alice in Accountingland," which concluded, "Everybody wants to get at the truth, but truth is not easily reduced to a set of generally accepted accounting principles."

Traditional sources of new capital dried up. Lenders and

underwriters saw only the company's bottom line. "They didn't care if it was a 'paper' loss," says Panic. "They just saw losses." The only solution was to sell off portions of the company to raise the cash necessary to pay the debts.

Eventually the FASB rule was changed, as more American companies invested abroad. But the damage had been done. Panic was forced to dismantle much of what he had built at ICN in the preceding years.

Selling off the foreign divisions did not, however, solve all of ICN's problems. Instead, the profits from the sales created new difficulties. Since they represented capital gains, ICN was presented with a hefty tax bill as a result of the sales. While the balance sheet showed a loss from the currency transaction, the company faced higher taxes for its troubles!

"It was a nightmare!" Panic recalls. "Our sales were almost $178 million in fiscal 1974. We sold everything, and dropped to $37 million in sales in 1983. So I had to keep selling, all over five, six years. But we paid off all the debt. Really tough program. Very few people would do it."

He shakes his head over the strange turn of events. "I had to sell the companies not for valid reasons, simply bookkeeping reasons," he says. "Every decision we made was correct. Still the result was wrong."

Despite the financial trauma, Panic never lost sight of the company's original goals. "I don't know by what virtue we continued to invest in research in spite of those losses," he says today. In the laboratories, shielded from the worst effects of the nightmare, ICN's scientists discovered more ways of using the basic elements of genes and proteins to turn out new products. Eventually, the labs produced more than 5,000 compounds, a number of which found their way into therapeutic drugs.

Panic also made some important decisions about the future of the company. New expansions would be financed through operations or equity. Some of the techniques that Panic and his financial advisers developed involving the use of subsidiaries and stock offerings raised eyebrows on Wall Street, but they enabled the company to get back to work.

They also provided Panic with the means of returning to the international marketplace. In 1987, after buying nineteen companies, he acquired a substantial holding in Hoffmann-LaRoche, Inc., one of the largest international pharmaceutical manufacturers.

"My objectives are very simple," Panic says. "We want to build a major worldwide health-care company. That's what I'm going to be doing in the next ten years.

"I am going from country to country and market to market. Basically, fifteen major markets in the world represent eighty percent of pharmaceutical sales. I was already in eight in 1972 (before divestment). Now we are in the United States, Mexico, Canada, Spain, and Germany — and a little bit in the United Kingdom. We'll be in all of those markets by developing the markets themselves or by buying major companies."

If Panic's education in international finance proved exceedingly painful, his growing awareness of America's political and social institutions provided some measure of relief. Despite his affectionate sense of gratitude for Richard Nixon's intervention when he was struggling to cross the Atlantic, Panic quickly discovered that his social and political conscience was more in tune with the Democratic Party than with Nixon's Republicanism, and he switched affilations.

He also became a close friend and student of then Senator Birch Bayh (D-Indiana), whom he describes as "my initial teacher of the American political system and how it *should* work. An extraordinary man! He really has the depth, an unbelievable depth, of understanding of what the government is and how it should be. I learned from him what American politics is all about, and I participate in American political life as actively as I can under the circumstances."

Over the years Panic has supported the Presidential candidacies of Bayh, Jimmy Carter, and Michael Dukakis, and he is a supporter of former California Gov. Jerry Brown and of California's senior U.S. Senator, Alan Cranston. More recently, he has been involved in the campaign of Birch Bayh's son, Indiana Governor Evan Bayh. Today Bayh and Brown sit on the Boards of ICN subsidiary companies, as do Francis Dale, former United Nations ambassador, and Robert H. Finch, former secretary of Health, Education, and Welfare.

"I really get involved," he says with a perceptible degree of pride. "More than just fund-raising. Strategy sessions — what's to be done."

Nor is his social commitment limited to politics. He has established the annual $50,000 "ICN International Prize in Virology," endowed university chairs, and contributed to a wide range of causes.

But in recent years, much of Panic's time has been taken up in the battle to gain approval for the antiviral drug, ribavirin.

Ribavirin was synthesized by Roland Robins, Ph.D., in 1970. It is the first broad-spectrum antiviral drug. Ribavirin has been shown in the test tube, in animals, and in an increasing number of human clinical trials, to have a broad range of activity against both DNA and RNA viruses. In the U.S., it was granted marketing authorization by the Food and Drug Administration in late 1985 for the aerosol treatment of infants and young children hospitalized with severe lower respiratory tract infection caused by respiratory syncytial virus. All children are exposed to this virus by the age of two. It can be life-threatening, especially when underlying conditions, such as cardiac conditions, exist.

Marketed under the name of Virazole, ribavirin penetrates the shell surrounding the nucleus of the virus and alters or destroys the nucleus itself.

In 1984, a report from researchers at the U.S. Government's Centers for Disease Control in Atlanta in the British medical journal, *The Lancet*, suggested that ribavirin might also be effective in treating the newly-discovered AIDS disease. Ribavirin had been tested against the human immunodeficiency virus (HIV) in the test tube. The report concluded:

"Our data suggest that ribavirin inhibits the replication of LAV (lymphadenopathy-associated virus) in human adult T lymphocytes in vitro...We feel that these initial data are sufficiently encouraging and the problem they address sufficiently serious to warrant an early report. However, we do not know whether these early laboratory experiments are predictive of a positive clinical effect in patients."

Panic immediately went into action. He arranged tests of ribavirin at eight renowned research centers. For Panic, and his initial belief that his company could make a significant contribution to health through genetic research, it appeared to be a triumph.

"The sequence was very simple. We tested the drug at Cornell on twenty-five patients with HIV, and found it appeared to be active. Then we organized the largest double-blind trial — to that time — ever done against HIV, involving approximately four hundred patients. With those findings, we came out in early 1987 with a very positive report. And yet, we faced an enormous — and unbelievable — avalanche of reaction. Negative reaction to a positive discovery!"

The FDA challenged the test results, claiming that the patient sample was incorrectly chosen and that the findings were not conclusive. Throughout 1987 and 1988, ICN provided additional data and analysis to the FDA. Today, the company and Panic are convinced more than ever that ribavirin may ultimately prove to have a place in mankind's arsenal against HIV.

But this experience has given Panic new perspective on the bureaucratic process, and its relationship to the pharmaceutical industry.

While ICN and the FDA try to sort out the AIDS issue, other teams of independent researchers are finding more uses for ribavirin. Recently, experimental studies have shown that it has efficacy against both A and B types of influenza and hepatitis B, and U.S. Army researchers have demonstrated clinical efficacy of ribavirin against haemorrag- hic fever. In all, ribavirin today is approved for marketing in over thirty countries for use in a variety of viral infections, including hepatitis A, herpes simplex virus, and measles. It is authorized for treating the respiratory syncytial virus in fourteen countries, including the United States. To date, the drug has been used to treat some five million patients throughout the world, and represents a research and development investment of more than $150 million over the past decade or so.

In the meantime, Panic has begun to look at new challenges. This is the question of aging, trying to determine whether or not the aging process — and ultimately, death itself — can be affected by genetic drugs.

Panic believes that "aging begins when the DNA code fails to send a message to repair itself. If we can assist the DNA in sending a message to repair itself, the cells will not age. If the cells do not age, you do not age. We have solved the problem," he says flatly, as if the solution were already at hand.

"We are on the brink of a biological revolution," Panic told an interviewer in 1987. 'The next five years may produce dramatic solutions to the problems of aging."

If Panic can indeed solve the problems of aging, it will simply allow him more time for his favorite activity: Work.

"There is so little to say about me without the company. This is my life and I like it," he tells visitors. "Work is a very important aspect of life, in my view. If you take that as a basic concept, then the rest really fits into it," he adds, noting, "If the company is the workplace, then this is life. Work is a major part of human existence."

His definition of work includes his community service. "This country was good to me. I decided to start giving back more, to work for the community and participate." He helped establish the Norton Simon Museum in Pasadena, and has given unstintingly to hospitals and cultural organizations including Orange County's Performing Arts Center.

When he is not at work, he spends time with his family. After the death of his first wife and young son, he remarried. He and his new wife, Sally, have raised two daughters from his first marriage and three others from her previous marriage. He now enjoys skiing with his grandchildren.

With all his battles, his achievements have not gone unnoticed. Despite his defection from Yugoslavia and subsequent renunciation of Yugoslavian citizenship, Panic's native country now honors him as a "son with vision." And, of course, he treasures the Ellis Island medal as a true symbol of his acceptance by his adopted land.

"What does an immigrant's medal mean?" he asks. "It means a lot to me, because if you are an immigrant you pride yourself on the concept of a country that allows people from anywhere in the world to come here and develop themselves, and still retain their ethnic values or to value their ethnic backgrounds. This is a tremendous idea.

"The world one day will become like America. Everybody

will be accepted everywhere. But the basis of that plan for a future world is going to be the American concept — not Russian, or communism.

"To be an immigrant and to be accepted and recognized means that I am part of a tremendous vision of a future where people will live like immigrants in the whole world and nobody will care where others come from as long as they contribute something to the life of everyone else. I think that is the American way."

Postscript:

ICN had reached sales of $178 million in 1973, before the international accounting nightmare forced Panic to sell off most of his company, driving sales down to $37 million in 1982. As a testament to Panic's determination, ICN sales approached $200 million in 1989, surpassing the previous plateau of 1973. It occurred on Panic's sixtieth birthday.

Jerry Whitfield
Pyro Industries

-10-

PYRO INDUSTRIES

"If a man write a better book, preach a better sermon, or make a better mousetrap than his neighbor, tho' he build his house in the woods, the world will make a beaten path to his door." So said American philosopher Ralph Waldo Emerson nearly 150 years ago, and the words still ring true today. And when one man, Dr. Jerry Whitfield, living in what most Americans would consider "woods" — Everett, Washington, population 55,000 or so — invented a better version of something Emerson himself probably owned, a wood stove, then the *New York Times* , representative of what many think *is* the world, did beat a path to his door.

"Wood stoves are back," heralded the *Times* in 1988, "and some stove manufacturers, like Pyro Industries based in Everett, Washington, have taken the technology of wood-burning appliances to a new level with the introduction of the pellet stove." The article quotes Pyro president, Jerry Whitfield, and credits him with having invented a wood-pellet stove for residential use in 1983. This new development, maintains the *New York Times*, could bring the lowly wood stove back into the same eminence it enjoyed during the oil embargo of the mid-seventies, when such stoves sold at a rate of nearly a million a year.

The wood pellet stove uses as its fuel wood pellets which

are approximately ¼ inch in diameter and are made from waste sawdust, a by-product of the saw mills. The pellet stove resembles a wood stove only in so far as it is a stand-alone room heater and provides a clear view of the roaring fire. In other respects, it is more akin to an automatic furnace as it stores its own supply of pellets (one to two day supply) and self-feeds the fuel and air to the fire as needed.

Jerry Whitfield, a good-looking man of forty-three, does not look like the mad inventor of comic-book fame; he is neatly bearded and academic-looking in his white shirt and pin-striped gray trousers. But as he talks his eyes light up with the enthusiasm of true creativity and his interest in his product is genuinely infectious.

The trouble with the old-fashioned wood stove, he explains, was that it was dirty, polluting, and ineffective. Ineffective because it emitted what is known as "radiant heat," which warms only the area around the source. "Your body reacts more quickly to radiant heat than to the heating up of the air around you with forced convection," he says, "so you can stand in front of a wood stove and get too hot. Then you back away ten feet and you're too cold. You get tremendous temperature gradients." Over time, he adds, as you get hotter you eventually open a window, by which time the fire in the stove has started to die. The room then gets cold, partly as a result of the window you've opened. And so it goes. "Whereas with a pellet stove," he continues, "you're feeding the fuel in continuously. Continuously, at a controllable rate, so it pumps out heat at the desired rate. Once you've got the house up to temperature all you're doing is a simple equation: heat output from the stove equals the heat loss through the windows, roof, and floors, in order to maintain a constant room temperature."

Simple. Brilliant, even. So why did someone not come up with it before? Perhaps because no one had pondered the problem for as long as Whitfield had, or worked with so many fuels for so long. Once, when employed by G.E.C. in the United Kingdom (no connection with G.E. in the United States, although they both make similar products), Whitfield tried out different fuels, from coal and wood to refuse-derived fuels, in a new combustion chamber. "Coal," he says, "was very dirty to handle, difficult to burn clean, with a lot of sulphur in it. Its only redeeming factor is that it's relatively cheap. Hog fuel, wood in sawdust form, was very wet, difficult to burn, and dangerous. It's stored in a big pile and can generate enough heat through the evaporation of the water inside to ignite spontaneously. Refuse-derived fuels have all kinds of toxic problems." As he worked with and rejected these different substances, Jerry (one cannot call him Dr. Whitfield for long; even his employees call him Jerry) thought about the ideal fuel. "Mentally, anyway, I tried to come up with a specification for the ideal solid fuel," he says.

This ideal fuel would be clean, easy to handle, dry, and would burn with a minimum amount of carbon monoxide emissions. "I didn't know what the heck it was," he says candidly, "until 1983." In 1983 a friend who knew of Jerry's interest in these matters introduced him to a small consulting engineering firm in Tacoma, just south of Seattle. This firm was in the alternative-energy field and was involved in the management of a wood-pellet mill. Commercially, the wood pellets were being used in large-scale boilers and furnaces at institutions like hospitals and prisons. "They were developed up here in the Northwest in the early seventies as a commercial fuel," says Jerry. This he knows now. Then, he had never even heard of pellets made from sawdust.

So it was pure serendipity, really, this meeting of man and fuel. As soon as he heard about the pellets, Jerry says, "a light went on in my head, and I thought, 'This is what I specified mentally ten years ago when I was searching for the ideal fuel." It was clean — people wouldn't mind handling the pellets; they were hard and round, which meant they could be fed easily with an auger-feed system; they were dry, therefore with forced-air combustion they could burn clean. Jerry was hooked. And thereupon he set about designing the perfect stove for the ideal fuel.

In those early days, after designing and testing a number of concepts, he decided to have a prototype built. "I got a local sheet-metal fabricator to make it," he recalls, "and when I felt that I'd got the design about right — the prototype looked good, it worked well — I said, 'Well now, what am I going to do with this?' I'd played with a lot of novel ideas and concepts in my life and this was the first one I felt had any commercial realism to it." Coming up in May of 1984 was the annual wood stove trade show put on by the Wood Heating Alliance. It was to be in Reno, and Jerry decided to get himself a booth and see if he would get a reaction.

He did. "For four days straight we probably never had fewer than twenty people around the booth," he says. "It captured their interest. The industry was just on the point of taking a big nose dive and the EPA (Environmental Protection Agency) was talking about emissions regulations. None of the manufacturers knew how to make a clean-burning wood stove. What were they going to do? The timing, in retrospect, was absolutely perfect." One company from Kansas was so impressed that they immediately placed an order for a thousand stoves and Jerry nearly panicked. "Well, I had no way of responding to that," he laughs. "I was employed full-time by Boeing and I had a small local sheet-metal fabricator." The last thing he would normally be building was wood stoves. "So, we talked this particular customer out of wanting a thousand stoves immediately and said, 'let this thing develop.'" Then some local people convinced Jerry that he should at least start manufacturing a few, if only to see how they would turn out.

The stoves sold. "I finally realized," he says, "that I was going to have to prepare for a decent-sized business, otherwise I'd never be able to keep up with the demand once it got going. So I put together a business plan, went to various people, and got some early investors. We put together $25,000 to give the thing a kick-off, then, by the winter of 1984-85, I got serious. I started putting together a dealer network and made plans to leave Boeing in early 1985. Up to this point, it had been only a hobby."

It all happened so smoothly that's it's difficult to believe that Jerry is no M.B.A., no businessman, but is what he himself refers to as "an ivory-tower engineer," a Cambridge Ph.D. in aero-acoustic engineering ("the noise made by jet engines," he explains).

Jerry Whitfield was born in London, England, and spent most of his early life in the south of England. "I went to college, did an aeronautical engineering degree at Southampton University, then did a Ph.D. at Cambridge." But his connection with the United States had begun long before that. "Before going to college I received an exchange scholarship to a prep school," he says, "so my first introduction to the States was at the Lawrenceville School in New Jersey. I had a super year there and it piqued my interest in coming back."

That opportunity came after Jerry's undergraduate study, in 1967, when the rapidly-expanding Boeing company came to Europe to recruit eager young engineering talent. "They came down to Southampton and offered me a nice job at three times the salary of any job in England," he recalls, "plus they offered to pay my way out here. I was twenty-one and single, and said to myself 'What a great opportunity!' When

Boeing agreed to let him ship his car, a Jaguar XK140, to New York so that he could drive it across the continent, he was totally sold. "I made a good trip of it," he smiles, "and I got to Seattle in November 1967." He immediately fell in love with the Pacific Northwest.

By 1970 Boeing's fortunes had dipped and Jerry, who had worked in the jet-propulsion division as a specialist on exhaust nozzles and inlets (for a new plane which would ultimately become the 767), decided to leave and travel around the world, with three other Englishmen whom he had met there.

"We pooled our savings and bought airplane tickets, and flew out to Japan and the Far East," he says. "We had bought an old Land Rover and had that shipped to India. We travelled all over India, Nepal, Pakistan, and drove all the way back to England. Took nine months, through places you can no longer go, like Iran and Afghanistan." In India Jerry managed to catch a virus. "We had gone to a restaurant, and the Ganges was right outside the door. We figured later that that must have been where they washed the dishes!" By the time they reached Turkey he was ill with hepatitis, and he was forced to fly home to England to recuperate.

Once recovered, he called Boeing to inquire about work there, but with no success. "They had dropped from employment of 107,000, bottoming out at 35,000. People were being laid off all over the place." So he went to work for Rolls Royce — which promptly declared bankruptcy....Those were not the best of times. But, since the bankruptcy seemed to have been merely a ploy to get out of a contractual obligation with Lockheed, Wilson's Labour Government lost no time stepping in and buying the company. Jerry stayed on, and ultimately found himself working on the Concorde project.

The major problem with the Concorde for many years had been acoustic; most major airports didn't want it to land because it made too much noise. "Working on the sound levels of the Concorde was one of the most interesting and challenging jobs in my life," says Jerry. "It was a very very difficult problem. We had some good ideas, and were well on our way to implementing them when the program was cancelled. The government had finally grown tired of pouring money into the Concorde." But it was during that period that Jerry got his Ph.D. Rolls Royce had set up a research unit at Cambridge, and Jerry had gone there as the company's representative. Not many doctoral candidates are so fortunate as to work with a Concorde as Jerry did. "A long way from pellet stoves," he comments.

Jerry's three-year involvement with Rolls Royce came to an end simultaneously with his doctorate and the end of the Concorde program. "No one was going to buy the Concorde, and the price of aviation fuel had gone through the roof," he explains. So he went to G.E.C.'s research laboratories. "I worked in nuclear-power stations — even in South Korea. In particular I was involved with developing a scheme to measure the performance of a full nuclear-plant steam-generator set." It was a good apprenticeship for someone who would later work with heating systems. Then, on the first work day of 1979, Jerry received a telephone call from his old boss at Boeing. Would he come back? By this time Jerry had been married and was living in the Midlands. They were expecting their first child, and it was not an easy decision. He had a good situation in England, but "I had fallen in love with this area and had made good friends here." That, and the fact that coming back would give him the chance to participate in a commercial program again, made him decide to return. "Because you do get very divorced from the real world when you work in research," he admits.

He says now that from a management point of view the move back to Boeing was the best thing that could have happened to him. "It was a good education for me," he says. Boeing needed Jerry for their 767 certification program. "They had learned from their previous disastrous experience with the 747," he says. "When they couldn't get it certified they couldn't deliver it. So their policy on their next plane was, 'we'll do our background work more thoroughly this time and we'll get more engineers to take care of it.' I guess the company did a good job on the 767; they had virtually no problems, so there were all kinds of eminently-qualified people sitting around with nothing to do." That experience stood Jerry in good stead with Pyro, for not only did he learn to focus on quality, he learned to try to foresee and solve problems before they became a major issue.

This approach is obvious in the company's attitude to quality control. At a meeting with Production Manager Don Schultz, Line Foreman Jim Martin, Sales Manager Drew McDaniel, and Marketing Director Ken Hussey, the men move easily from discussing the smallest details of the burn grates and burn pipes to the problems with noise and vibration. The influence of Boeing is palpable in the professional demeanor of the men in the room, in their attention to minutiae, and their intensity. The meeting is one of equals, of men who are all expert at what they do and who respect each other's opinion. What is obviously at stake is the betterment of their product, not the individual egos of the men there. It's refreshing, and rare in such a relatively small and new firm.

Marketing Director Ken Hussey says of the firm that it is a "team concept." He became involved with Pyro in 1986 and came on board officially in January 1988. "From the production people out there on the floor to management in here there isn't a door that's ever shut," he says. He then shuts the door, adding laughingly, "unless we're having a private meeting." He continues, "We *want* that open feeling. Any person in the plant can walk up here and talk to me, and vice versa.

"I'm not an academic manager, if you like," says Jerry. "I haven't gone through business school, don't know the names and the philosophies. I believe first of all in delegating, but at the same time putting managers in place who know every job they're 'in command of'. So the financial manager knows everything from the bookkeeping on upwards. The sales manager has been out on the road as a sales representative, that sort of thing." It's obvious from the attitudes and from the general atmosphere that even though the idea is Jerry's, the company style is democratic.

Pyro is structured quite simply; Jerry acts as CEO and chief engineer. "Under me I have a marketing director who covers inside and outside sales, a director of finance who also covers all the general office administration, a plant manager responsible for all our plant facilities and for developing and evolving the stove designs. A production manager has two shift foremen directly under him and is responsible for the day-to-day operations of the production line, hiring and firing of production employees, and so on. As chief engineer I also have research and development and production under me. We also have another production manager, who happens also to be my wife — she's responsible for purchasing all the parts that go into the stove, absolutely everything, keeping inventory control, advance purchasing, scheduling, that kind of thing. Then there are the sales staff, bookkeeper, secretary/receptionist, plus about eight or nine outside sales reps." All in all there are around ninety plant employees and ten office persons.

By and large Jerry has stuck to his original staff, and the

formula works. "We've doubled our business every year so far," he says. "We were just over $2 million two years ago, and $700,000 the year before that. Last year we were over $5 million, and in 1989 we will exceed $10 million. The figures speak for themselves."

The story of Whitfield's coup in the pellet-stove industry reads a bit like the "how-to-succeed-in-business" section of a textbook. "First of all, I think, we were in the right place at the right time," he says, "with the right idea. We've introduced a new technology and we've been recognized as the leaders, which is a good position if you can maintain it. You've got to be technically and financially capable of holding onto that position, but you *get* there by being there first and by being credible. Credibility is vital.

"It's a question of doing things right," continues this perfectionist engineer. "Developing a good product, following up with better products, being prepared to have others come along and try to overtake you — but keeping one step ahead of them." One of Pyro's advertisements says: "Who's our toughest competitor? We are," apropos of a new stove they have launched. For Jerry, what this translates to is the time and energy devoted to research and development, which too few firms tend to take seriously.

And, simplistic as it sounds, it is important, says Jerry, that when one is in the manufacturing business one be *good* at manufacturing. "That entails a lot of things," he points out. "It means having the right equipment, the right process design in your plant in order to make the product at the right price. Furthermore, it is not enough for a product to be functional; it also must *look* good. Packaging and external details matter. "Customers assume that every product will work as well as the next, but if one product *looks* better, people will buy that," he says. "Looks sell. And you have to consider sales, first and foremost."

He doesn't scorn the so-called "basic" management techniques either. "I've taken on good-calibre staff, and they've worked well," he says. "They've supported me and we've formed a good close-knit team. I think this has been perceived out in the field. You go talk to our dealers. They say 'this is a company that sticks by its product — and performs as they say they will.' That's the kind of image we're trying hard to create, not by advertising but by going the full ten yards: Doing what's necessary to support the product and to keep on improving it. Then to have the best salespeople out there who will give the service and who are knowledgeable. In short," he finishes, "Being a good, *professional* organization."

This is especially important since they are in what Jerry laughingly calls a "low-tech" industry, particularly at the retail end. "Retailers are not necessarily good business or technical people," he says. "They need to be assisted and trained in marketing our products." This came as a bit of a shock to Jerry who had been accustomed, at Boeing, to dealing with airlines who often knew as much about the planes as did the engineers themselves and possibly more. "Here," says Jerry, "you spring something on them and it's 'What's a pellet stove? I've never heard of it — how do I sell it?' We've had to relearn our sales technique a lot. We definitely do not do the 'hard sell'. So when someone comes to us and wants to handle our line we can give them the whole package and then be confident they can go out to do a good job for us."

Jerry may not have known too much about business, but he had realized in his years at different corporations that the key to any successful business is its personnel, which must comprise knowledgeable individuals capable of filling in the cracks. Ken Hussey, who has been in the wood-stove industry ever since he left school and has seen it grow "from infancy to multi-million dollar business" is one such person.

He says Jerry's idea drew him from the very start. The concept of self-feeding, the cleanliness of not having the mess of a wood stove, not to mention the constant heat the pellet stove provides all attracted him. "Since 1983, when the company started, and 1984, our first year of real production, we have come a long way," he says proudly. "This last year we have built more stoves than in the previous two years. We're growing as fast as we can without losing control. When you're a company that's in a growth period," he adds, "well, I have seen so many go out and destroy their market and their product by failing to provide good service and good training for their dealers. Also, when companies are in a growth period like that they often over-borrow. Banks, believing in them, give them money and they over-extend themselves." Ken Hussey sees one of his roles at Pyro as overseer, making sure that Pyro "grows within its means."

It often happens that companies founded on one idea, with a brilliant inventor at the head, find themselves unable to cope with expansion. Larger companies cannot be run in the same casual and haphazard fashion as smaller ones. Jerry, having worked for large companies, and having the intelligence to see the pitfalls of a company that revolves around him alone, has avoided this thorny issue.

Hussey says there is no reason why Pyro cannot continue to expand, given the market that exists. He simply realizes there will be more competition, and therefore they will have to keep their edge by remaining better than the others. "When Jerry started he was 'It'," he says. "Now, there are approximately twenty other manufacturers, probably only about six or seven real competitors, but nothing is going to slow this industry down." Jerry adds that they must maintain their head start with high quality control - not just advertising it, but by providing it.

The highest standards in the world cannot ensure that all problems can be foreseen, however. Jerry's horror stories all have to do with some detail they managed to overlook. "You think you've done all the testing," he says, "and you get into production; then, six months later, you find a problem. For instance, the stoves don't operate quite the same at high altitudes as they do at sea level — really we should have a high-altitude lab as well. *Those* are the kinds of things I lie awake at night worrying about," he concludes.

One has to keep a sense of perspective, though. One simply has to come up with a solution to each problem, multiply it by a ten or a hundred, depending on how many units are affected, and go out there and "retrofit" everything. "That's a nightmare," he admits, "but you've either got to pay the dealers to go out and do it or you've got to send out someone from your own company." Dealers don't like doing that sort of thing, it's disruptive of their time, so it's usually the company that deals with it. It has to. This is the sort of attitude that ensures buyer confidence and advertising by word-of-mouth.

"In some ways, the worst part of being innovative and creative is the need to get enough testing under your belt, under all conditions you hadn't thought of. Other horror stories have less to do with the product than with bad judgement in picking dealers. You make a bad mistake in choosing a dealer; you get one that doesn't understand the product even though you've trained him.....I'm not too far off if I say eighty percent of problems in the field come from the way the stoves were installed. The exhaust wasn't hooked up right, or wasn't hung right."

In some ways Jerry might agree with P.T. Barnum's cynical observation that one never went broke underestimating the intelligence of the public, but unless Jerry decides to do his own distribution and direct sales he has to work with the outside dealers. (Most of whom, he hastens to add, have been intensely loyal and extremely capable.) Buyers, too, blithely disregard directions and do silly things like attempting to start the stove with a flammable liquid — "because they had a can of gasoline in the garage." "How do you protect against that sort of thing?" he asks rhetorically.

Then there is the funnier side. "We had one stove, one of the built-in ones," relates Jerry. "It was summer and the stove was not in use. The owners heard a noise coming from it. They opened the door to investigate and two birds flew out! They had nested in the exhaust pipe and couldn't find the front door to get out. They had gone backwards through the blower impeller right back into the stove." But this story had a happy ending; the birds flew out unharmed.

Naturally, lacking a crystal ball one cannot predict events, but it seems likely that Jerry Whitfield, and Pyro too, will have a happy ending. Partly because theirs is a product for the time, but also partly because Pyro works at being a good business with a good product. "We take a very conservative approach wherever we can," says Jerry bluntly. "We know it's a risky business. When we go through a design we always test for all the worst-scenario possibilities; we try to document everything; we review the data; we don't jump to quick conclusions but go back and test and test and retest." One must be thorough. "When the production line starts rolling, if you've made a mistake you've suddenly got a hundred mistakes, a thousand mistakes to be dealt with.

Safety comes first, no matter what. "We may make a very conservative technical decision; the stove might work better if we did *this* rather than *that*, but if 'this' is safer than 'that', then this is what we'll go with. You try to anticipate everything people will do to mess up the stove, but you can't. So it's still a learning process."

For Jerry Whitfield, the learning process is the business.

Which is why he will continue to build a better stove; and why the world will continue to beat a path to his door. Soon, that path will be a highway....

Janie D'Addio
Security Manufacturing Corporation

-11-

SECURITY MANUFACTURING CORPORATION

"Neither rain nor wind nor dark of night...shall keep them from their appointed rounds." So goes the motto of the U.S. Postal Service; and the Post Office has always done a pretty good job of moving the mail. But where to deliver it is another question. As the population has grown, so has the volume of mail, and there have not always been sufficient locations to which it can be delivered conveniently. That's why the private mail-receiving business has come into being. In recent years, this business has grown into a multi-million dollar industry, thanks in no small part to the efforts of an energetic and determined woman from Orange Country, California.

There are millions of women in this country who married early, had children, and spent years keeping house for a husband, only to find themselves approaching middle age, faced with a divorce and with no way to make a living. It happened to Janie D'Addio. But she did something about it; she believes any woman can, even if it takes some time to find that out.

Born Janie Henson, the youngest of seven children, she grew up on a farm outside the little town of Cassville, not far from Joplin, in the hill country of southern Missouri. When she was old enough to go school she walked four miles to school and four miles home daily, and never missed a day. And every year she received a silver dollar for her perfect attendance. It was the first money she would earn, but it was to be far from the last.

Lonely, as a child, Janie turned inward to discover a world of imagination, and developed an avid interest in art and literature. When the bookmobile from the county library came by, she would check out a whole armload of novels and bury herself in their pages for days. "I'd read anything," she recalls, "and I loved to draw." Her artistic talent inspired her sixth-grade teacher to enter her work in a national contest. When she won a scholarship to study art, the embarrassed college had to reconsider when they discovered they had awarded it to an eleven-year old girl.

As her sisters were considerably older, and her brothers were generally off pursuing their own pleasures, Janie spent much of the time by herself. But she was aware that there was a world out there, and she yearned to be part of it. Her father used to tell her she could do anything she wanted to do, if she would only put her mind to it, and over the years, she has indeed proved the wisdom of his counsel.

When she reached her teens Janie felt she could wait no longer. She quit school at thirteen, packed what little she had, and hitch-hiked her way to California. She shakes her head now thinking back on it. "Can you imagine, a thirteen-year-old girl hitch-hiking across the country, all the way from Missouri to California? When I think of my own daughter doing the same thing, it scares me to death." But she made it. When she arrived, she went to the factory where her girl friend worked and got a job.

Three years later, barely sixteen, she was married and almost immediately started having babies. "I was raised to think that you had to get married," she says. "You got to be sixteen, seventeen years old, you married somebody, and you had to have two kids, at least. That was what a woman was supposed to do. Where I came from, that is what you did. That was the way it was, you know — Southern Baptist, Missouri, the Ozarks. So I thought, 'Okay, I'm sixteen, I should get married and have a couple of kids right away, right? So that's what I did, got that out of the way."

During the next twenty years, she would raise her family — and wait. "Well, after I had the two kids, I looked around and said to myself 'Here I am, twenty years old, a wife, a mother, with no education. What am I going to do now?' It took me about fifteen minutes to clean the house every morning. What was I going to do all day? So I started doing charity work."

Her husband was an electrician. He was from Montana, and was definitely of the old school; among other things, he didn't believe in women working. "Oh, he believed in me working for free, doing charity work, all right. But he didn't believe I ought to get paid for it.

"I had always been very energetic, so when I got into anything I was very active. I was active in the church, and I was active in every charity that came along. I helped in a lot of the public schools here; I would do all kinds of art work for them. The parents were interested in what kind of things their kids were working with in school. I'd go in and help the teachers make up all kinds of programs for them, especially in the inner city and in Santa Ana.

"So, for about fifteen years I was doing all this charity work. I mean, I was *working*. I was working all day, every day, I was taking stuff home to work on at night, I was working weekends for these people. I was working a full-time job. Plus doing all my housework on top of that. And I wasn't getting paid for any of it. Finally I started realizing I wasn't even getting a 'thank you' for it.

"Then my father got sick, so I went back to Missouri. I was very, very close to my father, even though I had run away from home. I was his daughter, more than my mother's. He never would allow me to get spanked, or anything like that. He always told me I was something special. And I was always treated as special, because I was the baby. Well, he got real ill, with stomach cancer, and didn't recover. And I spent ten weeks with him at the hospital, I stayed at the hospital and took care of him. Until he died.

"When I came back I was devastated. The day I got home from the funeral, I got a phone call. It was from the school, from this teacher, who demanded, 'Where have you *been*? I've been trying to reach you for six weeks. We need you down here to do this and this and this.' And I said, 'No kidding. I just didn't think I had to report to you that I was burying my father.' She acted like I was employed there. I hung up that phone and I said, 'That's the end of that.' I never did another day's work for nothing."

After some research in the local library, Janie decided to get a real estate licence. She went to real estate school, but she didn't want to take the time to attend all the classes she was told she would need to get her licence. Impatient, as always, she obtained all the tests and studied them, and then went out and passed her examinations in record time. Now she was a licensed real estate salesperson.

At that point, she traded in some of the equity in her home and bought a second house. She knew this property would appreciate in a very few years as Orange County continued to grow. She went to work for Red Carpet Real Estate as a novice agent, a position that would scarcely last through the first year.

Then her natural impatience exerted itself. She didn't want to work for somebody else. But it took two years to get a broker's licence in California, and, as you might expect, Janie did not want to wait two years. So she "rented" another person's licence and opened her own office. It was not an unusual or unethical practice; she would simply open what amounted to a branch office for him.

She did just that, hiring ten people (mostly women) to work for her. In no time she had turned her operation into the best office in the entire Century 21 network. They won practically all the awards in the company, every month. The office was finally sold, for the highest price any office had ever brought in, and she thereupon started her own investment company.

When that company was up and running, and her financial future no longer in doubt, Janie told her husband she wanted a divorce. She was ready; he was shocked. But, as with most matters there was no stopping her; she flew to Haiti and got her divorce in fifteen minutes. She already owned more than he did, so she decided to give *him* a settlement. She bought a place of her own, near the water in Newport Beach and now, at the age of thirty-eight, she was free to pursue her own interests, and determined to enjoy every minute of it. To celebrate, she decided to treat herself to a vacation.

She went to San Juan, Puerto Rico, to enjoy the sun and the gambling in the casino there. She loved to play the horses, to play poker and, most of all, to play blackjack. "I do *love* to play blackjack," she says with a grin, "especially if I'm winning. I do love to win." And winning does seem to be a natural state for this woman. On this trip, however, she would win more than she expected.

She had taken her sister with her. Much of the time the sister was off with some man she had met, having a great time. But Janie just wanted to relax, forget about men, and enjoy herself. Little did she suspect that she was about to meet the man who would become her second husband, and who would eventually work for *her*.

One night she was in the casino, at the blackjack table,

when she felt someone's eyes on her. She looked up and saw a man a short way across the room, staring at her. She thought, "What a jerk!" But then he smiled at her — and she smiled back. When she looked up again, he had disappeared.

"Pretty soon I felt somebody was staring at me again," she says. "When I turned around, he was behind me, over on this side staring at me again. He was talking to some guy, who I found out later was his attorney. They had come to Puerto Rico together for a weekend. Then they walked over and went into the lounge. So I said to myself, 'Well, hell, I might just go have a drink.'

"So I cashed in my chips and wandered over to the lounge and looked around. Now, you have to understand that I have never ever picked up a man in my entire life, before that or after. But I was curious. So, I'm looking around and there he is. He came over and said, 'Are you looking for your husband?' And I said, 'No, I'm not married.' He said, 'Oh, I thought you were. I saw your wedding ring.' Do you know I had forgotten to take my wedding rings off? That's how little they mattered to me. In fact, I was shocked to find that I still had them on.

"So I said to him, 'Would it matter to you if I was married or not?' And he was so flustered. My husband is so shy about some things. He said, no, it really wouldn't matter to him. I said 'Why don't you buy me a drink?' So he bought me a drink and we talked. We hit it off right away. I ended up taking him back to my hotel room. Kept him there for nine days, without going out at all, not even for food; we had a room-service bill you wouldn't believe. But it was sure worth it."

Sal D'Addio was a successful businessman in his own right, with property, investments, and other business interests in the Northeast. But after nine days in Puerto Rico with Janie, he flew home to Connecticut, sold his apartment houses and businesses and headed west to join her. They've been together ever since.

Meanwhile, she flew to California to do the same. She closed her real estate office, and gave everybody back their licences. Whatever deals she had pending, she transferred to other brokers who she knew could handle them. Then she liquidated all of her holdings, selling all her apartment houses and property. By the time Sal arrived, she was ready to go. And go they did. For the next three years, they travelled all over the world.

Returning to Southern California, they bought a motor-home, intending to travel some more. Because they needed a way to get their mail they went down to get a Post Office box. Here they learned that there weren't any available, and probably wouldn't be for months, even years, not only at their local station but all over Orange County.

Problems don't stay without solutions for long in the world of Janie D'Addio. Around the corner from the Post Office, she discovered a man running a private mail-receiving service, out of a storefront. Recognizing a good idea when she saw one, Janie decided to go into business for herself.

Purchasing several sets of boxes from a company that supplied the Post Office, she opened three mailbox stores of her own. They were instantly successful; so much so that, hardly a month after she'd opened their doors, she sold them for three times what they had cost her. "We started up in early December of 1979," she recalls. "By the first week of January, we had had such a response I said, 'This has got to be the best business in the world.' So I ran a three-line ad in the *Orange County Register*, and sixty-four people came and wanted to buy them. I sold two of them to the first guy, and the third one to the second guy, and I used the office there to start the manufacturing company."

She had decided she really belonged in the other end of the business, supplying the boxes, so she started out in her garage, and subcontracted most of the work. "I didn't have the faintest idea how to build mailboxes," she says with a laugh. "But orders were coming in and I had to get them out. So I went to a man who owned a small factory, showed him a prototype, and said 'This is what I want. I have no idea how to put this thing together, but I know you do. Can you make it for me?' He probably wondered what I was doing in this business." Little did he know. But he did know how to make the boxes she wanted, and her fledgling business, Security Manufacturing, was up and flying.

By the time the first boxes were built and ready to ship, Janie found it necessary to rent an office, so she leased a 3,000-square-foot plant and started building. Although she quickly established her own production facility, she still had to subcontract part of the work out, because so many orders were coming in. For the first year, she and her crew worked in that 3,000-square-foot plant in Costa Mesa, but by Christmas of that year, it too was inadequate.

So she bought another building near the first one, a 10,000-square-foot structure, and spent the 1980 holiday season moving the plant. The business outgrew that one in about three years, but they stayed there for a time, leasing extra space elsewhere as needed. Then, in January of 1988, she bought the building the company is in now, a cavernous structure of 40,000 square feet, in nearby Garden Grove.

The necessity of asking men for help didn't bother Janie one bit — and still doesn't. She's known for years that there are men who think that women aren't quite up to doing business properly, and that when a woman asks for assistance it is proof she is not as capable as a man. This archaic attitude doesn't in the least disturb the chief executive and sole stockholder of Security Manufacturing, who knows better. As she points out with a smile, "You know, when all is said and done, I'm the one who takes the check to the bank."

As for the politics of some of her contemporaries, Janie has a few less-than-kind words. "There are some women, especially those who think of themselves as being in the liberation movement, who would say, 'You don't ever want to ask men for help, because that makes them think they're smarter than you are.' To that, I say, 'Let them!'"

The results are self-evident. "What happened is that now, ten years later, I'm ten times, maybe a hundred times, wealthier than they are. So, I ask you, who's smarter? What does 'smarter' really mean? They do their job well, I do mine. I make it, and I sell it. If I believe in the product, I can sell anything. And that's what it's all about, isn't it?"

In the case of Janie D'Addio, that certainly *is* what it's all about. "I don't know how many boxes we made that first year. But the demand started off strong and kept getting stronger. It's easier to think of it in terms of stores. The number kept doubling every year, to the point where now we've set up stores all over the country."

Most of Janie's business, probably eighty-five percent of it, according to her estimate, is with people who are running a business out of their home. They don't want to use their home address, and they don't want a Post Office box number because it makes them look like a fly-by-night organization.

Some of their concern has its roots in history. "A long time ago, they had these transient hotels, where people could get their mail. That's where the CMRA's — the Commercial Mail Receiving Agencies — got their name. Trouble was, there were people dodging the law and things like that, which gave it a bad name. We don't deal with anybody like that."

Her records indicate that her customers are now operating

about ten thousand offices across the country. Indeed, they are all over the world, in about twelve countries so far. There are stores in Canada, Puerto Rico, Hawaii, Guam, even the Philippines; and she knows practically all of them. "You know, the day Aquino took over in Manila we had a guy open a mailbox store there."

Janie D'Addio not only knows her people, she believes in doing everything she can to support them. To help her new customers to succeed in their new-found ventures she wrote a book. She called it *"Turning Mailboxes Into Cash Boxes,"* and to date has sold tens of thousands of copies. In it she lays out a complete plan for setting up and operating a private mailbox facility, complete with sample forms, rate schedules, and floor plans. She even has a section with ideas for ancillary services, like word-processing, fax, or copy machines. Written in the same straightforward way its author talks, the manual is a nearly-foolproof guidebook to success. It should be. It is based on the experience of someone who not only knows the business, but who practically invented it.

Janie is proud of what she has accomplished. "I created this business," she states with no false modesty. "Oh, there are other box manufacturers, of course. But they don't understand what these entrepreneurs really need. I do. After all, I am one."

Part of the reason she has come to dominate her industry lies in the product she puts out. "Nobody else makes the box we make. First of all, their prices are higher, and their quality is lower. Also, they sell mostly to the Post Office. They just were never into this kind of an industry. Some do sell to private businesses, but very few. That left the field to me. The result was that, for all practical purposes, I was the only one making the boxes these people needed."

Over the last ten years, Security's product line has

expanded. "We make every style of post-office box that anybody needs. We have four models for the private mailbox industry. First, there's the standard aluminum box, that looks just like the new ones in the Post Office. Then we make the gold box, like the old ones the Post Office used to have, but without the window. The windows were always getting broken and people could see into the box, so we redesigned it. We also have a special Eagle edition, a reproduction of the antique boxes with the eagle on it, which is beautiful. And there is also the front-load box. Plus the apartment-house boxes. We got into making a line of vertical boxes for apartment houses about two years ago; now we're a major force in that part of the industry, too. And, finally, there's the cluster box for the Post Office. So we make six different kinds of boxes."

In 1981, she met some people in San Diego who wanted to start a franchise operation they called Mailboxes, Etc. She liked their idea, and decided to help them get started. She bought stock in the fledgling company, and eventually owned fifty percent of it. As the business grew, she kept investing in it, first by supplying them with the boxes, and then occasionally supplying them with cash. Like so many businesses when they first start out, they had cash-flow problems, and one thing Janie had was cash. "It was a pretty sweet deal," she says, "for both of us, actually."

Then, in 1985, Pak-Mail came along. It was a little company, started in Denver. Two or three other little franchise operations had started up, but this one caught her interest. It was right in the middle of the country and, in Janie's opinion, perfectly situated for expansion. "I figured they needed a little exposure back there," she says. So, after thinking it over, she sold her interest in Mailboxes, Etc. and invested in Pak-Mail. It has since become a public company, and she now owns thirty-seven percent of it.

"I got a five-year contract to sell the company all its boxes." That contract, which is still operating, amounted to several million dollars' worth of business for Security Manufacturing and, of course, more profit for Janie.

"I made the same kind of deal with Pak-Mail, too. I have a five-year contract to sell them boxes. I had bought into the company, and they decided that they might as well get their boxes from someone who just happened to be a major shareholder. Besides, I'm the only person in this business that services this industry as well as it can be serviced." This assessment is supported by the fact that so much of her business is from regular clients.

There are approximately eighteen franchise companies in the private-mail business, with fifteen who provide turnkey operations. They go in and put the whole shop together and tell you how to do it, and then they're gone. You're on your own, and whatever you make is yours. There are no royalty payments.

Recently, Security was approved to do business with the Post Office. "They want to start using a new box, it's called a cluster box. You've probably seen 'em. They're out in front of offices, or on street corners in new tracts of homes. They have a group of boxes on a pedestal. It's like a return to the old row of mailboxes on a post, only slicker. But that's the direction the Post Office wants to go; and if they want 'em, we'll make 'em."

There used to be about twenty-five companies that sold to the Post Office; now the number is down to about six. Of these, only four companies have qualified to make the new box "....and mine is one of them," grins Janie. "There are a lot of companies, some of them eighty or a hundred years old, that wanted that contract, but they couldn't get it. I could."

Even though her company does millions of dollars worth

of business every year, her staff comprises only two salespersons, one accountant, one shipping and receiving person, and one secretary. "I run a tight ship. But I have very good employees. In fact, I've got the most efficient staff in the business. Right now, I'm one of the major suppliers in the country of post-office boxes of all kinds. And according to the financial information I've received, I'm also the most profitable company in the country.

"We really pride ourselves on making a quality mailbox. The Post Office sends people out to inspect the plant and the boxes and everything, and they'll vouch for the kind of product we make. I was in Washington recently for a meeting on women-owned businesses. While I was there, we got a report from the Post Office that we were making the best mailbox in the country, the best quality. We've done it. We're the best."

Besides justifiable pride, one thing Janie definitely has in plentiful supply is enthusiasm. When asked about any aspect of the mailbox business, she waxes estatic. "This is the hottest little business I've ever seen in my life. I've put so many people in business, people that never thought they could have a business. Women whose kids grew up and they didn't have to be home all the time, women who didn't know anything, didn't have any education to speak of. Like me. I never even went to high school.

"A lot of women my age — I'm fifty years old — got married very young and never went through school. They had kids, and stayed home, and never did learn how to do anything except keep house for some man — who was probably going to leave 'em some day, anyway. So when I first got in this business, that's who I went after, those women. It was a natural. It gave them a chance to make it in a world that was stacked against them.

"Of course, I think the whole system was made wrong to

start with. I think we should have done something else, about training women to work, about encouraging people to run smaller businesses. More smaller businesses is what I think this country needs, not big conglomerates. With more small businesses, each one could have a reasonable number of clients and serve its share of the market, instead of one monster company that thinks it has to take up the whole world.

"My real interest in life has been to help women that don't think they can do anything; I show them they really can. I get calls from women who say, 'I just can't believe it. I just love this business. It's just what I wanted. I get to socialize with my customers. They all love me because I give them such good service, and they had such a miserable time at the Post Office.' It's become a business they can relate to. It's not a high-stress job to do. It's not a regulated business. There is no regulation on the private postal industry, except for a few rules about forwarding and sizes. Basically, it's a very, very simple business, and of course you can add anything to it. We help them with everything — from a manual that shows them the business start to finish, to supplying all their equipment to open their store. That's the nice thing. It's made this a real happy job, for me.

"These mailbox stores have changed things for a lot of people. They've become a neighborhood service center. People are realizing they can get so many things there that they can't get in a Post Office. You can't get welfare checks in a P.O. box. You can't get the record-of-the-month; how they gonna put it in your P.O. box? You can't get a UPS package there; you can't get a Federal Express. You can't get any of the other carriers there. The only thing you can get in that box is what goes through the U.S. Postal Service.

"That's one reason private boxes have become so popular. UPS has outpriced the Post Office. In our shops, with a package up to about thirty-five pounds, you're still cheaper than the Post Office, even with your service charge for UPS on top of it.

"It's been very interesting. We've been at it for about ten years now. In fact, now that I think of it, this is our tenth anniversary. We'll be at for another ten years, too. Or twenty. We've had a lot of fun, we've made a lot of money, and we've made a lot of friends out there. We can't go to a city anywhere in the country that we don't have people in now.

"It's virtually an unlimited market. And the competition isn't increasing, like you might think, it's actually decreasing. A lot of box companies get in trouble. In fact, two of them went out of business just this year, two big ones. One is a major company that has been in business for years, but it's in bankruptcy now. I don't know if *they* call it bad management, but *I* sure think it is. They got too big and didn't control their company."

That isn't likely to be the fate of Security Manufacturing. If nothing else, Janie D'Addio is firmly in control of her company. "Some people think I seem pretty aggressive. I think I'm pretty easy on people. I just expect the job to be done." And she feels that good work should be well rewarded; she pays her employees very well. "We pay the workers in our shop better than any other company in Orange County pays its employees. We have no trouble getting people, we have people who would love to come to work here." Janie knows just how she wants her business run. "I want the place clean, the offices, the factory, everything. It's kind of a joke around here; we have inspectors come in and tell us it looks like a house back there. But that's how I want it.

"I expect a lot out of people. I expect to be able to call them at night, or on weekends. And they can call me, too. If they need money for something, they know they can come to me for it. And they know they won't have to pay interest. We took our entire office staff and their spouses to Cancun for ten days last Christmas. We took them to Cabo San Lucas the year before. We all go as a group and have a great time. It's our way of giving everybody a Christmas bonus.

"I just love this business. And I love being able to help people help themselves." Her customers are well aware of her outlook, and have benefitted from it. The company maintains an 800 number for customers to call her, about anything that comes up in their business. The number, not surprisingly, is 800-PO-BOXES. "I found that, when I spoke to people, they always wanted to be able to call me. So I got that number for them, both in California and around the country. It's the only place, by the way, that we can actually use the term 'P.O. Boxes.' And we do use that line a lot. We talk to our clients all the time. We've got friends all over the country."

Those "friends" are now running some 8,000 stores around the country, many of them run by women. "The first five years, I would say eighty-five percent of them were run by women. Then we started getting into the mini-stores business, like print shops — people that were dealing with other small-business people on a daily basis already, but wanted to tie them to their business all the time. And the mail ties you to someplace; you have to come back to pick up your mail. So if they have to send a package, where are they going to go to send it? You run a print shop, and they need letterhead. Where are they going to go to get their letterhead printed?"

After Janie began selling to all these related companies, she found the approximate percentage of women owners had dropped from eighty-five percent to around sixty-five percent. Then, as she started going around the country, she discovered another phenomenon: husbands were starting to work in their wives' shops. "He starts out just giving her a hand. First thing you know he's quit his job and he's working in her shop. Suddenly the wife's little business isn't so little, after all. It's growing so fast they need another employee, and it's making more money than he was making on his 'regular' job. So they end up in business together."

As always, Janie has an anecdote ready about one of her many successful customers. "The other day, there was a guy in here who has a store out in Irvine, who told me he has four full-time employees and he never even goes in the shop. And this last year after taxes, he made a hundred and fifty-some thousand dollars. On one little shop. It's a very lucrative little business."

Janie says her customers have a failure rate of less than one percent. Three years ago she did a survey. "I sent letters to all the people we had put into the business up to that point, to ask how they were doing and if they were still in business. Do you know that less than one in a hundred weren't there any longer? And that included the people that had moved their offices!"

The reason for the failures, invariably, was that the operator had gone into a place with the lowest rent in town. "The ones who failed always were in that kind of an area," she maintains. "That's not where this business works; it works in the highest-rent areas. That's where people want a business address. They should be next door to the local post office — there's still a chronic shortage of boxes at most post offices — or in a shopping center or near a college campus.

"People are now looking for our centers. We try to locate them predominantly in a shopping center, with a grocery store. Lots of women are working now. On their way home, they may have to stop and get something, and they can run in and get the mail or ship a package at the same time. That's the best location, in a residential area, with some businesses, and lots of homes. Upper-middle and upper income areas have been the best, because so many of those women are working.

"Speaking of women working, I said that I wanted to encourage women to go into business for themselves. I've had a chance to talk to a lot of women's groups, and done a lot of TV shows, maybe fifty or sixty TV shows. Everywhere I go, people ask me the same questions. So I wrote this little book, called *Every Woman Can*." Early in 1983, she printed the first edition of it, with the idea of just giving it away. But again fate intervened.

Before the book was off the press Janie went on the television show *Hour Magazine*. She talked for only about six minutes, about the postal-box business, how she got started and so on. Then the show's host, Gary Collins, said, "It sounds as if you want to help women get started in business." Without hesitation, Janie responded, "Yes, that's right. I do. And not just this business, but anything they want to do. Matter of fact, I've written a little book about that very subject." And he said, 'Oh really? What's the name of the book?' And she told him, "*Every Woman Can*."

During the interview, the location of the business was given only as Huntington Beach, along with the name of the company. No street address was given, and no phone number.

The show was taped, and was to be aired in three weeks, and during this period Janie flew off to New York for a meeting. One day, while she was still there, she realized that the show was supposed to air that very day. Her first impulse was to call home and tell her people that it was to be on, but after a glance at her watch, she decided it was too late. "Well," she thought, "I'll call them in the morning." And she went to bed, not suspecting the storm that was brewing.

Next day, when she tried to get through, she discovered to her surprise that all the lines were busy. They stayed that way all day long. At about eight o'clock that night she finally got through; all the girls were still in the office, answering the phones. People had called *Hour Magazine*, they had called the Building Department in Huntington Beach, they had called the Library, the Chamber of Commerce, even the Post Office, to get her phone number and address.

Hour Magazine called the next day and they said "We are just swamped. We've had to add a bunch of people to our phone room, because we're getting so may phone calls about that segment." Janie was shocked. "What in hell did I say?" she wondered.

The staff of Security Manufacturing was equally amazed. When the first person called in, the phone was answered by the company's secretary. When the caller inquired about the price of the book, she didn't know what to tell them, so she yelled to the back of the office, "How much is Janie gonna sell that book for?" No one knew; she hadn't discussed it with them. So the secretary said to herself, "Well, it's a book, I guess $9.95 sounds about right," and "The price is $9.95," she told the caller.

Janie laughs "You know, we've been selling them for $9.95 ever since then. And we've sold thousands and thousands of them." Not bad for a little booklet she had written and had had printed herself. It drew so much attention that eventually even major chains like Dalton's and Waldenbooks carried it.

Three days later, *Hour Magazine* called again. The show had been aired on a Monday. By Wednesday, they said, they had received more calls and more letters than they had ever had concerning any person who had ever been on the show. By Friday they had received more calls than they had in the entire three years they'd been on the air. Janie herself was the recipient of more than 30,000 letters. It was amazing some of them reached her at all. Some had just her name and the words "Huntington Beach" on the envelope, no state, no zip, nothing else. But the Post Office somehow deciphered all the abbreviated addresses and delivered bags of mail every day.

At first, she planned to read every one of them, but she quickly discovered that her plan, however well-intentioned, was not practicable. She also discovered there were definite patterns to the letters. "An incredible number of them were basically the same," she says. "Women who had been caught in a divorce, who had no education, no way to go out and work. Or even if they did have some kind of a job before, it now didn't pay enough to keep up their life style. It was a situation I knew well."

There was another group of people from whom she received a great many letters, people over fifty-five years of age, couples too old for anybody to hire, too young for Social Security. People who had been fired by companies they had worked many years for, leaving them with no pension plan, people that had had to sell their homes to have enough money to live. "There are millions of people like that out there. People who need something of their own, some way to make a living. And I've got just the thing for them." she says.

When President Reagan began the Women's Business Ownership Program, Janie was asked by the SBA (Small Business Administration) to participate. "They were encouraging women to go into business and they picked me, as one of the three most successful entrepreneurial women in the country, to be on a videotape." They came out to the plant and interviewed her about the business, and put it all on tape. The completed video has been used for the last seven years to encourage women to go into business.

"It's really been a lot of fun," says Janie in retrospect. "We've toured all over the country, meeting with women's groups, telling them that the SBA would help them get loans, and so on. We'd use me as an example, a middle-aged divorced woman who became successful. And you know," she smiles, "I think a lot of women could see that if an uneducated runaway like me could do it, they could, too. And that's okay with me."

John Ortega
CLOTHESTIME Stores, Inc.

-12-

CLOTHESTIME

The music is upbeat, impudent. The sometimes sexy, sometimes cheeky model kisses her man and leaves him; she saunters into a boardroom; she rollerskates up a hill. Her clothes are alternately funky, trendy, classic....but always fashionable. Always right.

"Nordstrom?" asks the announcer. "Broadway? Neiman Marcus? Saks?"

"CLOTHESTIME!" she answers, as if imparting an enormous, delightful secret.

CLOTHESTIME. One of the shooting stars of women's fashion, with over three hundred stores in seventeen states and sales approaching $200 million. Two-times on the *Forbes* magazine list of 200 Best Small Companies. An award-winning distribution center — 140,000 square-feet of technological finesse — which originated with three teenagers divvying up clothes like marbles.

CLOTHESTIME, the little company that grew; that plans to comprise one thousand stores by 1994; that, despite certain set-backs, thinks it can.

The model in the new ad campaign is smiling because she looks so good, and paid so little to look so good. Sitting in his modest but ample Anaheim, California office, co-founder John Ortega is smiling too, because he and his crazy company have come so far.

In just fifteen years, the business that started as a weekend gig in the Southern California flea markets has come to pit itself against the major league department stores. And the nineteen-year-old who spent long hours in the sun peddling T-shirts can now afford long hours in the sun on his own boat.

A flush of mischief colors his boyish face when Ortega, now forty, talks about the growth of CLOTHESTIME. "We always kept it lean and mean," he says. "That was our secret."

Lean and mean. It sounds more like a football cheer than a fashion motto. But the story of CLOTHESTIME is like that. CLOTHESTIME is like a Sunday pick-up team that went semi-pro, then found itself in the NFL. (In this case, read the "National FASHION League.")

The year was 1970, and swapmeets were still glorified garage sales. Twenty-year-old Ortega was working with his father and brothers selling picture frames from Mexico at weekend flea markets and mid-week cattle auctions. They bought them for a dollar a piece in Tijuana, added prints and oil paintings, and sold them as complete *objets d'art*. It was a nice little business but, for John Ortega, it was short-lived.

"I'm kind of a hot-headed guy," he admits. "I got in a fight with my dad, and that ended the Ortega Art and Picture Frame Company for me."

He quit with $500 in his pocket and, since the same hot temper had landed him in his own apartment at the age of sixteen, he now found it expedient to start looking for a way to pay the rent. What he found was a back door to the clothing industry.

Those were the early surfing days, and surf styles were *hot*. The hottest was a company called Hang Ten, whose logo was a pair of bare feet. The factory was making shirts too fast to take time to fix "irregulars" — shirts with the feet of the logo upside down or with mismatched stripes. They just tossed them aside, half a million of them in one large room. A man named Lou Falcowitz, who had a store, made a deal with the Hang Ten Shirt Company: all the irregulars for twenty five cents each. He hired Ortega to sell them for whatever he could get at the flea markets with the agreement that they would split the profits.

"So I went out to the Orange Drive-In Theatre," Ortega recalls. "I had a whole station wagon full of these Hang-Ten shirts. That first day, I think I did about $2,000 business, because I was selling three shirts for five dollars. I had great mark-up on them, but they were eight dollars each in the store. It was right close to Christmas, so it was the best selling time, and I had the hottest item there.

"A couple of friends of mine were out there selling pool sticks and hand-carved artefacts from Taiwan; their dad had owned a pool hall and he still had all the old pool sticks and some new ones. And those guys who used to be out there became my partners in CLOTHESTIME: Mike and Ray DeAngelo."

When the supply of T-shirts was exhausted, Ortega bought a load of shirts from Mojave Manufacturing. He wholesaled some to the DeAngelos, who had entered the clothing business too — with 25,000 pairs of Wrangler jeans, financed with their father's credit. A simple deal evolved: John sold Mike shirts; Mike sold John pants. Soon they were pooling their money to make better buys.

John Ortega pushes his chair back and laughs at the memory. "These Wrangler jeans had fourteen-inch bell-bottoms, with cuffs," he says. "And they were plaid! We sold most of them at the Paramount Drive-In Theater, and we got rid of all 25,000 pairs. But it took so long to sell them, we decided we couldn't make these monster buys.

Out there in the open the sun would attack the edges where they're folded over. It would bleach out the fronts of all these pants, so we had to go out and buy canopies to protect them from the rain, the wind and the sunshine. We learned everything by making mistakes. We had started something just because we wanted to start something, because we *had* to start something."

He pulls a photo album off his bookshelf and opens it to a snapshot of a canopied table of merchandise. Every juncture of CLOTHESTIME's growth is recorded in these albums and scrapbooks, and when the story becomes tangled, he draws maps and diagrams to illustrate it.

"So, Mike and his wife, myself, and Ray and August DeAngelo were out in the flea markets in 1972," he continues. "Every Monday we'd put all of our money together and go to L.A. and buy merchandise. Tuesday, I'd go out to the Chino auction. Wednesday, we'd go back to L.A. Thursday, I'd run back to the Colton auction. Friday, we'd get ready for the weekend. We'd split up: I'd buy some of Mike's pants or take the pants for him, or we'd divide up a bunch of shirts we'd bought during the week: a third of them for me, a third for Mike, and a third for Ray and his dad, who were partners."

This was not a company, he points out. They were not all partners, "Just guys at flea markets. And we were using Mike DeAngelo's garage for distribution because he owned a house!"

But, alone or united, that business took root. Instead of four stands, they had six or seven, sometimes two at the same swapmeet. "I had a couple of kids working for me," says Ortega. "It was like getting eight days of selling in!"

And it grew! More stands, more people working, bigger trucks to hold the merchandise. The trick was to keep everything "lean and mean."

"We'd live on five dollars a week and put all the money we could into merchandise," he explains. "We would stretch and stretch, and buy things and owe people money. We always paid our bills on time — we were never late in payments — but we would put every nickel into it. We'd always over-buy. You'd go into one of our stands, and we'd have 5,000 pairs of black pants. If you needed a pair of black pants, we certainly had a great buy on black pants!"

They bought 20,000 Western men's shirts at a crack, a $50,000 deal, and sold every one. They added the Fresno auction, they added Bakersfield. Ortega opened a stand in San Jose with his brother. It was an unbridled, wheeling-dealing non-partnership; a swapmeet selling frenzy. Then Mike DeAngelo started talking about — dare he say it? — stores.

"At that time we thought that stores were the worst thing," says Ortega. "We could always undercut the stores because we had less overhead. Sometimes, with stores, the stuff's in transit for two weeks. Here we're buying it and selling it the next day. The turnover on it was fabulous."

But Mike's neighbors were complaining, understandably, about all the trucks coming in and out of his garage. The police wanted to know what he was up to since this was not a warehousing district. And because he only went out on the weekends, the merchandise just sat all week. So, in 1974, Mike DeAngelo opened a 1,200-square-foot store in Orange, California.

"Actually, Mike was the founder of CLOTHESTIME, because he opened the first store," says Ortega. "He named it Clothesline."

Not to be outdone, Ray and his father, August DeAngelo, opened their own store in Costa Mesa. It was completely separate from Mike's, but they called it "Clothesline Two." Immediately, Ortega opened Clothesline Three in La Habra.

It was only 900 square feet, with a cement floor and pipe racks on the walls — the same pipe racks they had used at the flea markets. Clothing hung on wire hangers, and nothing was priced at more than six dollars.

"That was the beginning of the company in 1974," he says. "Three separate little stores and the flea markets." Except that it wasn't yet one company; it was three companies: DBA Clothesline One, Clothesline Two and Clothesline Three. They went to the city and got three separate business licences and opened three separate checking accounts. What didn't sell in the stores went to the flea markets.

At the time, says Ortega, there was "no such thing as 'off-price.' There were just a few companies on the east coast starting to do this: Marshalls, Hit or Miss, and T.J. Maxx. So when we did it, it was unique; We were the first one on the west coast. The only competitor we had was a company called 'It's a Dilly/Pick a Dilly.'"

Then Mike opened a second store. So did Ray and "Augie". So did John. They added women's merchandise and advertised together in the *Penny Saver*, a local advertising circular. The full-page ad listed all six locations. And they continued to pool their resources in the garment district, dividing the clothing at Ortega's store in La Habra.

"In the back was a dirt field," he recalls with amusement. "We'd set up a big long pipe, put all the merchandise on wire hangers on this pipe: One for you, one for you, one for me, and so on." They would flip a coin for the last piece of merchandise. It was, he says, "...a very sophisticated system of distribution."

Store followed store and they made up the rules as they went along. For instance, no one could open a store within three miles of someone else.

"So we used to have a big map, and on it we'd draw a

circle around each store, with a diameter of three miles on them. None of us could move inside that three-mile circle." He starts drawing circles on a pad of paper. "If you opened up a store, you could draw a three-mile ring around it. And if I opened up a store, my three-mile ring couldn't touch your three-mile ring. We had this one big old map with all these dots on it. And there were Mike's green dots, John's red dots, and Ray and Augie's blue dots, all with rings around them."

At the same time, they were their own biggest competition, each trying to beat the other's price on everything — carpeting, rent, employees. "Everything was low and go. Lean and mean. We were doing $16 million and still we'd fight over that last garment."

The schedule was gruelling. Up early. Work all day. They would wrap up the last deal in Los Angeles at seven, eat dinner and return to La Habra by nine. Then they had to unload everything because Ortega was going to the Chino auction, thirty miles away, at 6:30 a.m. Once the merchandise was divided, Ortega split his own portion between his stores and the flea markets. He was in bed after midnight and up again at 4:30 a.m. to pick up his helpers and hit the swapmeets. Then it started all over again.

"We went to the flea markets until we had twenty-five stores. Every Tuesday, every Thursday, every Saturday and every Sunday. That's how we got started, just perseverance."

Not that hard work was new to Ortega. As a child, he had a monster paper route — 240 houses at age thirteen, which made him the number one paperboy for the local paper.

He considers himself a self-made man, having had little assistance from his family, but traces his tough work ethic to this Lithuanian mother, who met his father, a Mexican-American Air Force provost marshal, during World War II.

By the time Clothesline had grown to ten stores, they decided they needed a common warehouse; the dirt field had become too small. So, although they were still three separate companies, they joined forces to rent a 4,000-square-foot building, incorporated it and called it "Clothesline, Inc." It was a simple arrangement, they thought, with limited liability: "One checkbook at the warehouse bought all the merchandise from L.A., then three checkbooks paid back their share into this one checkbook."

By now they had found their fashion niche: the trendy, volatile junior market. Women's clothing simply had a faster turnover than men's, says Ortega. Besides, "We were young guys and we knew what we wanted to sell."

It was a clean sweep of sales and stores until Ortega opened his first store in Los Angeles County and came chin-up to a lawsuit. Someone already had two exclusive stores called Clothesline in Los Angeles, and had incorporated the name for all of California. "This guy started to sue. We had this little Mickey Mouse commercial that we did for T.V.; he said we were invading his marketing territory."

Faced with six to eight months of legal wrangling and the possibility that they could lose, the non-partnership decided to proceed with caution and call any new stores "CLO-THESTIME."

They incorporated the CLOTHESTIMEs — Numbers One, Two, and Three, just like the Clotheslines — and opened new checking accounts. Now there were seven companies: three Clotheslines, three CLOTHESTIMEs, and a warehouse, Clothesline, Inc. And, true to form, they advertised Clothesline and CLOTHESTIME in the *Penny Saver*. "Oh, what a job just transferring all this money around, every week!" he recalls.

There were thirty-eight stores by the time the lawsuit came

to a head. Nineteen were still Clothesline, and the possibility of losing loomed on the horizon. So they found an even simpler solution: to change all the stores to CLOTHES-TIME. "So we went out a week before we had to go to court, tore off all the Ls and the Ns, physically, and glued on Ms and Ts with tape. Hey, we're not Clothesline, we're CLOTHESTIME!"

They changed all their advertising to match, and the suit was dropped.

But while the name change solved their legal problems, the competitive trinity had new obstacles to tackle. Their inadvertent weekend business had mushroomed to forty-two stores (fourteen each), three owners and seven checkbooks (two per company plus the warehouse). They were still buying together and advertising together, but no one knew they were still three separate companies. The result was total confusion.

The real estate people didn't know whom to call on at CLOTHESTIME. They finally decided that Mike DeAngelo was responsible for signing leases. But that was bad news for Ortega "because nobody was calling me and I couldn't expand my stores."

The customer was baffled because if she wished to exchange or return merchandise it could only be within the same owner group.

And the creditors were bullish; in fact, they couldn't get credit outside of San Francisco and Los Angeles. New York manufacturers would deal with them only in C.O.D. or cashier's checks. And, once they had a cashier's check, "they wouldn't always honor the deal, Ortega recalls. "You'd buy THIS, and they'd send you THAT. They'd cherry-pick whatever you'd bought, and they'd take all the good stuff out. What can you do to them when they are holding all the money? Nothing after the fact."

The problem wasn't bad credit, it was no credit. CLOTHESTIME, Inc., the fourth company, that did the buying, had no assets.

Says Ortega: "The assets were these stores. Our Dunn & Bradstreet rating was weak because this corporation had no money in it. It was just a checkbook in an empty warehouse that split up all this merchandise with these three companies.

"A couple of people came by and said, 'We can't even sell you guys merchandise. You're doing $16 million, and we can't give you credit from New York.'"

They called in an accounting company, which took one look at the books and recommended that they take all seven checkbooks, dissolve them, and merge the three companies into one.

But sandlot competition dies hard. For one year they fought over how to divide the stock, arguing over "who has better stores, who works harder, who wakes up later, who has better real estate, who goes home early." They finally agreed it would even up in the long run, and did a straight three-way split. And, in 1979, forty-two stores merged into the new corporation: CLOTHESTIME, Inc.

Meanwhile, someone else had been watching the company grow. In 1980, the new corporate officers received a letter from Utah. Gordon Nielson, former chairman of the west coast division of Marshalls, was impressed with CLOTHES-TIME, but saw the need for computerized systems like merchandise control.

"We didn't have any of those systems," says Ortega. "In the typical entrepreneurial fashion of most small retailers, we wore all the hats: we made the bank deposits, delivered the merchandise, hired and fired, worked the sales floor, whatever it took."

They hired Nielson as a consultant manager and, within a

year, made him president of the company. It was like hiring an education.

Because all three men had started working the swapmeets right out of high school and junior college, and because they never worked for anyone else, their secondary education took place in the "dog-eat-dog" world of the flea markets and the garment district.

Ortega, who had been accepted at Stanford, had postponed college for a year because of business. "Well, next year didn't happen," he says, "because we had fourteen extra swapmeets and four or five more stores." So he planned on going next year, at twenty-one. "Then, we had twenty-five stores, so I never did go."

Instead, says Ortega, they hired their education. "When we realized the growth potential the company had, we surrounded ourselves with bright people who are pros at what they do, and we gave them enough space to do their jobs. We hired our president, who taught us how to become retailers; we hired our chief financial officer. You might say we got our Masters Degree in Retailing in the program of 'teach along the way'.

"It's a very scary thing for any entrepreneur to let go of the reins," he adds, "but it's absolutely essential. When you visit your stores every day, you've got a pulse on the business. You know what sells and what doesn't. But as you open more stores, it gets harder to wear all the hats."

Nielson helped launch a computer system to handle inventory and merchandising. The $5 million-worth of programs took seven years to write and allows the home office to audit each store daily. He brought them up to an eight-week turn around, equal to the most successful specialty retailers, and helped push their earnings ever higher.

By 1983, CLOTHESTIME had scored with 126 stores

and $46 million in annual sales. They went public the same year. The sale of 1,615,000 shares at $11 each brought the company $17,765,000, of which $12 million went to the founding stockholders.

"It was the first time we ever got any real money," says Ortega. "We took every nickel and dime from 1974, when we opened our first store, and we just kept putting it back into the company."

Sales and store-counts continued to sky-rocket. In August of that year, they opened twenty-one stores in one day. Profits had increased by an average of 98.3 percent since the company went public, and they had projected $500 million in sales by 1991. *Business Week* ranked CLOTHES-TIME 18th of the nation's 100 Fastest Growing Companies. *Forbes* ranked them 22nd of 200 Best Small Companies and moved them up to 16th the following year.

They even weathered an unsuccessful attempt at courting career women, hoping that working mothers might shop in the same stores as their teen-age daughters. After eighteen months, they refocussed on the junior market and decided to invade the midwest and east coast, but on a smaller scale than the typical 4,300-square-foot California stores.

Low prices and convenience have been the key strategy in the CLOTHESTIME appeal, backed by the old team cheer, "lean and mean".

First, they keep a low overhead. All the stores are leased, and most are opened for less than $100,000. Rents in the strip centers are lower than regional malls, and the sheer volume of their team keeps advertising costs down. For instance, there are 88 stores in the Los Angeles market. "So everytime we run one commercial, it's being paid for by 88 stores."

More important, says Ortega, "We have no long-term debt. We don't believe in it. If we had a bad quarter, we wouldn't open any new stores. We only open stores with money that we've made, and we pay cash for it. That way we don't have to worry about long-term debt — debt that's over a year. We have a $40 million line of credit with five leading banks, and we pay them right down."

Then they only purchase goods below wholesale. Buyers in New York and Los Angeles scout the department stores for the hottest fashions, then watch for manufacturer close-outs and cancelled orders. They also create private-label copies of brand-name designs.

But there's a skill to buying opportunistically; it's volume and timing.

Most stores buy styles three dozen at a time and mark them up sixty percent over cost. CLOTHESTIME buys 27,000 pieces of one style and only marks it up forty-five percent. Because they don't ask for advertising or mark-down allowances, and pay quickly, they get a large percent cut from the manufacturer up front. In fact, with a four to eight week turn-around and billings every thirty to sixty days, they actually pay for the merchandise with the money from its sale. Says Ortega: "Get 'em here quick, get 'em out quick and sell 'em quick, before you have to pay the vendor."

And if they wait until the last few weeks of a season, the industry starts itching.

"It's like being in the produce business," he notes. "There's spoilage. This is a fashion business. They cut too many garments because the department stores get mad if there's nothing to re-order." And when they don't re-order, CLO-THESTIME picks them up at half price."

Then there is what Ortega calls "Time Poverty".

"People don't have any time left to shop, not like they did fifteen years ago," he explains. "It was a big deal on Saturdays or Fridays, you went and you shopped. You window-shopped. Nobody does that anymore. They want to run into the store and get their outfit. They've got a date an hour from now."

CLOTHESTIME's strip center locations are the answer. There are simply more strip center possibilities than malls in any given area, and they are much more accessible.

"You can run in and be out within twenty minutes," says Ortega. "What mall can you run into and out of in twenty minutes? It takes you twenty minutes to find a parking stall, and twenty more minutes to walk to the store you want."

But not even a lean, mean strategy prepared Clothestime for the apparel industry shake-out in the summer of 1987, particularly in the junior market. More off-shore manufacturing, increasing copy-cat designs, created an epidemic of "sameness" in the market, and the ever-fickle junior buyers got bored. Stocks dropped by twenty to thirty percent throughout the industry, says Ortega; even The Limited and The Gap, two of the most successful specialty retailers, reported dragging sales.

CLOTHESTIME, working on a short mark-up and expanding rapidly with sixty-five brand new stores, wasn't ready for the slump. Sales dropped twenty-five percent and the stock price dropped from $14.00 to $5.00.

"I personally lost $60 million," says Ortega. "The market evaluation was $350 million, and it dropped down to about $100 million."

Faced with a $2.2 million loss for the year ending 28 January 1989, the CLOTHESTIME triumvirate called a huddle and reassessed their game plan. It was a lesson in demographics.

They noticed that stores with an older clientele suffered less in the slump, that the size of the youth market was shrinking and that their own customers were outgrowing them.

"The population is shifting; there are less and less

teenagers," Ortega explains. "These gals that were in CLOTHESTIME in 1979 were fifteen to eighteen years old. Now in 1989, the same gals who were seventeen years old, they're twenty-seven! They don't want all that bubble-gum merchandise."

Career women reappeared in the playbook then, along with higher-priced merchandise, and the advertising followed suit.

"We decided to keep both," says Ortega. "To have some junior merchandise and have some of this career, because our customers want the playwear on the weekend, but they need something to wear to work and we never had it for them.

"Now we're getting better merchandise. Our average price point in 1988 was $14, the year before that it was $12; today our average price point is $23, almost double in 2 years. We used to sell dresses for $19.95; now we have dresses for $59, which retail for $100 at better department stores.

"And you know what? The higher priced dresses we put in our stores blew out. You mean we could have been selling these dresses for $59.00 all this time?" he asks himself. "We didn't have to be selling them for $19.95! So our price points will continue to increase, enabling us to sell better merchandise, with the emphasis on value."

The stepped-up ad campaign reflects the new career move. It's all upscale — the models, the music, the styles. It lets the straying customer know that her teen-age fashion source has grown with her. And it compensates for one thing the strip centers lack: foot traffic.

Says Ortega: "You've got to make your own business in the strip centers. That's why we've got the direct mail pieces. That's why we're on TV. That's why we have three million customers who've signed up on our mailing list. We have to spend that extra four, five, six percent of sales to bring them to CLOTHESTIME. We're pretty much a destination-oriented retailer now; people are going to come to that center because they know they're going to CLOTHES-TIME."

It seems to be working. The 1989 advertising budget, for print, TV and mail order, is based on projected sales of $200 million for the year. And in the first three months that the new commercials aired, sales in the Los Angeles market increased forty percent.

Ortega is proud of these commercials. While CLOTHES-TIME has always looked at the department stores, but not other discounters, as its primary competition, this campaign puts them in the big league. "In a nice way."

So, the flea-market mavens are competing with Nordstrom and Saks. But, says Ortega, "There is a method to this madness. You can't do it overnight." It is all a question of customer perception, he says. Upscale advertising creates an upscale clientele. "Maybe in another one, two, three, four years we'll be a little Nordstrom...maybe we'll be selling things for more money than anybody else..."

Not that Ortega would work any less. Success breeds its own demands, and CLOTHESTIME is on the fast track.

"When your company is small, you're not involved with too many outside things," he reflects. "You don't have any money, and you've got your eyes on one thing: opening up stores." Now he is involved as a speaker for the International Council of Shopping Centers, as well as making appearances for a variety of charitable organizations. Also, with a goal of one thousand stores by 1994, expansion is more a priority than ever.

Not that all Ortega's time is devoted to the company. He maintains his 58-foot Bertram, "The C.Time," in Cabo San Lucas, Mexico, to which he escapes for five days at a time to relax and indulge his love of big-game sport-fishing. His passion for cars takes the shape of a $6 million collection of classic Ferraris and occasional jaunts to Europe for vintage-car races. And his fervent belief in real estate makes it almost a side-line business, if not a calling.

"Buy real estate!" is his advice to any young entrepreneur. "Because it's always going to be worth more money than it was the year before. And buy it as young as you can. The first thing you should do is buy your own house."

At nineteen, he put five percent down on a $40,000 four-plex and sold it four years later for $79,000. He continued to buy wisely, doubling his investment each time. A $900,000 house sold for $1,350,000 within eighteen months, allowing him to purchase his bayfront dream home in Newport Beach.

His own philosophy is a unique combination of shrewd business sense and simple good will. On the one hand, he believes that "in everything you do, you've got to save a nickel here and a nickel there. You can get a deal anywhere, but you'll never get it unless you ask. We do that buying cars, we do it buying real estate, we do it buying desks for computers. We barter, barter, barter."

At the same time, he believes in karma. "Do unto others what you want done unto yourself. If all your life, you're a cheating and lying type of person, you'll get paid back at the end of your life by bad health, bad marriage, those type of things. I believe in good karma in business; being fair with people always seems to work out better."

When John Ortega was seven years old, he sat down one day and wrote the story of his life. He said that he would raise horses and would become a millionaire by the time he was twenty-five. "One out of two isn't bad," he comments laughingly. Then the boyish face turns serious. "The limit," he says, "is only how hard we want to work."

Bud Fabian
For Better Living, Inc.

-13-

FOR BETTER LIVING

In 1969, when Francis G. Fabian, Jr., left a successful employment as president and chief executive officer of Hunt Foods and Industries, he had been a corporate executive for over thirty years. Yet he did not hang up his resume and jet off to Tahiti or Palm Beach, there to luxuriate in a less-harried lifestyle; nor did he reap his accumulated benefits and investments. Instead, he stepped right back into corporate life by founding and running a diversified corporation called "For Better Living, Inc.," with headquarters in San Juan Capistrano, California.

"I have a high regard for business," he says with conviction. "It has always proven an exciting and fun occupation. It's creative and constructive, and when properly done it can help people grow. I find I usually end up helping people to grow stronger, and to believe in themselves and in their ability to be more effective than ever."

A quick glance through the annual reports of For Better Living, Inc., reveals Chairman and President Fabian's realistic no-nonsense approach to management. Other companies' annual reports tend merely to provide glowing information. For Better Living's provide an account of increased earnings, coupled with a philosophical discussion of problem-solving and tightening controls, aimed at getting a better job done next year.

"Why a conglomerate? I guess, with all the different businesses I've been in, there are things a central management can do that can be helpful to the various divisions of such an organization," he explains.

For most of his life, diversity has been Fabian's watchword. When he founded For Better Living, Inc. in 1969, he had already been president of several extensively-diversified corporations. With For Better Living, he pulled together several private concerns too small to go public by themselves which, when banded together, formed sufficient critical mass to support an effective public offering.

Fabian chose the name "For Better Living" to represent the company's purpose — to provide a mix of products and services that would serve the customer more efficiently than the competition did. During the 1960's, diversity was viewed as offering strength to offset any momentary weakness that might develop in any one sector of a company's operations. Fabian organized his staff to provide optimum skills and experience promptly. As it grew, For Better Living acquired a concrete products company, a home-fixture concern (since sold), a retail camera store (also sold), an engineered fasteners company - Circle Bolt, and *Surfer* magazine, which later acquired other magazines.

Fabian says, "When we are unable to help a company grow vigorously and profitably, we feel we must turn it loose; usually we turn it back to the people we bought it from. In most cases we had brought the companies in with their own management and they were able and delighted to carry on alone again."

The company's earnings have increased over the ensuing years, and in 1987 For Better Living's net sales were $81,078,000, up from those in 1986, when they were $71,640,000. Much of the company's success can be attributed to the key executives, who have continued to develop better products and services. Such products and services include manufacturing and distributing precast concrete and plastic products, the publication of specialty magazines, investment in oil and gas exploration operations, sales of automotive radiators, and several distribution activities.

Today, For Better Living owns Associated Concrete Products Inc., which is grouped with DeKalb and Dalworth Construction Inc. Its products are sold, primarily to utility companies and general contractors, by twelve plants in California, Texas, Arkansas, Georgia and Florida. Raw materials are obtained from nearby domestic sources for the manufacture of products such as containers to house distribution boxes, manholes, and underground transformer structures. The concrete division is one of the largest producers of underground precast structures in the United States.

The plastics division, under Associated Plastics Inc., has two plants, located in California and Arkansas, that produce designs using a "structural foam" process developed for injection molding. These products are sold primarily to electrical and telephone utility companies throughout the United States and parts of Canada.

For Better Living's Magazine Publications Group publishes *Surfer* and *Powder* magazines, both circulated worldwide. *Surfer* is published monthly and *Powder* seven times a year. Both feature extensive coverage of their respective sports, with an in-house staff that designs and produces the magazines, including photography, photo lab work, writing, editing, and advertising sales. The staff also supervises the printing and circulation of the end products; the trademarks of both magazines are licensed to certain manufacturers of sportswear and accessory products. *Surfer* is in its twenty-

seventh year of publication, and *Powder*, which was
acquired shortly after its launch, is in its fourteenth.

For Better Living decided recently to make significant
write-downs of its investments in its oil- and gas-producing
properties. Located mainly in Texas, Louisiana, and Arkansas, these properties will not undergo any future exploration,
due to their reduced ability to produce profits at price levels
about fifty percent below recent historic levels. Fabian's
no-nonsense scrutiny of his Western Stock Exchange Over
The Counter stock is the hallmark of his method of doing
business. For Better Living stock today commands a price
between $12 and $15 a share, some 874,398 common
shares outstanding. About forty-six percent of the stock is
held in a trust, of which the trustee is Richard G. Fabian, the
chairman's son, an Episcopal priest and a member of the
board of directors. Over seven hundred people are employed
by the company.

Fabian's confidence and interest in his corporation are
total. When, for example, his magazine subsidiary started a
new publication called *Sailboarder*, Fabian decided to learn
sailboarding so he could understand the lifestyle portrayed in
the magazine. Today he still sailboards, though not as
vigorously as before.

He believes in the profit motive as a valid discipline for all
business operations and he strives to see that For Better
Living key employees have a continuing interest in the
corporation's profit-making ability. "They need that type of
interest if the company is to profit and grow," he says.

Monitoring a profitable course requires the institution of
control points along the way. These points are the beacons
that show how well the planned goals are being achieved.
"Each manager is expected to have controls which tell him
promptly when he is in trouble. Each manager knows that
his boss also has his own controls, and he soon learns that

when he has a variance from the plan, he should have corrective measures already installed by the time his boss's controls indicate a variance from the planned course. Only thus can he prove he has his part of the job under control," Fabian says.

"Our policy in business is that every company and profit center must earn its profit by meeting the customer's true needs — with a plus of being better than the competition. And we want that plus designed to be hard to copy," he adds.

Fabian does not believe in simply drawing up profit plans and then letting nature take its course. He stresses to the members of his staff that each of them must be in control. "If you really take responsibility for any project, you must first establish a definition of your strategy — how to win, the tactics, and the specific action plan," he says. "A plan of action is the foundation of control. Then you can always check to see how your plan is progressing. Always insist that your subordinates know and understand the plan's factors clearly before they start a day's work, a trip, or a visit to a customer. Successful control requires constant feedback.

"If you are in charge, you have to be able to think things through — to know where the problems lie and what's going on. Anytime you're surprised by what happens, you've lost control. And if you can't get it under control, you can't justify being in charge," he says with finality.

Fabian requires his managers to forecast profits for every product and service every month, and even for shorter periods. His approach to the magazine division is unorthodox, to say the least. It is generally assumed throughout the magazine industry that profits cannot be predicted until six months, or sometimes a year, after the magazine has hit the newsstands. Some publishers believe it is impossible to determine profitability before printing an edition. "We cannot accept that assumption," Fabian says firmly. "My publishers have to know a close range of the profits before they give the orders to print."

Fabian is not afraid of pulling out of an unprofitable project. In 1984, two magazines were started in an effort to cash in on the then prevalent skateboarding and sailboarding crazes. They were called, naturally, *Skateboarder* and *Sailboarder*. After almost four years of publication, neither magazine was showing a satisfactory profit and they were promptly folded, by decision and order of their publishers.

A key to Fabian's success is his strong reliance on defining a project before it is started, and establishing its objective. "Where do you want to be? How do you plan to get there? These are questions we ask ourselves," he says. "And we write the answers down."

It is important to ask the right questions, he cautions; ill-formed questions will sidetrack operations. His strong belief in definitions, controls, plans, and strategies indicates a man with a penchant for problem-solving. Fabian has a degree in Industrial Engineering from Yale University. Although a graduate of this respected university and, before that, of a prestigious college-preparatory institution, The Choate School, Fabian was not born with a silver spoon in his mouth. He was graduated *cum laude* from Choate, and on a scholarship.

His highly-principled parents worked hard to insure that he and his siblings all went to good schools that prepared them for university, which they all attended on scholarships during the Depression. His father was a mining engineer and his mother a housewife. "The major influences in my life were being born in this country *and* the coaching I received at home and at school. It was 1931 when I made the decision to go to Yale. I didn't especially want to go to that college, but at that point the Depression had wiped out my family's fortunes. I knew I had to handle my college education completely on my own, by scholarships and outside student employment." He says, "I found Yale offered me the best opportunity to work out a definite plan to pay my own way."

So, meticulously and methodically, he planned his college career. Down to the last cent. He smiles slightly as he reminisces. "I had to plan everything. I knew I would need to be completely self-supporting."

When he got to Yale he worked in various capacities on campus. "I waited on tables," says Fabian, "And I had jobs in newspaper distribution and the student offices. I also worked with people who were supplying goods and services to various campus activities. There were never enough hours in the day to work."

His busy workload did not stop him from trying for and winning positions on the Yale rowing and wrestling teams. Somehow he was able to cope with the stress of juggling his work, study, sports practices and social life. He is especially appreciative of his parents, and of some unforgettable teachers who were dedicated to getting him through school and giving him a principled view of life, no matter how adverse conditions became.

He remembers an incident that took place when he was young, about five years old. Feeling very sorry for himself one day, he complained that life was so difficult that he wanted to die. His mother heard him. She pushed him up against the wall and told him, in no uncertain terms, that he was never to say that in his life again. "She said, 'You don't quit. No member of this family quits. You keep trying. You may not be successful but you are *never* totally defeated by anything in this life.' I can still feel those hands on my shoulders," Fabian smiles. "I figured what she said was right and I've never forgotten it."

One of his first mentors was his sister Dorothy, now

Dorothy F. Sullivan. "She was quite brilliant, and a good coach for me," he says. Just before he left for Yale, Dorothy took him aside and told him that he would come into contact with many professors who could add to his understanding of life and living. But in the long run, she warned, it would be up to him. He could just sit there and listen, or he could become really turned on by whatever energized these motivated educators. "Dorothy told me I could become fascinated with what excited the professor so much about his subject, and thereby double my pleasure in hearing the lecture about it. And in turn, the professor's enthusiasm would act as a spur to encourage me to learn more. In addition, as a natural by-product I would earn higher marks when my instructors saw my enthusiasm. When it's sincere, it's a two-way street."

He has not forgotten his sister's advice. Today, when most people would think Fabian must surely have learned all he can about life and business, he still finds excitement in learning, and in communicating new ideas. He says, "It doesn't take more time, probably less. Whatever time it takes, it will return ten times the benefit and pleasure."

This firmly-ingrained belief is applied when he works with his For Better Living management and staff. However, he is realistic; he knows that sometimes they will want his coaching, and at other times they won't. "That's just the way it is," he says, matter-of-factly. "You can't force learning. You have to wait until the person's ready to accept your coaching."

Another person who played a major role in shaping his principles and motivation was his wrestling coach in college. Fabian wanted to become an intercollegiate champion, but he seemed unable to achieve sufficient skills and timing. His coach took him aside. He told Fabian that he might have the ability to become champion, but he was never going to make it if he didn't learn that his best friend was failure. "He convinced me that when I got beaten, I'd better be sure I found out how and why it happened and what I was going to do about it, then do it right there no matter how beat up I felt. If I didn't, I would fail again. The result? I became intercollegiate champion three years in a row. Not a big thing now, but at that point in my life it convinced me I could make it, and that I must always try to forge my own destiny. It proved to be of lasting value in the times ahead."

Another memorable coach was Yale Professor Elliot Dunlap Smith, who taught a course called "Psychology for Executives." It was a mandatory course and Fabian enjoyed every minute of it.

Professor Smith taught him many of the management techniques, skills, and work habits he has since applied throughout his work life. Fabian also worked for Smith as a student aide and so was able to observe the professor himself applying the same principles. Smith maintained that problems had to be defined thoroughly before any solutions could be reached.

"He would get me into a box, where I had to find a way out myself. What I learned was that you *can* work your way out of almost anything when you get boxed in tight enough," Fabian says. "I learned that one must be able to pierce through to the heart of any problem."

In many ways Yale was a pivotal learning experience and a break-through for Fabian. It was at Yale that he devised a method of using those too-short hours in which he had to cram school, work, sports, and social obligations; he decided to make his subconscious mind work for him. While this may seem commonplace today, it was not so then; that was a time of rugged individualism, not of New Age concepts. But Fabian was able to make his subconscious his ally.

"I wouldn't let myself go to sleep until I had written a few notes defining the heart of the project I had for the next day's class, whether it was a test or something else. Then I would go to sleep. The next day, I would wake up — and the problem was solvable!" he says, with a snap of his fingers. "You can do it too, but in your own way. Your subconscious is the most loyal friend you have — you must get it trained so that it will work with you."

Fabian is aware of the danger of tenaciously clinging to a certain way of solving a particularly tough problem. "There is a gray area between where tenacity stops and stubbornness takes over," he says. "It is important to recognize this gray area and to notice when it becomes stupid to keep on trying in a no-win situation. The best approach I have found is to ask myself, 'How can I justify continuing on this route?' If I can't answer logically, I abandon that method and go to another."

Following graduation from Yale in 1937 and until he joined the U.S. Navy in 1942, Fabian worked for Al Morey, who later became chairman of Marsh and McClennan, Inc. "It was a delight to work for Al Morey. I learned many lessons, and had many humorous, stimulating experiences as we worked to develop better and better solutions to our customers' industrial insurance problems. Al had been a professional hockey player, and he taught me that above all I must keep the play in focus at all times. *He* sure did! He also always required that we figure out a better play for the next time. Our bond of mutual respect is one of the finest in my business life."

When it was time for Fabian to join the fight in World War II, characteristically he learned much from his years in the U.S. Navy. Welcoming many of the stimulating challenges, he learned to meet them head on. Yet there were moments of uncertainty. "In some cases, I was in shock; but I finally realized that I could probably do the job as well as the next guy if I would give it everything I had, even when the task seemed virtually impossible!" he says.

In retrospect, he believes he accomplished many missions effectively because of his teammates' cooperation. Early on, an older officer taught him that "an officer who takes care of his troops well will find that his troops will do exactly the same for him; and, inevitably, the converse holds true." "It is a golden rule that can be demonstrated with immediate and diabolical thoroughness by the troops once they get going," Fabian says with a wry smile.

When he resigned from the Navy at the end of World War II, he had reached the rank of Lt. Commander and his last command was that of Chief Engineering Officer on board an escort aircraft carrier.

On leaving the Navy, Fabian went to work for Lindsay Structure Inc., a manufacturer of patented prefabricated buildings and truck bodies. "It was my first direct participation in a small business," he says. "I loved it. I loved the product, the problems we faced of finding new ways to apply it to different end uses. And I really enjoyed working with the people at Lindsay. There were terrific camaraderie and humor ever-present — thanks to my boss Hunter Lindsay." He eventually became vice president at Lindsay. In 1950, he left and joined the management consultant firm of Booz Allen & Hamilton as a consultant, where he was later promoted to the level of associate.

In 1953 he joined Dresser Industries as assistant general manager of Dresser Manufacturing Division and he eventually became the president of that division. In 1959, he was moved to the corporation's headquarters in Dallas as one of the two executive vice presidents. Later, he became president of Dresser Industries and a member of the Board of Directors.

But in 1966 he accepted an offer from Hunt Foods and Industries to be its president, and he moved to California. (Hunt Foods and Industries subsequently became Norton Simon Inc.) Three years later, Fabian left Norton Simon Inc. as president and chief executive and founded For Better Living, Inc. where he is still working.

He believes that his corporate effectiveness was usually due to productive teamwork; it was the basic focus of all his administrative effort. In order to make such teamwork succeed, he stresses, all team members have to know and understand the team's goals, strategies, assignments and controls.

"Each member has to know that if he or she drops the ball, everyone in that team will know about it, and that if he can't prevent that happening again, someone else will have to replace him. In my company, we all agree that we must strive to win over the competition by meeting the customer's true needs better than competition. And our controls require that each of us learn from our failures or be replaced." Fabian says.

He is a firm believer in the old corporate saw, "no surprises." "Our team members realize that this does not mean that there will be no surprises. It means they have to be *ready* for surprises by managing their part of the business with anticipation of all kinds of surprises that may come their way. You must have the corrective measures already conceived and practised — so that by the time you face a new problem and report it to the rest of your team, you have corrective action underway already.

"A classic example of such a problem is the effect bad weather can have on construction. A competent manager will anticipate unexpected weather, whereas an incompetent boss will hope for a break and gamble that there won't be any inclement weather."

Fabian believes a related value of well-assigned teamwork is the "stand-by strength" that exists in the team when members know about each other and their job responsibilities. "The other members, including the supervisors, represent an added source of knowledge and experience in the area you are handling. They will be available to back up your actions and check your thinking and problem-solving," he says. "They will provide strength as the *square*, rather than the sum, of the team's ability."

To this end, Fabian believes that one of the worst maxims in the world is "What he doesn't know, won't hurt him." It is fallacious and disastrous to team effort because it sets the team up to flounder and fail. It is better to face the light of truth and deal with it than to hide from the possibility of what's likely to happen.

But he believes a team's most effective work lies in its coaching. "Everybody here is a coach and we all know the toughest person to coach is your boss, of course," he adds with a smile. "The best hope for that is for the boss to convince staff members that such advice is welcome.

"Now there are two good ways to do that. The first is for the boss to say, 'If you realize I'm doing something that can let me fall through the ice, I *need* to have you tell me.' The second and basic approach is for us both to have agreed beforehand on our objectives and agree to speak up whenever circumstances are endangering those objectives." Fabian points out that if a subordinate wilfully withholds such warnings, he must realize that that is counterproductive. Fabian has employees who tell him when they see that the course he is charting is prone to danger, and he believes in expressing gratitude when that happens. He has learned to ask, "What's the danger in this course?" And he will expect an appropriate response.

While he may seem to present a slightly distant demeanor,

Fabian strives always to be open to ideas and suggestions as long as they have been thought through. This melding of ideas and minds is only possible if both parties are willing to speak openly. According to Fabian, if a person lives vigorously and alertly, and believes that the interaction between two brains offers the square instead of the sum of the effort, then there will always be a person with whom such an interaction can be attained. But this melding has to be a voluntary mutual exchange of logic, otherwise it dies.

"This mutuality also holds true with criticism," Fabian says. "Some people have such a highly-developed sensitivity that they find criticism hard to accept. Even so, if you give them time to digest it, they can realize it is for their own good. But the basic need is to keep your agreed mutual objectives clear so you can see you are only discussing *how* to reach them.

"It is universally accepted that motivating others is part and parcel of management. We must agree that each person on the team will be counted on to perform well and efficiently, otherwise he will cause the team to fail. And the manager can be considered to have failed too.

"In order to live with this team administration, all members must do their parts or be replaced," he says. "I've got to have employees here who feel that they've got to deliver their part of the job. That's the teamwork rule. In the process of doing this, I upset some people — usually people who got up the ladder through political influence. But here at For Better Living, we believe in a "results" attitude. We are a *results* operation."

However tough such a results-oriented attitude may seem, Fabian believes that is the essence of fairness to all members of the team who depend on each other. Most of them have already learned from athletics that the coach must replace poor performers or the team will fail again and will all suffer.

Like many successful people, Fabian tends to crowd his calendar. He is an example of that old adage, "If you want to get something done, give it to a busy person." He admits that while his major load now concerns the future of For Better Living, he tends to accumulate added workloads. "I always have," he says, wryly. "You know, the busier you are the more you try to do."

A fast thinker who must think on his feet, Fabian finds it easier to arrive at solutions but harder to bring them to fruition when they involve other people, other performances, other functions. "Then you have to break them down into individual problems," he says, "and solve them one at a time."

Fabian is ready to put in long hours, whenever necessitated by his workload. He works from 8 a.m. to 5 p.m., then he usually has some work at home to complete during the evening hours. He is comfortable with his ten- to fourteen-hour workday. However, he is likely to jot down a few ideas before he goes to sleep each night, as well as jotting them down all day long.

His long hours and dedication to his company do not prevent Fabian from taking days off. A consummate athlete, he enjoys skiing most of all. Each year, he sets aside at least fourteen days when he can hit the slopes. However, he can be called back to his San Juan Capistrano desk at any moment by telephone — or in person if needed.

Fabian believes it is important to live a constructive life. "Business is a constructive worthwhile contribution to the world," he says, "If you owe the world something, and I think I do, then I feel business is the way for me to repay it. If you do it right, then it is good for your teammates and customers too."

When asked for a final word of advice he does not

hesitate. "Figure out what you want to do," he says. "Be sure it is a satisfactory goal and then figure out a strategy for getting there. Don't allow yourself any excuses. Just remember you may fail, and if you do, make failure your friend by learning from it, and you'll always end up a stronger, happier and more useful person for it.

"Most of the work of a manager is coaching and teaching members of the team. That's how business becomes a constructive worthwhile life's work. For when you think on it — teaching has always been mankind's highest calling and superior teaching is probably how our forebears became the ones who developed the knowledge necessary to put a man on the moon."

Fabian reflects, "As I think over all the foregoing experiences and lessons and principles, I must pay homage to one human characteristic that always proves the most valuable of all, in good times and in bad. It must always be kept alive and well. And that is—a sense of humor.

"If the leader is wise enough to support *humor* in the group and to stimulate it, it makes the whole job *fun*. You and I have seen it so often — it indicates the stature of a man, his perspective — his humility — his love of mankind and his enjoyment of the human comedy we're all acting in.

"For when he sees the humor in the situation and shares it with the team, he makes it fun to come back tomorrow; even in the worst conditions. It is probably the most effective, most subtle stimulant of all."

Jim Slemons
Jim Slemons Enterprises, Inc.

-14-

JIM SLEMONS ENTERPRISES, INC.

"A chicken in every pot and two Mercedes in every garage," could very easily be the credo for residents of Newport Beach, the Shangri-La of Southern California good living and the crown jewel of Orange County, where new money and conspicuous consumption have redefined what the American dream is all about. In a city where minuscule plots of land on chic Lido Isle are snapped up for millions, Mercedes dealer extraordinaire Jim Slemons sits on eight acres of some of the most valuable land in Southern California, eight acres that he bought eighteen years ago when businessmen derided his decision, friends laughed at him, and the Mercedes Benz office told him he was a fool.

Today those eight acres alone push Jim Slemons' personal worth up by about $14 million, an impressive return on a $2-a-square-foot investment made back in 1971. But Slemons doesn't take his personal wealth — or himself for that matter — seriously. He neatly sidesteps any discussion of his personal assets. "People think I'm rich, but it's an illusion," he insists. "Because my name's on the building, people think that if I sell a car for $70,000, I'm going to put $50,000 of that in my pocket, and it's just not true."

Even so, Slemons has been able to indulge his taste for the good life — homes from Tahiti to Palm Springs, a luxury yacht and 30-foot speedboat, and a multi-million dollar antique car collection — thanks to a diversified mini-fiefdom that includes dealerships for Mercedes, Acura, Volvo, Jeep/Eagle, and Honda, an auto-leasing firm, a wholesale parts distributorship, a boat-manufacturing company and a small commuter airline. He even publishes his own magazine. It is estimated that projected total gross earnings for Jim Slemons Enterprises for 1989 will top $190 million.

In terms of car sales alone Slemons is ahead of the pack. He has been the nation's top agency for parts and service for the last three years, and he was rated the eighth biggest car dealer in the United States in 1988 in dollar volume and the No. 2 Mercedes dealer, moving over 150 new and used Mercedes every month. His 50,000-square-foot parts warehouse does $2 million worth of business each month in wholesale parts alone, making it one of the top parts distributorships in the country.

But in spite of his diversification, and in spite of his successful dealerships for other makes of car, in Orange County Jim Slemons's name is synonymous with Mercedes. It would be easy to wave off his success as simply one of luck, of sitting on the right product in the right place at the right time. But when Jim Slemons bought his Mercedes franchise back in 1961, practically no one had heard of the car, no one was interested in it and no one was buying it. And that was all Jim Slemons needed to know to fire a notorious stubborn streak he had displayed since his youth.

That stubborn streak had pitted him against his successful father throughout his career, and if Slemons has one regret today, it is that his father died in 1973 and never lived to see how successful the son he derided grew to be. "All my life my father used to say I would never amount to anything, that I never had enough sense to get in out of the rain," he says.

If Slemons Senior had been able to prevail over his son, young Jim would have followed him into the farming business, and indeed for a while it seemed that he would. He studied agriculture at the University of California at Davis where he did quite well, although he adds with typical self-deprecation that the only reason he studied hard was that there was nothing else to do — in those days the male/female student ratio was ten to one. He then returned to work on his father's farm in the Coachella Valley, where the primary produce was citrus fruits, alfalfa, and cotton.

It was clear from the start that farming and Jim Slemons were not an ideal match. "The first month after college I drove a tractor on the farm, but I was always getting it stuck in the sand and another tractor would inevitably have to come to pull me out," he laughs. Undefeated, he purchased two diesel trucks with trailers, and for the next year he hauled grapefruit to the Mexican border town of Calexico and brought steer fertilizer back with him to Indio. "I loaded and unloaded it all myself," he says. "It wasn't a pleasant job — especially with temperatures that reached $120°$"

Those long hauls gave Slemons time to ponder his life, and he realized he would never be happy as a gentleman farmer. As long as he could remember, cars had been his passion, and he had often dreamed of becoming an automobile dealer and selling cars. "I wanted to be around cars, to be out meeting people," he says. "Even in college I was the one making spare money by going round to Ford and Mercury agencies selling those "Continental Kits" for fastening a spare tire kit to the trunk lid like the old Lincoln Continentals."

He finally bit the bullet, told his father he was leaving the family business, and found himself a job selling cars. Not just any cars, mind you. Jim Slemons's first job was selling Edsels.

Slemons has no patience with the smirking 20/20 hindsight that the name Edsel evokes today. Back in 1957, when the car first hit the market, it carried behind it the full marketing force of America's top automaker. "It was new on the market and it was the coming car," he explains. "I went to the introduction and got real pumped up on it — you know how they can pump people up on cars when they want to."

Even so, Slemons felt a real affinity for the Edsels and managed to sell them at a healthy clip. "I liked Ford products," he says simply. "The Edsel was funny-looking and everybody made fun of it, but I believed it was a good car and the price was right, and when you believe in something, you can sell it."

That uncanny salesman's knack — the ability to sell an icebox to an Eskimo — is a rare trait and one that has served Slemons well, but insiders add one more dimension to the man who eventually became one of the top Edsel salesmen in the country. "He's the archetypal entrepreneur," says one close associate. "He likes the challenge of being told it can't be done." This philosophy has put him at odds with the prevailing wisdom since his first day on the job.

That first Edsel dealership was in Slemons's home town of Newport Beach, then a sleepy little seaside village of less than three hundred persons whose population was to swell to over five thousand each summer with the influx of well-heeled vacationers. The Slemons family was one of the few year-round resident families, and it was from here that Jim's father commuted to the farm in Indio a few days a week in order to escape the searing heat of the California desert.

In spite of Jim Slemons's salesmanship the Edsel itself was not faring well on the market. He rued the day he sold one to his father, for on the latter's first trip to Las Vegas the car required eighteen quarts of oil because the rings had been installed backwards. "My father called me and began cussing me out about what did I sell him that damn thing for," laughs Slemons. "The oil was coming out as fast as he could put it in." His father didn't keep the car very long, and indeed, the dealership in Newport Beach began to founder. The time came for Slemons to ponder his next move.

"My father was a very dominant man, extremely hard to get along with," says Slemons. "I was married at the time, and my wife and I lived in a house that was owned by him, and we paid rent to him. He kept track of where I was, what I was doing. We had no freedom of our own, and he began to insist that I go back into business with him. So we made our decision in the middle of the night to just pack up all our belongings, take off, and not tell anybody where we were going."

Jim and his wife went to Las Vegas, where he knew he had a job waiting for him at the Edsel dealership, and his wife went to work as a showgirl. "This was the tail end of the Edsel market," he says. "These guys were buying Edsels from other dealers who were going out of business." In spite of the Edsel's declining favor, it was during this time that Slemons rose to become one of the top Edsel salesmen in the country. But soon he began to lose his taste for the car-selling business, for it was in Las Vegas in the late fifties that the industry was reaching new heights — or depths — of shysterism.

"In those days, automobile dealers could get away with all sorts of borderline legal or even illegal activities that would land them in jail today," he says. "There were literally no controls or restrictions, and car dealers would try just about anything they could to sell a car."

Slemons, who is celebrated among his friends as an incomparable raconteur, can't resist running down a list of stories from the car dealers' chamber of horrors. One of his favorite instances is the way a prospective buyer would be shuffled to two, three, or even four different finance companies ("there was one on every street corner in those days") to borrow money against the same furniture again and again until enough cash had been drummed up to make a downpayment on a car.

"Contracts were forged...it was 'anything goes'", says Slemons, shaking his head. "I felt uncomfortable doing business that way, and I simply gave up selling cars." In his heart he knew he would one day go back to being a car dealer, but he wanted to do it on his terms. So he made a deal with the devil; he trained to become a casino dealer.

The casinos in Las Vegas were at their prime in the late fifties. The high rollers played for big stakes and tipped handsomely, and in those days tips were not taxed. "The way for a dealer to make it big was simply to be the best," says Slemons. So every moment of his free time was devoted to bettering his abilities at the tables — he practiced shuffling, memorized combinations, and honed his precision by throwing cards into a hat on the bed. It paid off.

Dubbed "The Killer" by comedian Lou Costello, he was celebrated as Las Vegas's top 21 dealer. He appeared on the syndicated television show "What's My Line?" and was the favorite dealer of big-name celebrities like Eddie Fisher and Elizabeth Taylor, who would hire a plane and fly into town if they heard that Jim Slemons was dealing. Tips were big — up to $400 and $500 in cash on good nights — and within three years, Slemons had put together a tidy cash pile of $40,000. He walked away from Las Vegas in 1961 without ever having played the tables. "Me gamble?" He pauses to laugh, adding, "Sure. I gamble in business every day."

He returned home to Newport Beach and, after attending a trade show in Los Angeles, toyed with the idea of opening an automatic car wash, which struck him as a business venture that would not require a large cash outlay but had the potential to earn him a lot of money. But it was not in the cards, for he bumped into an old friend who offered to sell him a car dealership in Santa Ana — lock, stock and barrel — for a mere $27,500. His dream of becoming an automobile dealer was confronting him again and Slemons seized it.

No matter that the dealership sold little-known slow-selling foreign cars like Mercedes, Renault, Peugeot and DKW (now the Audi), and no matter that his friend admitted he was losing $3,000 a month on the business, Slemons jumped in feet first and put everything he had on the deal.

He shakes his head now at his own business naivete back then. "I figured if I started selling cars right away I would have enough money to sustain myself. I didn't realize that I had to *buy* used cars, or that contracts could get tied up at the bank and I wouldn't get paid straight-away." Even so, he still believes his decision was a smart one. "It was a bargain in terms of buying a dealership," he explains. "In those days, a Volkswagon dealership would have cost you a million dollars, for example, because the Volkswagon was something everybody wanted."

Inevitably, Slemons began to run out of money. "I nearly went under daily," he remembers, "and I was continually out of trust at the bank." Because his father had heaped ridicule on him for buying the dealership, he knew he couldn't approach him for a loan. So he turned to his mother, who lent him $25,000, and then another $25,000 not long after.

"When my father eventually found out, he was furious. We had a lot of family fights, but I was literally at their mercy," says Slemons. Over the next two years, Slemons was forced to borrow a total of $150,000 from his parents to keep his dealership going, in exchange for which his father took eighty-five percent of the stock and left his son a mere fifteen percent. Father and son quarrelled continually over the running of the business. One night, in the depth of despair, Slemons calculated that it would take over two hundred years to buy his father out on his humble salary.

For his $27,500 investment Slemons inherited six employees and a staff drinking problem. "I discovered vodka bottles stuck down behind the toilet one day. I literally had to clean up and start over." He recalls his first five years as an endless round of sixteen-hour days and six-and seven-day weeks where he juggled the roles of sales manager, lot boy, janitor, and salesman every day.

All he needed on top of these woes was to be selling a car that practically nobody had heard of. "In 1961, the Mercedes was like an antiquated car," Slemons says. "To roll the window up you had to crank thirteen times — I counted it myself. The cars had no air-conditioning, no automatic transmission." He was selling more Renaults by far, and it occurred to him that if he got rid of the Mercedes and devoted himself exclusively to Renaults he could make a lot more money. But he didn't. In fact, he kept the Mercedes, inexplicably, and got rid of all the other cars he was carrying.

It proved to have been a pivotal decision, and it was based more on a belief in the car than anything else. "I thought the product was good," he says simply. "It may have been antiquated, but it was built like a tank." The man who wasn't defeated by an Edsel was certainly not going to be defeated by a Mercedes.

"I'm a stick-to-it kind of guy," he explains. "I swore to myself that I was going to make this car a success even if I had to sell it to my friends, and that's what I proceeded to do. I was out there ringing doorbells. I gave every customer I sold a car to my home phone number, and sure enough there'd be some nights in the middle of winter at 2:00 a.m.

that somebody would get a flat tire and call me, and sure enough I'd go out and fix it."

According to Slemons, while American car companies offered a variety of incentive and advertising programs, dealers of imported cars were virtually on their own. "What Jim has wrought," says one insider, "he has wrought himself. He owes no one for his success — not even Mercedes-Benz."

In 1965, in debt to his father, working extraordinary hours and selling Mercedes cars one customer at a time, the man who had taken the hard road of selling imported cars when the country was in love with Detroit did something that to this day astonishes industry chroniclers — he bought a franchise to sell Japanese cars. Jim Slemons had not learned his lesson; as far as he was concerned there was no lesson to be learned.

"My philosophy in business is that you can't stand still," he says simply. "There's no such thing as a mom-and-pop grocery store these days because the supermarkets are so big the little ones can't compete with them. And the car business is the same way. You've got to be a supermarket, or you can't compete. Just look at the price you pay for personnel — you need a full-time CPA and high-priced general managers, and unless you can share their expertise with other companies you own in the same area you can't stay competitive. You have to expand, so if one product has a bad year, then another will pick up the slack."

But Toyota?

In 1965 Japan was still considered a place that manufactured nothing more sophisticated than plastic gewgaws for gumball machines. No one had ever driven a Japanese car. "Well sure I would have liked to buy a Ford dealership," admits Slemons. "But who could afford one? My Toyota agency cost me all of $650. I was only the third Toyota dealer in the country — they needed me more than I needed them!"

But to the salesman in him the cost was not a factor. "I honestly liked the product and felt I could make it go," he explains. "I liked the price, and the cars had a lot of features that other cars didn't have — they were well-made, gave a comfortable ride, and were economical to run."

Even so, he had a hard time persuading the bank to take the venture seriously. "They told me I was nuts," he said. "In their opinion, nobody in their right mind would buy a Japanese product, so they were not going to finance any automobile dealers that *sold* Japanese products." After a month of cooling his heels outside the manager's office, however, Slemons's inimitable salesmanship won out and the bank reluctantly agreed to "floor" two cars — industry jargon which means that the bank literally owned the cars until they sold, at which point the dealer paid the bank back. "There was one proviso," adds Slemons, grinning. "I had to sell one car by the end of the first month or they would not renew my flooring line.

"So here come the two Toyotas, and at the end of the first month I had not yet sold the first car. A friend of mine was considering buying a Renault as a graduation present for his daughter, but I told him I would make him a better deal if he bought a Toyota. I sold him the car for $500 over my cost, but I sold the car." It is clear Slemons relishes the telling of the story. "When his daughter saw the car she cried for days, and asked her father, 'What are the kids going to think about me when they see me in a Japanese car?' " Slemons allows himself the last laugh. "These days," he says, "all kids *want* is a Japanese car."

Within two years, Slemons was selling over one hundred Toyotas a month, and had his first million-dollar year. Even so, he admits, the going was tough. Educating the public while trying to sell them a product is pioneering work, no matter which way you cut it. "A lot of Toyota dealers didn't make it," he says. "It's your own stamina and the salespeople you have. You drive them. That's why I worked such long hours — I was the one selling most of the cars. I was the one picking up the phone, getting people in, making the deals.

"Look," he says energetically, "I'm simply more of a salesman than I am a businessman. I'm a born salesman. You can't learn that in college or out of books. There are people in the business who know more about the car than I'll ever know, but they're afraid to hand the customer the pen and ask them to sign the order. They'll show the car and demonstrate it. Their product knowledge is excellent. But there's that fear of asking someone to sign an order. That's the difference between a salesperson and a clerk.

"I used to sit in with the salesmen. I never let a customer walk out of the showroom unless I talked to them. Where a salesman couldn't sell a car, I would." Edsel in 1958, Mercedes in 1961, Toyota in 1965 — Slemon's track record obviously speaks for itself.

"He can sell a new skin to a baby rattler," agrees Malcolm McCassy, Jim Slemons's general manager. "To this day he still loves to sell cars to people, and he'd be the first to admit to you that he'd rather be selling cars than sitting in an office. He sells fifteen automobiles a month every month, and he gets the greatest thrill out of doing it."

Ten years after he started in business, in 1971, Slemons made a crucial decision to sell the Mercedes agency. But in a shrewd market move, he placed both his dealerships on the market at the same time. To his surprise, the Toyota agency sold first, and for more money, and suddenly Jim Slemons was back to being a Mercedes dealer. More important, he finally had enough cash in hand to buy out his father. It cost him $750,000, but he feels it was worth it. "It would have been easier doing business with a bank than with my father, but that was the deal that was made," he now says philosophically. "Still, I felt all the chains had been taken off me when I gave my father that check. I could finally say, 'Now I own one hundred percent of the company.'"

That year proved to be a significant one for the Mercedes as well. Slemons remembers it as the year the car finally came into its own, and owning a Mercedes suddenly became the "in" thing to do. "That was the year the 220 SE 3.5 convertible took off," he says. "It was a good-looking car then and it is still a classic today. It was expensive even in those days, and the fact that you had to put the top down by hand rather than electrically gave it immense snob appeal." Hollywood fell in love with the Mercedes — thanks in part to the Mercedes factory's lending cars to the film industry for use in movies — and what Hollywood fell in love with, the public fell in love with. If the affluent and well-heeled young luminaries of the silver screen were tooling from mansion to nightclub in a Mercedes, that was all the public needed to know.

Mercedes sales took off in a big way for Slemons that year, and although he sold many cars to the Hollywood crowd he noticed that more and more of his customers were coming from Newport Beach, whose population was now exploding with overnight millionaires and prosperous entre-preneurs who were turning the town into the wealthiest community south of Beverly Hills.

In a flash of inspiration, Jim Slemons purchased his legendary eight acres "in the middle of nowhere" in inland Newport Beach. He was cautioned by Mercedes-Benz headquarters that the property was too big to support a dealership, and his friends scoffed that 'nobody was going to come all the way out here to buy cars.' Today his dealership (now subdivided to carry his Acura agency) is surrounded by skyscrapers bearing some of the biggest names in American industry.

It would have been easy for Slemons to coast at this point, but he couldn't resist setting himself the challenge of reviving sales for Mercedes diesels, an unlikely push even by Slemons's own admission. "They were slow and kind of sluggish, they cost a little more than the regular cars and although the diesel fuel cost less, people still had to pay the road tax on it. But the car's mileage was good and they were dependable — they ran forever. If I could just see another way to move them..." He breaks into a hearty laugh as he remembers the day he discovered that farmers bought diesel fuel — tax-free — to use as weed-killer. "So I told my customers to call the large oil companies and order a fifty-gallon drum of No. 2 diesel oil, purportedly to be used as weed spray. I was selling more diesels to places like Newport Beach and Balboa Island, where people were storing fifty-gallon tanks of 'weed spray' for yards that barely measured 10' x 10', and they were driving around for fifteen cents a gallon instead of fifty cents a gallon."

Slemons's diesel bonanza didn't stop there. The two gasoline crises of the seventies (1974/75 and 1979/80) brought the spectre of endless lines of frustrated motorists waiting at gasoline stations. Yet diesel-fuelled trucks — and Mercedes — could simply zip in and out in moments at the uncrowded diesel pumps. "It didn't take them long to figure out what was going on," says Slemons, "and in no time they were coming in to buy diesels. I made more money during those gas crises than I ever made in the car business before or since. These people didn't care what color the car was or even how much they had to pay for it — as the trucks came in to unload the diesels, there would be people standing in line to buy them."

Jim Slemons's penchant for original marketing has hardly

abated, but today he says he markets himself. "It's my name that's on the side of the building and on the licence-plate frames — I've come to be a symbol of my company. So I'm highly visible in the community, and although I'd rather sometimes just sit at home quietly, I make a point of going to as many functions as I can."

That includes devoting time, energy, and money to charitable work. Since 1985 he has sponsored the Jim Slemons Pro Celebrity Tennis Tournament to help children fight drug abuse. He also co-sponsors the Children's Classic, which benefits Camp Ronald McDonald for Good Times, a camp for children with cancer. And in 1988 he sponsored wheelchair tennis to help raise $75,000 for the handicapped. It was for these philanthropic endeavors, as well as for his continued commitment to the Cystic Fibrosis Foundation, the Rotary Club, and other local charities that he was inducted into the Sports Illustrated Hall of Fame for Outstanding Dealer Accomplishments in 1987, an honor based on his community involvement, commitment to charities, high ethics as an automobile dealer, and his public perception. "It's your duty to put something back into the community you live in." he says simply.

It is to the Coast Guard, however, that Slemons is most committed. He calls it his "favorite charity". "I'm into boating, but the yacht club doesn't help people," he says dryly. "The Coast Guard helps people and saves lives, and they are also into drug enforcement, which I strongly support." He joined the Coast Guard in 1974 and has risen to become a lieutenant commander, but he prides himself more on having personally brought in over 250 new members. He also founded the annual Coast Guard Ball seven years ago as a fundraiser, and with his expertise in public affairs he hooked up with the Hollywood Liaison Office, and increased the Coast Guard's exposure dramatically by arranging for the use of their boats and helicopters for chase scenes in movies.

If having a high-visibility name works well as a marketing strategy, Slemons also understands the downside of having his name outside his buildings and on those licence frames. "I'm very conscious of the fact that it's me my customers hold accountable because of that," he says. "And when you have close to five hundred persons working for you, you hope they'll do the right thing by you." Slemons personally selects his staff based on abilities and business ethics, and likes to compare each of them to a *maitre d'hotel* at a fine restaurant.

These days Jim Slemons does very little advertising, but relies for the most part on word of mouth from satisfied customers. "Each customer is phoned the evening after having a car repaired, for example, to ensure that the service was satisfactory," he says. "Backing our products with that kind of service is why people come back."

Except for his Volvo dealership, all his other business interests are located in Orange County. The Volvo agency, his smallest and yet his second most profitable dealership, is in Honolulu, Hawaii. "I have always loved Hawaii and planned to retire there someday," he says, "But I wanted a small business interest to give me something to do there." Back in 1977, Volvo was the only automobile manufacturer not represented in Hawaii, which was all Jim Slemons needed to know. "My nearest Volvo competition is 2,500 miles away, which is a long swim," he jokes. "It's a nice position to be in." He is currently gearing up to open a second Volvo dealership on the island of Maui.

In spite of his enormous success, Jim Slemons is quick to admit that he doesn't have an infallible Midas touch. "I could always remember my father saying, 'Don't be a jack of all trades and a master of none'," he says. "I'm a believer in that adage, that you should do one business well and stay with it. Yet I don't practise what I preach. It seems every time I have gone outside the car business I have not done well." He is referring specifically to his Pan Am Commuter, which has hit financial turbulence. "The airline has been a major setback financially," he admits candidly. "It's going to take me a lot of years of hard work to get out from under that. In one year I lost on the airline what it took me six years to make in the car business."

He feels he may have spent much of his life simply trying to prove his father wrong — just once — but instead finding himself at the helm of such dubious business ventures as a take-out Chinese restaurant that delivered by rickshaw. He also blames the frantic pace at which he pushed himself for imposing a toll on his personal life, which included several unsuccessful marriages.

It wasn't until 1984, in fact, that the last piece of Jim Slemons's life finally fell into place, when he met and married his present wife, Diane. "This is the one I trust," he says with a smile. They met at the opening of his Honda dealership. A businesswoman in her own right, Diane plays an active role in his business life, running her own boating and sportswear division and editing their quarterly magazine "SL", which they call 'The Magazine of Superb Living'. "She's good at business, she likes the business community, and she wants to make a success of herself," says Slemons proudly.

Unfortunately, with two workaholics in the family dinners are almost always at a restaurant, and quality time together is limited to long weekends away — from Friday noon till Monday morning — at any one of their resort homes. Slemons may talk wistfully about retiring to his beautiful house in Hawaii, or even just having a little more time to indulge his passion for travel, but he knows himself too well. He is his own worst enemy. "I don't plan on growing much more. But," he adds, without missing a beat, "I'm looking — possibly — at another auto franchise and a dealership to handle the Italian truck line, Iveco, one of the largest truck manufacturers in the world." He shrugs. "I guess I just love business," he says.

When Jim Slemons was a boy, he was so passionate about cars that he could correctly name car models in the black of night simply by looking at their headlights. Today his collection of antique cars is his pride and joy. "I own a mix of about twenty old cars that took my fancy," he says, beaming, "from a 1919 fire engine to old Packards and Cadillacs and an old Rio tow truck." The collection's crown jewel is a 1935 500K Mercedes, believed to have belonged to Nazi propaganda chief, Joseph Goebbels, and now valued at over $2.5 million. "The story goes that it was hidden in a Swiss farmhouse by Goebbels's chauffeur," says Slemons, who has loaned the car for use in movies like "The Hindenburg" and "The Winds of War".

As he spins tales about each of his cars it becomes clear that Jim Slemons would rather talk about automobiles than about spreadsheets any day. In some ways that small boy with the big passion for cars is never far away from the man who made it big doing what he loved best.

Jack McNaughton
National Education Corporation

-15-

NATIONAL EDUCATION CORPORATION

"Come with me," says John ("Jack") McNaughton. "I want to show you something." The man who parlayed a gamble into the world's largest private educational concern has a twinkle in his eye, and a visitor can't help but wonder what could possibly still excite this man who has seen it all and done it all.

"Look," he says. He opens a pair of double doors onto the *sanctum sanctorum*, the Boardroom on the top floor of the National Education Corporation Building in Irvine, California. "Isn't it something?"

Indeed it is. Reminiscent of the aristocratic private clubs of yore, the Boardroom is serene, elegant and heavy with an atmosphere of power and success. Deep plush leather chairs surround the burnished ebony and rosewood table, and McNaughton can't resist running his hand over its exquisite finish. A penumbral light filters down from the Tiffany skylight.

If McNaughton is proud of his Boardroom, it is because it reflects the calibre of the Board itself, which counts among its members such luminaries as former Senator Barry Goldwater and General David Jones, former chairman of the U.S. Joint Chiefs of Staff. "The Board is like a reflection from the outside on the quality of the company," he observes. "These people wouldn't associate with a company that wasn't qualified."

When Jack McNaughton retired as chairman of the board in 1988, National Education Corporation (NEC) had grown from a one-room mail-order operation in 1954 to an international conglomerate operating in nearly forty countries around the world, with revenues of $458 million dollars in 1988 and annual earnings of $46 million.

Today National Education Corporation is the world's largest provider of education and training to business, industry and governments. The company's subsidiaries include correspondence schools, vocational schools, educational publishing, and state-of-the-art training and consulting services used by more than eighty-five percent of Fortune 500 companies.

Jack McNaughton's boyish good looks belie his sixty-seven years. His ruddy cheeks and unlined face, his youthful figure and energetic gait are those of a man twenty years younger. He has taken to his retirement like a duck to water. As far as he is concerned, the thrill of the game has been edged out by the ponderous technocratic infrastructures that inevitably weigh down a corporation the size of NEC. No, it was better in the good old days.

"You don't fly by the seat of your pants any more," he muses. "It just doesn't work today because things have become too sophisticated, too complicated." According to McNaughton, the free-ranging creativity that helped build the company has gone, replaced by number-crunching expertise and technological "know-how." "The young bucks have taken over and the company is now run by accountants," he laughs, pointing out that even H. David Bright, the company's CEO and the man who replaced him as chairman of the board, is a CPA.

The good old days began back in 1947, when Jack

McNaughton, fresh out of the Navy, began working in the Los Angeles office of J. Walter Thompson, then the largest advertising agency in the world. He had fallen in love with the advertising business while still in high school in Burlingame in northern California. At the time, his cousin was working for J. Walter Thompson in San Francisco, and one day young Jack accompanied her into the office. From that moment, he was hooked. "You couldn't find a more exciting business to be in at that time," he remembers.

University courses in advertising and marketing were practically non-existent forty-five years ago, so when he entered the University of Southern California in Los Angeles, he chose the next best thing — merchandising. But in February 1944, with the world at war, his NROTC class was called out early.

After the war he began looking for a job, and discovered there were two openings in a special training program at the J. Walter Thompson office in Los Angeles. His creative application landed him one of the slots.

In McNaughton's view, the unusual structure of the training program paid off in spades for him. The two trainees were assigned to work in each of the company's departments for six months at a time, acquiring invaluable hands-on experience in all facets of the advertising business — copywriting, production, media, account servicing. "By the time you finished," he says, "you had a pretty well-rounded education. It was an excellent, excellent service."

He soon discovered that there was more to a career in advertising than just collecting a pay-check each week. "One evening, I was working late with the other fellow who had been selected for the training program, and we ran across the salary schedule which had been left out. We were appalled at how little the account executives were making.

The man who worked on the Douglas Aircraft account was only making $30,000 a year, yet the account at that time was worth something like $10 million. It was simply unbelievable."

Right then and there, McNaughton decided that there certainly was serious money to be made in advertising, but not as an employee. He completed his training and worked his way up to the position of junior account executive, but all the while he kept one eye open for the right moment to strike out on his own. That chance came in 1950.

When the opportunity to acquire a small but lucrative advertising account came up he decided to grab it. He formed a small company with Wally Hunt, a superlative salesman and life-long friend from San Francisco. Today, Wally Hunt is better known as "The Pop-up King". As the head of Intervisual Communications, he oversees an empire that produces the majority of pop-up books in the country as well as creative pop-up display ads in magazines.

McNaughton and Hunt got the account and never looked back. "In those days, the advertising agency business was fantastic," says McNaughton. "You had the opportunity to make an awful lot of money." Back then, the standard fifteen percent commission on all advertising placements was still in full effect. This changed as clients became more knowledge-able and demanded more accountability from their agencies, who now have to account for their hours in order to justify their fifteen percent.

"The accountants got involved and took away most of the incentives," says McNaughton, shaking his head. "But back then you could reap a harvest of money. You could take a small account and build it up from peanuts to maybe five or six million dollars. You still earned fifteen percent but the service time was about the same."

That first account was with Todd's Clothing Stores, which

McNaughton describes as "one of those walk-up/save money operations." The clothes were inexpensive and the owner advertised his twelve locations heavily. The one account literally paid all the bills of the fledgling agency.

There was more to the account, however, than simple income. McNaughton greatly admired the owner, Wolf Weinberg, whom he considers to have been one of the major influences on his professional life. A self-educated New Yorker, this elderly gentleman passed on a lifetime of business acumen to the eager young entrepreneur. McNaughton also adopted Wolf Weinberg's business philosophy for his own and has adhered to it ever since: "All through your life, keep a fourth of your money in the business, a fourth in cash, a fourth in stocks and a fourth in real estate, and from time to time look at your portfolio to see if you're in line."

Adman Gordon Van der Boom soon joined the partnership, and the business flourished. "When you're new in the business, you take what accounts you can get," says McNaughton, reflecting on the growth of the agency. "For some reason or other, we attracted many mail order accounts, like Weatheby Guns, Frederick's of Hollywood and Studio Girl Cosmetics. In fact, we had most of the major mail order accounts west of Chicago that were worth a darn. We were noted for that, and word got around."

Jack McNaughton particularly enjoys telling the story of how the agency helped launch a young man named Dave Bushnell, a fellow tenant in their building on Lafayette Park Place, into the mail-order binocular business. Bushnell, who was just starting out in the import-export business, had suddenly found himself the owner of a windfall shipment of binoculars from Japan, and he came into McNaughton's offices to ask what he could do with them.

McNaughton suggested selling them by mail order, and

helped Bushnell place a tiny ad in *Outdoor Life*. The binoculars sold out instantly, Dave Bushnell found himself in the binocular business, and the name Bushnell was on its way to becoming a household word.

According to McNaughton, when you are that close to the mail order business, you can't resist the urge to try it for yourself, so he and Van der Boom (Hunt had left the company by now) looked into finding a product which they themselves could sell. Since archery and bow hunting were extremely popular at the time, they decided to import the hand-laminated bamboo bows and arrows from Japan that world champion Howard Hill was using, and in February 1954 they set up shop in an abandoned 500-square-foot barber shop under the name of the Malibu Archery Company.

"We were too busy at the agency to run the new business ourselves," says McNaughton, "so we hired a guy to handle it for us. We'd go over after work every day or so to check the mail, see how many orders had come in and have a beer before we went home. It was a lot of fun, and a relief from the high pressure at the agency." The business did well, and soon other products were added.

Meanwhile, business was also booming at the advertising agency. Wallace Laub joined the company in 1955, bringing with him the advertising account for the Purex Corporation.

Then one day an employee, an avid outdoorsman, showed McNaughton a three-line classified ad in *Popular Science*. "Get a job in the great outdoors," it urged. "Positions available everywhere." The employee assured McNaughton that just about everybody who liked outdoor activities would love to be able to get a job outdoors. McNaughton smelled a tremendous untapped market.

He contacted the California Department of Fish and Game and learned that, sure enough, a range of jobs from fire-watcher to game warden was literally going begging. So he hired a retired game warden to write a correspondence course for these jobs, and the agency proceeded to advertise them. The response was staggering.

New courses were added and the business became, in McNaughton's words, "extremely profitable." Soon correspondence courses had edged out products as the mainstay of the Malibu Archery Company. There were profits to be made, obviously, and there was no room for sentimentality, so the archery division was sold in 1957, and emphasis was then placed upon the acquisition and distribution of accredited correspondence courses to serve the needs of America at the time.

McNaughton echoes the credo of the successful salesman when he explains the new direction the company was taking. "Most people find a product and then hope there's a market for it. But salespeople, especially in the advertising agency business, know that if you find a market for something you can always manufacture the product to suit that market."

A canny mix of solid business principles and an instinct for emerging social trends has marked the growth of the company ever since. By the late 1950's, at the height of America's love affair with television, the company's TV-servicing correspondence course was accounting for twenty-five percent of all sales. Fifteen years before today's day-care crisis struck, the company began to offer courses in child care which have since become so highly regarded that now ten states automatically grant licenses upon their completion. And even today, as national levels of illiteracy and innumeracy (minimal ability to work with numbers) approach crisis point, NEC has picked up where the education system has failed by working closely with private industry to bring up to par employees' basic reading and mathematics skills.

"We kept abreast of things by reading and being aware,"

explains McNaughton. "The Department of Labor also supplied a great deal of information on job openings in various categories. Then we would sit back and have brainstorming meetings, where we would ask ourselves, 'What kind of course can we have next? What do they need out there?' We had to determine where the need was."

By 1958 the name Malibu Archery Company had become irrelevant. The hot buzzword of the day was "systems", so the company's name was changed to National Systems Corporation. Gordon Van der Boom sold out his share of both companies to Jack McNaughton and Wallace Laub, and the agency changed its name to McNaughton-Laub, Inc., heralding a partnership — and friendship — that has lasted over thirty years.

Sales for the first six months of 1961 were less than $150,000, and the partners decided to take the National Systems Corporation public with an initial stock offering of $300,000. Mortgage bankers Gregory-Massari had only one condition for the deal — that Jack McNaughton devote most of his time to the new company. They didn't have to ask twice.

"The advertising agency business was extremely demanding," he says. "We were very successful, but the idiosyncrasies of some of the accounts could drive you up the wall. I was a little bored, a little burned out. I had always liked the idea of having a public company, of dealing with the investment community." Indeed, while still in high school, he had worked summers as a runner for a stock brokerage firm in San Francisco.

"I would deliver certificates all over and got to meet many interesting people, like the president of Greyhound and the president of Bank of America, because I had to walk into their office to get their signatures. I thought it was pretty exciting, and I was the kind of kid who made it his business to ask a lot of questions and find out what was going on."

As McNaughton moved in to run National Systems Corporation, Wally Laub continued to run the McNaughton-Laub advertising agency. Today, Laub sits on the board of NEC, and is the company's executive vice-president in charge of marketing. "We're still as close as brothers," says Laub of the friendship that has spanned divorces, remarriages, and a career-long mutual passion for golf.

The company expanded rapidly, by using capital from the stock offering to acquire correspondence courses as diverse as drafting and interior design, and they soon found themselves competing head on with other companies offering correspondence courses. Jack McNaughton knew the credibility of his company depended on his being able to separate National Systems Corporation from what he calls those "fly-by-night outfits" with very poor reputations, and the first step was to become fully accredited by the National Home Study Council in Washington, approved and recognized by the U.S. Department of Education.

The second step was to make a clear commitment to quality education by bringing in renowned educator Dr. Eugene Auerbach as the company's director of education. At the time Dr. Auerbach, who had a Ph.D. in Education, was teaching at the University of Southern California and writing a syndicated weekly column for the *Los Angeles Times*. He had always been a strong supporter of vocational education, and his relationship with the company lasted twenty-five years, until his retirement in 1986. He retired from the board of directors in 1988.

In 1965 McNaughton moved his operation south from Los Angeles to Newport Beach in Orange County, where he had kept a boat for many years. In those days Orange County was a quiet backwater, with no freeways and no industry to speak of apart from the cultivation of oranges and lima

beans. Today the burgeoning county ranks as one of the top
thirty five industrial powers in the world, in terms of its own
GNP.

The move was a signal, indicative of the aggressive new
changes the company would soon embrace. In May 1968
the company bought its first group of residence schools,
Anthony Schools of Real Estate. "We acquired residence
schools because you could only go so far with home-study
courses," explains McNaughton, pointing out that it was
simply a logical progression for a company devoted entirely
to education.

Other acquisitions soon followed, marking a decade of
explosive growth — Patricia Stevens Finishing Schools,
Bryman Schools of Nursing, Innkeepers Institute International, RETS Electronic Schools, E.I. Electrical, the prestigious
Spartan School of Aeronautics in Tulsa — the list is a long
one.

Today, nearly sixty different schools operate under the
umbrella name of National Education Centers and make up
the largest chain of proprietary vocational schools in the
nation. While enrolments at traditional two and four-year
colleges and universities have remained flat, National
Education Centers have been seeing enrolments increase
nine to twelve percent annually. "Not everyone can attend
college," says Jack McNaughton. Nor do they need to,
obviously — ninety-five percent of their vocational school
graduates find jobs.

Jack McNaughton may like to think of himself as a
gambler, but like any true entrepreneur he has made his own
luck. The litany of acquisitions and growth could read quite
differently but for the hard business principles behind each
decision; no school was acquired on its potential alone, but
was subject to tough scrutiny. "We would look at their
graduation rate as well as their attrition rate, which is how

long a student actually stayed in the school," explains McNaughton. "We also looked at the books to find out how much they paid for each enquiry from advertising and where it came from — what publication, radio or TV advertisement."

The year 1978 was pivotal in the history of the company, beginning with its third — and final — name change, from National Systems Corporation to National Education Corporation. "When we chose the word 'systems', we didn't know what we were going to be in," says McNaughton. "But since we had become an education company it made sense to call it National Education."

In the years between 1978 and 1982, a period of high interest rates and a sluggish economy, NEC quintupled its sales, from $26 million to $134 million. Aggressive activity in acquisitions accounted for a great proportion of these sales figures, but McNaughton learned early on that a weak economy, paradoxically was literally his company's trump card.

"We are virtually recession-proof," he says with obvious satisfaction. "When there's high unemployment there's a lot of retraining necessary, and business increases. We may have more trouble with collections, but it's more than offset by the added enrolment." Buying distressed companies at bargain-basement prices was also profitable. "We *never* paid retail," he jokes, adding, "We were like the fair-haired boys who could do no wrong. The stock market valued our stock at such a high multiple it gave us a chance to do the things we wanted to do."

Some of NEC's most significant acquisitions came in during those years, including Steck-Vaughn Company, the Austin-based text-book publishing company, Bauder College, Arizona Automotive, and International Correspondence Schools (ICS), the largest such school in the country.

Founded in Scranton in 1875, ICS was, in McNaughton's words, the granddaddy of them all, and the prestige that came with the acquisition was a coup.

Words like "prestige", "credibility", and "quality" are Jack McNaughton's mantras. His personal crusade to create a prestigious board of directors began in 1977, when none other than former California Governor Edmund "Pat" Brown accepted his offer to become a board member and chairman of the nominating committee. Brown, a Democrat who had run the state with autocratic panache from 1958 to 1966, had scored wide successes in the area of higher education, and he was pleased to serve on the board of a company dedicated to education.

Jack McNaughton credits Governor "Pat" Brown with teaching him a lot about the value of honesty and integrity. He also learned from him the importance of expediency: "Just Do It" became one of the most important maxims in McNaughton's business philosophy.

"Southern California wouldn't have enough water today if Pat Brown hadn't pushed through the Central Valley Water Project when he was governor," says McNaughton. "It wasn't perfect, but he just fought that thing through."

That sense of urgency is what McNaughton believes separates him from the rest. He admits he's not a perfectionist — far from it — but he understands that this is the *quid pro quo* for being able to strike while the iron's hot. Ask those who have known Jack McNaughton longest and they all agree that his canny sense of timing is his trademark.

National Education Corporation's entry into the prestigious New York Stock Exchange in 1980 was also the source of enormous personal satisfaction for McNaughton, and he relishes telling the story of how the company first made a step toward this goal.

"To qualify for listing on the major U.S. stock exchanges, you must tailor your business to suit certain stock listing requirements — so much stock trading, so many stockholders, so many shares outstanding and so forth before they even consider your company for listing," he says. "We had brought the company up to where we satisfied every requirement but the number of shareholders. We still needed a couple of hundred. So Wally Laub and I made a list of all our friends and we sent each of them a free one-share certificate of stock with a short letter explaining that we wanted them to become a shareholder." The ruse worked and they were able to satisfy the requirements. Today, each of those little $1.00-value stock certificates is worth about $200.

The eighties have marked NEC's entree into the high-tech arena of what McNaughton calls "advanced teaching techniques." The company, under the presidency of H. David Bright, led the way in the development of sophisticated training systems through the use of enhanced videodisc technology, video-text systems with advanced graphics, and computer-based interactive technologies. Courses were developed in such emerging technologies as robotics, aviation maintenance, and information processing. Even correspondence courses entered the Brave New World with such enhancements as instant interface with instructors and electronic testing through computers linked to a home telephone.

The biggest change, however, came in the direction taken by the company itself. Industrial training was slated to become the next growth area, and the company geared up to meet the new market.

In 1986 NEC acquired Chicago-based Deltak, Inc., the teaching arm of Gulf + Western Inc., for $84.5 million and combined it with their own National Education Training

Corporation to form DELTAK Training Corporation. With annual revenues of more than $66 million, the new entity became a dominant industry-training company, specializing in white collar training programs like information processing and technical data-processing equipment.

A new industrial-training subsidiary, Applied Learning International (ALI) was formed in 1987 when DELTAK merged with Advance Systems, Inc., a provider of diverse training materials and services, thereby creating the broadest-based training company in the world. ALI's library encompasses 20,000 hours of training and over 7,000 courses, most of them on laser disc interactive video. Today, more than eighty percent of Fortune 500 companies and a host of government agencies are ALI clients, and with twenty-six international offices stretching from Stockholm to Sydney, a client's needs for training material can be met virtually anywhere in the world within twenty-four hours.

In December 1988, Boston-based Spectrum Interactive, Inc. was added to ALI. Spectrum was especially known for its client consulting services, and the acquisition has given NEC the leading edge in the newest branch of industrial training — developing and installing customized training programs for industrial clients.

Today, industrial business represents sixty percent of the company's revenues. Training modules consisting of video tapes, floppy discs and touch-screen consoles are leased to industrial giants like General Motors, hundreds at a time. Complete training programs are customized for other corporations like Federal Express, who maximize productivity by continually testing and retraining their 12,000 employees. And companies like Motorola Corporation are budgeting to spend tens of millions of dollars over the next few years just to raise the levels of their employees' mathematics and language skills.

Jack McNaughton delights in discussing these new technologies and the new direction of the company, but as he skims over the details of NEC's growth in the eighties, it is clear that the thrill of the chase has lost its edge for him. Even advertising no longer holds the magic it once did, and the man who says he always put in his two cents' worth on all major decisions now finds the creativity has gone, stifled by the fragmentation of the advertising industry into ultra-specialized fields. Mail order, for example, has become a precision art of computer-generated minutiae, and television advertising is now the realm of deft media experts whose main talent lies in cutting deals.

National Education's 1988 advertising and marketing budget of $140 million represented nearly one-third of its revenues. But, as Jack McNaughton points out, with so many different products and such diverse advertising requirements, NEC now uses up to seven different ad agencies around the country, and these are in turn overseen by the company's in-house agency, W.O.L. Advertising (Wallace O. Laub).

McNaughton's face lights up, however, when he manages to turn the subject of conversation around to his favorite topic and the great love of his life — horses.

Horses have been in his blood since his junior high school days, when he earned extra money by working as a "hot walker" at the local race track. He promised himself then that he would one day breed horses, and he finally got his wish in 1971.

"That was the first time I felt I could afford a horse," he laughs. "I bought it as a sideline business." Today McNaughton owns six mares and has interests in three others. He has produced a string of winners, including the 1989 million-dollar Santa Anita Handicap winner, Marshall Law.

Like a personal metaphor, McNaughton's interest in horses shows the cool hand of a businessman who can temper passion with the bottom line. By the time he could afford a horse, he had found out enough about horse racing to know that there was no money in following the prevailing practice of racing colts.

"If a colt doesn't perform at the race track, he's virtually worthless to anybody," he explains. "Nobody's going to breed to him, and you end up selling him to a riding stable. But I noticed that if you buy a filly you can have just as much fun...without the downside. With a well-bred female, you can always breed her to a good sire and you're still in business."

That logic earned McNaughton a comfortable annuity with his very first purchase, a mare called Satin. Not only did his $65,000 investment bring in winnings in several stakes, but Satin's pedigree also formed the foundation of his lucrative breeding operations back in Kentucky. "I sell off most of the offspring, but every now and then if I have a good filly that I want to keep to breed later on, I'll bring her out to California and race her. Then I'll send her back and breed her. It's a helluva business, and fun, too."

When he is not overseeing his horses, Jack McNaughton is either playing golf or travelling with his wife, Nancy. They share a magnificent 7,000-square-foot home, complete with indoor and outdoor waterfalls, which overlooks the ocean in exclusive Crescent Bay in North Laguna Beach. They are both active in charities, and are deeply involved with Interval House, a shelter for battered women and children. Jack McNaughton is also Governor at the Balboa Bay Club in Newport Beach.

But Jack McNaughton is by no means out of the picture at National Education Corporation. Now bearing the title of Founder-Director he attends all board meetings. The company has provided him with a plush corner office and a secretary, and he comes in frequently, as he puts it, to keep his finger in the pot. He doubts if he will ever be able to divorce himself completely from the business, and plans to continue coming in occasionally "until they kick me out."

He is quite content to let the new generation of "young turks" take the company into the next century. "They'd like to acquire the world, really," he says with admiration.

In 1986 the corporate headquarters were moved to the top two floors of a gleaming mirrored skyscraper overlooking the bustling 405 freeway. The five-foot-high letters of the company's name are clearly visible to the twelve lanes of north-south traffic as well as to all incoming planes that are landing at nearby John Wayne Airport, the nation's fifth busiest — a boon for business. "We always had such a low profile," laughs Jack McNaughton. "But now, it's amazing how much that sign has done for us!"

As he contemplates the view, he pauses to consider his legacy to National Education; an extremely modest man, he does not indulge easily in self-approbation. Those who know him well call him a visionary.

"He's a dreamer," says his good friend and fellow director, Wally Laub. "He can look at things and see them as they could be, and then plough in and get them done. In business, if one out of five ideas work you're usually very good. Jack would average three out of five because his timing was so exceptional. He always had great ideas which he would start and then turn over to other people to handle for him while he went out and started another one."

Jack McNaughton says he modelled his business philosophy on Walter Chrysler's admonition always to hire people smarter than yourself. Among those he likes to name are current Chairman and CEO, H. David Bright, who came on board in 1972 as a finance and management whiz, and

Wally Laub. Such long-term loyalties create what he likes to call "hustle and bustle."

"But you can't gather these kinds of people around you unless you make it worth their while," he explains. "Sometimes you have to sacrifice in doing it, too." He points out that most of the people who have been with him since the early days are millionaires today. "I didn't take large options myself because I held a lot of founder's stock anyway, but I always made sure that they had the options."

That generosity of spirit is legend among those who know him — once Jack McNaughton befriends you, he is your friend for life. If in fact he has one fault, they say, it is his difficulty in letting people go. Says Wally Laub, "We've hired some turkeys along the way, there were even a few backstabbers. But Jack always had a hard time getting rid of them. He's one of the nicest, finest human beings I have ever met." McNaughton simply preferred to overlook any wrongs done him, moving onward and upward rather than letting such things get him down.

The future looks bright for the company that Jack built. The National Education Corporation has enjoyed fourteen consecutive years of growth, most of them record-breakers.

"I don't think there is any other business area with more growth possibilities than education," says Jack McNaughton. "It's such an explosive business and we're suddenly the leaders. More than anyone else in the world, we are poised to take advantage of that mammoth market. I believe in five years we may be a billion-dollar company."

With Jack McNaughton's track record, that's no idle threat.

Mel Haber
Ingleside Inn

-16-

INGLESIDE INN

"I cannot overemphasize the fact that I never know what I'm doing."

This remarkable statement is made by Mel Haber, the Brooklyn boy who grew up to become, without knowing what he was doing, the owner and operator of a world-class establishment — the Ingleside Inn in Palm Springs, California.

He is seated at his favorite corner table in his elegant Melvyn's Restaurant and Lounge at the Ingleside Inn, trying to explain how he happened to make his first fortune. This is not easy to accomplish, because staffers keep interrupting with important questions, and guests drop by to shake their host's hand and exchange a few words.

Then there is an unexpected interruption. A man appears at the table and abruptly thrusts a check at Haber for $1,000. Somewhat embarrassed, he tells Haber that several years ago he cheated him out of some money, but he's doing better now and he can afford to make repayment and amends. The two men smile, shake hands and wish each other the best of luck. Turning to his guest, Haber shrugs off the incident. Things like that happen all the time. Back to the story of his life.

"The story of my life is really a series of stories," Haber

says with a grin that lights up a lean, celebrity-tanned face framed by dark wavy hair that is debonairly gray at the temples. His muscular frame is evidence of his conversion to physical fitness at age forty-nine.

"I did everything backwards my whole life," he explains. "I never exercised. I never ate a square meal. But four years ago I discovered health. That's a story in itself."

Mel Haber's life is indeed a collection of stories. In fact years ago, in response to numerous guest inquiries about the Ingleside Inn in its early Haber years, the hotelier dictated his favorite remembrances and had the stapled photocopied manuscripts placed on the night stands of the guest rooms. *"Bedtime Stories of the Ingleside Inn,"* was an immediate hit. Years later, in 1988, a frequent guest surprised Mel Haber with five hundred professionally published copies of *"Bedtime Stories."* Upon request, a delighted Haber will sell personally-inscribed books and donate the proceeds to his favorite local charity, Angel View Crippled Children's Foundation.

In his book Haber recalls the awe he felt on the fine spring day in 1975, when he first passed beyond the wrought-iron gates onto the ground of the then rundown Ingleside Inn, a stucco-walled two-acre private estate barely two blocks from downtown Palm Springs. With a lily pond gracing the central courtyard, a promenade of cypress trees shading the stone benches and walkways, and the scent of flowers filling the air, the hotel exuded a genteel, old-world solitude. Haber has carefully preserved the ambience so each new guest to the Inn can savor the welcome as he once did.

"My first impression was that the world had somehow forgotten about this property. It had charm and atmosphere as only a piece of property could have that was built fifty years before. The first thing you saw when you entered was a charming, Spanish-style hacienda, complete with tiled roof and lovely vines on the walls. There were several Spanish-style bungalows situated lazily around the property. It was a scene out of old-world Spain, or perhaps even Mexico.

"Orville's, the restaurant, was located in a little house at the edge of the property. It was oppressively decorated in rose-colored flocked wallpaper with burgundy drapes and carpeting."

Haber recalls seeing about twenty couples, average age about seventy, eating lunch. "Each lady was dressed 'for tea' in a long dress, and each man was wearing a jacket and tie. I commented to the manager that I felt awfully warm, even though dressed only in shorts, tee-shirt and sneakers, and he said there was no air-conditioning. My thoughts were that either this was a stage-setting and they were shooting a movie, or these people were dead and had forgotten to fall down!"

The future hotelier was struck dumb by the sight of some nameless and faceless senior citizens eating lunch and sweating, but he was even more flabbergasted by the information contained in an old dusty card file he found in the basement. The guest list, so carefully preserved by the previous owner, practically glimmered in the dust. Palm Springs is the playground of world and Hollywood royalty and the Ingleside Inn was the courtyard. Previous guests included Howard Hughes, Clare Boothe Luce, Mervyn LeRoy, Elizabeth Taylor, Gene Tierney and Rita Hayworth, to name just a few luminaries from a very long and very distinguished list.

Apparently the Ingleside Inn would rival its newest owner with its own colorful stories from the past — not to mention what the future held.

Some people recount their lives as if they were reciting from the text of a junior high school history book, factually but so blandly as to make even the extraordinary ordinary.

Not so with Mel Haber.

When Haber talks about himself, he lives his life again before your eyes. The storyteller feels again the excitement of preparing for the next business scheme, one that would undoubtedly let him support his wife and family in grand style; and then his disappointment and desperation at each new failure. He experiences again the bone-tired weariness but also the supreme satisfaction of surviving twenty-hour days jammed with hard worktime and equally hard playtime. There's still the wide-eyed wonder over the first Rolls Royce, the first big house on Long Island's South Shore, the rat-race of the high life — then the relief, subsequently, of giving it up in laid-back California. Above all, there's the genuine appreciation of the irony of a mid-life career change that resulted in fame and fortune in the unlikeliest of places, Palm Springs.

Haber firmly insists that not only did he never plan to buy and run a hotel and restaurant, let alone create a world-renowned establishment, but until his opening-night party, in September 1975, he never even considered the hospitality business to be a real business. Where he came from that wasn't what real men did for a living.

Born in 1936, Haber is the son of a New York City garment-center salesman, who died of a heart attack at age fifty-two. Bad hearts ran in his family. The boy was thirteen years old at the time, the only son in the family and the baby by eight years of three older sisters. The son idolized his father and his father's friends. To him, the garment center was the center of his universe.

"To be a man, and to be a big shot, you had monograms on your shirts, the cigarette hanging out of the side of your mouth, you gambled and you ran around and partied with your friends. I grew up with all those values," Haber explains.

A Californian since 1974, Haber still *tawks* Brooklynese. Speaking at a rat-a-tat-tat machine-gun pace, he crams more facts and more stories into casual conversations than the average human being could possibly manage. But that's also how he thinks, and how he works, and that, he claims, is how he got to be where he is today.

"My philosophy in business was very clear," he says. "I figured I was half as bright as the next guy therefore I had to work twice as many hours to do equally well as he did. I said I have no control over my ability or my talent. The only thing I have control over is how hard I'm willing to work, how many hours I'm willing to put in. I used to work unbelievable hours. I got by on sheer guts. And luck."

To support his claim of naivete, Haber tells the story about building the bar at Melvyn's. He claims it was typical of the entire renovation project for Ingleside Inn.

"It's 4:00 a.m. and I'm so nervous I can't sleep. I went down to the restaurant area to inspect the bar itself. I was seated at the bar and, for some reason, I found I was not able to face where the bartender would be standing. I had never been a great one for bars, but I knew that whenever I sat at a bar I was facing the bartender. I was really confused, and sat racking my brains as to what was wrong. My stool was right next to the bar and I could only sit sideways and not face the bartender. It took me an hour and a half to discover that we had forgotten to put the ledge on the bar and, consequently, if you were sitting flush against the bar, you had no room to put your legs in front of you and therefore face the bar.

Rather than being discouraged that someone had forgotten the ledge, Haber was thrilled that he had found a solution to the problem — and the problem itself — in under two hours.

Haber had tumultuous adventures with his hotel in its

pre-opening days. They represent a telescoped version of his early life. The days and nights of Mel Haber the gracious host weren't always as simple as they now appear to be. He could have been an elevator operator for all the ups and downs he's had.

When Haber graduated from high school in Brooklyn, his personal goal back in 1954 was to earn $200 a week, preferably in the rag business, as the garment center is called by its intimates. He enrolled in New York City's Fashion Institute of Technology, knowing at the time that you really don't need academic preparation for work in the garment industry.

Then Davy Crockett came along and changed everything.

When Haber was twelve years old he worked on and off for a friend, the son of a furrier, who sold raccoon tails as bicycle accessories. He combed fur, cut the excess skin, stapled ends and put the tails in plastic bags for sale, Not exactly exciting work, but something that earned him a few bucks.

Virtually overnight the demand soared for raccoon tails when the King of the Wild Frontier appeared Sunday evenings on Walt Disney wearing his trademark coonskin cap. It seemed like every boy and girl in the country needed a coonskin cap.

Haber was swept up in the Davy Crockett craze. He quit college and joined his old employer as the company's production boss for $85 a week, a rather princely sum at the time. Unfortunately, the job lasted as long as the supply of raccoon tails held out, which wasn't very long.

After a brief stint as a salesman at an exclusive women's shoe salon on Manhattan's Fifth Avenue, that was owned by a brother-in-law, Haber returned to his furrier friend. This time the company was concentrating on its bread-and-butter business in the bicycle trade: locks and chains, decals, plastic streamers and the occasional raccoon tail. But after a while Haber, now a husband and the father of a baby boy, wanted more money. He was making $95 a week and had asked for a $10 raise. Instead, he was offered a small percentage of the profit if the company exceeded its sales of the previous year. Unfortunately, the previous year had been the best ever and Haber was certain the company could not beat its record high. He was discouraged. It was 1961 and he was twenty-five years old.

Using some connections, Haber teamed up with a woman who wanted to own and operate a bar. She would put up the money and Haber would get a liquor licence and run the place. They would split the profits. Unfortunately, the liquor board rejected his application. Worse, Haber had quit his job during the waiting period.

"And I had no money and no place to go. It was the first time in my life I was out of a job," he recalls with a sigh.

"I remember it was a weekend. I was at home, sitting out front, wondering what to do when a guy drove up in a taxicab. We started talking. He owned the cab and he told me that you can really control your own destiny once you pay the $25,000 to buy your cab and medallion (licence to operate). You put down ten percent and a broker financed the rest. I thought this was really the business for me. I was good at working incredible numbers of hours so I thought I'd work hard for two or three years and make the money, pay off the medallion, sell it, and then start my own business.

"That's all I talked about the whole weekend. I had the whole thing planned, including borrowing the down payment from my sister with the shoe-store husband. I couldn't wait for Monday morning to come so I could get my hack licence!"

But on Monday morning the licensing bureau rejected Haber. When he was two years old, he lost his right eye in a fall down a flight of steps. To drive a cab in New York, you need *two* good eyes.

Crestfallen, Haber left the licence bureau and glumly wandered a few blocks until he came to the office of his wife's cousin, who ran a small stock-brokerage house.

On a sudden whim, the man gave Haber 300 shares of a four-dollar stock and told him to sell them. Haber made three telephone calls and got three hits: his best friend, his former boss and his mother. Within minutes, he had earned $75 in commissions.

"Unbelievable!" he exclaims. "So I became a stock broker. I became a big shot."

In the first six months on the job, Haber earned about $15,000 working with only fifty over-the-counter stocks.

The market was booming. Unfortunately, Haber's stocks were not.

"I never had one winner," he says quietly. "I didn't know it, but I was working for a boiler shop. I buried everybody — including myself, because I bought every stock I ever sold. I had my mother in there too. My only justification to myself was that I was honest and that I didn't intentionally do anything wrong. I wasn't that kind of guy. I wasn't a rotten guy. I wasn't a sharpshooter. I was the guy who sold his stocks to his mother!"

So Haber, now the father of two children, made his third return trip to his old boss. This time he got his offer of $200 a week. This time he rejected the offer. Instead of a raise, he demanded a percentage of the business. The company had expanded into the automotive business and the future looked very bright indeed.

"We were quite a combination," Haber says of his former boss.

"Everything that I was not, he was. Everything he was not, I was. If you put the two of us together, you had every possible facet of a human being. He was mechanical; I couldn't turn a screw. I was athletic; he couldn't throw a ball. I worked inside; he worked outside. I got up at 6:00 a.m.; he got up at 11:30 a.m. It was the most amazing combination. Business started to go great. I worked my tail off; he wanted to play."

Knowing his strengths and betting on his instincts, Haber cut himself an excellent deal. He was on the payroll at $64 a week but, based on his take of the profits, his annual income reached $250,000.

Haber is now an old hand at managing money so he can objectively analyze how the nouveau riche spend their dollars.

"Wealth is interesting," he comments. "You have a lot of needs — or a lot of wants — I should say — and a lot of holes to fill with the first few dollars you make. You buy your first big house, a Rolls Royce, diamonds and furs for your wife. But after you get beyond your initial rush of money, you don't buy your fortieth Rolls Royce. Now the money starts to fall off to other things that hold intrinsic value. You buy a piece of art, a rare car, things that will hold their value and appreciate."

With his first big money, Haber bought a large house in the town of Atlantic Beach, on Long Island's opulent South Shore. To celebrate his thirty-sixth birthday, he bought himself his first Rolls Royce.

He also used some of his money to make investments. These side deals negate his public claim as a stumbler who relies on blind luck for success. While continuing as a salaried employee, he made solo forays into the world of the entrepreneur. One of Haber's first businesses was a company that made vacuum-formed blister packs for packaging consumer products. One deal led to others over the years until Haber found himself juggling nine small unrelated businesses such as an importing company, a boiler cleaning service, a front-end repair shop, a belt buckle manufacturing firm and a factoring company for a medical center.

"If I were an analyst, I'd say I was looking for a Mel Haber so I wouldn't have to come to work. My boss had found a Mel Haber. I was looking for a young guy to serve me. But I never found anybody."

That meant Haber put in a lot of hours every day. On the plus side, it also meant he had plenty of excuses to get out of the house and away from a marriage that was not working particularly well.

"In hindsight, I don't believe I lived that life. I was getting up at 6:00 a.m. and taking on all the automotive work because I don't know how to delegate responsibility. All I know is how to work hard and long hours. Smoking five packs of cigarettes a day and drinking four pots of coffee a day. Then out to dinner to party with friends. Drive to Long Island in a haze. Go to bed at 2:00 a.m. Get up at 6:00 a.m. and start all over again.

"But there was nothing unique about what I was doing because everyone in New York seemed to be doing it, although not to the extent that I was. I also had a tremendous desire to do everything because I knew I was going to die by age fifty-two like my father and my aunts and my uncles."

About that time Haber, a voracious reader, hit upon a personal truth in Robert Townsend's bestseller "Up the Organization Chart — How to Stop the Corporation from Stifling People and Strangling Profits."

The maxim that struck home was, "Concentration is the key to economic success." His secretary committed it to needlepoint.

"Realizing the accuracy of that statement, I made peace

with myself. I was not after the economic gain; I was after the action. I wanted to be an action guy," he says.

The frenetic pace of daily life didn't change appreciably but other changes came. Haber's company was bought out, so he went to work for a new employer. The parent company sent him to California where he bought an automotive products manufacturing firm in Watts. As president of Wallfrin Industries in Los Angeles, Haber became bicoastal.

In 1971 Haber's faltering marriage finally ended. The couple's two sons were twelve and five years old and their daughter was two.

After three more hectic years of bicoastal commuting, he finally decided he'd had enough, and on July 4, 1974, Mel Haber accepted an invitation from his board of directors and shifted his operating base to the west coast. He became Californian and took a furnished apartment in Marina del Rey for himself and his girlfriend. In keeping with California's celebrated healthy lifestyle, Haber gave up the fast life, including the drinking and the smoking. Five months later in December, while visiting friends in Palm Springs, he bought a condo for weekend getaways and relaxation. Then in April he passed through the portals of the Ingleside Inn and into a completely new life. It was the stereotypical mid-life career change.

At first Haber looked for partners for the Ingleside venture. He talked about turning it into a spa, a "fat farm" or even a private playground for himself and his co-owners, but he failed to find anyone who saw any merit to a deal for an aging hotel property. Still, his gut instinct was to put down the $100,000 and buy the place for $300,000 even if it was just ground in Palm Springs. One week after setting eyes on the Ingleside Inn, Mel Haber became the latest on a short list of owners.

He soon discovered that the Inn itself is as celebrated as

its former clientele.

The Humphrey Birge family, of Pierce Arrow automobile fame, built their palatial mansion and playground on the property in 1922. Fond of lavish parties and lavish spending, the Birges decorated their home with antiques reflecting their eclectic tastes. Haber inherited an assortment of antiques, such as a sienna bust of Laura by the Italian Renaissance poet and artist Petrach, a commode once owned by Mary Tudor and a carved wooden vestment chest used by 15th century priests. They're all back on display in the guest rooms and villas.

In 1935 the property was purchased by Ruth Hardy, a wealthy Indiana expatriot, who saw its potential as a private club for her type of people, White Anglo-Saxon Protestants, and for the Who's Who of the world.

"Hardy" is a familiar and beloved name in Palm Springs. As the city's first councilwoman, she is remembered for having had lighted palm trees placed along downtown's main boulevard, Palm Canyon Drive. A grateful Palm Springs named a park for her after her death in 1965.

The Indiana widow also had a rather inelegant side, which Haber discovered from the fifteen drawers of 5,000 index cards she kept on her former guests.

Mrs. Hardy pulled no punches in her pencilled notes about who was acceptable and who was not. Mr. and Mrs. Samuel Goldwyn of Hollywood, California were "NG" for "No Good" and "J" for "Jewish". The hostess could also be quite arbitrary. She would turn thumbs down on people who were too loud, too risque, too ugly. A certain Harry B. was blackballed forever because he "came in with bare tummy and a paper soldier hat — No, No, No." An Earl Martyn who registered on October 12, 1946 was Howard Hughes but "wants no one to know." Hughes later earned an "NG" when he arrived with Ava Gardner. Elizabeth Taylor

(Movie Actress????????) was a "lovely young girl" who registered at the Inn in 1959. Others on the Hardy-approved list included Katharine Hepburn, Bette Davis, Cyd Charisse, Dr. Norman Vincent Peale (who stayed as her guest), Salvador Dali ("I believe he is a painter!!!"), Peter Folger of the coffee fortune and Lily Pons, who kept the same suite for thirteen years.

In the ten years after Ruth Hardy died and left a void where the personality had been, the Ingleside Inn hit a downward spiral, falling into total disrepair. Years passed before Haber could laugh about what he got for his money.

"I had inherited, along with the hotel, a staff consisting of a funny-looking fifty-year-old fat man with a limp, a toupee, who was my manager; a twenty-year-old boy from Arkansas with an incredible drawl who was my bell captain, bellman, bookkeeper, front desk clerk; a chef who was temperamental, totally absorbed with pornography and who had never cooked for more than fifty people at a time; a lovely housekeeper who picked fresh flowers for the rooms but who had a bad back and had difficulty making beds; and four little sixty-year old waiters, one of whom was an Englishman who called everyone "Mum" and "Dad" with the net result that most customers were offended." Despite their unprepossessing appearance, however, Haber's staffers managed to keep the Inn functioning during their boss's weekday absences.

On July 4, 1975, Haber declared himself independent of the past. Leaving behind twenty-two years of life with a paycheck, he quit his job and moved to Palm Springs to be a full-time hotel operator.

Finally Mel Haber had found a project, a single pursuit, that could consume all his energy and time, not to mention money, which was being spent at an incredible rate.

Haber would spend that summer totally renovating his jewel of an inn and at summer's end open a dazzling new establishment with class and style that would make even Palm Springs glitterari take notice.

That Haber completed his task by summer's end is a testimony to his fabled ability to work at a furious pace for hours at a stretch. Back in 1975, the go-get-'em attitude so prevalent in New York City was an anathema in Palm Springs.

"When I became successful I used to make the statement, which was not very popular, that in New York, to be in the race you gotta run the mile in four minutes. In California, if you run the race in twenty-two minutes, you win the race. Guys who came to Palm Springs didn't come to work eighteen hours a day like I did. They close one night a week, three months a year, ten o'clock every night. They came here to enjoy the sun and play golf and if that moron Mel Haber wanted to work eighteen hours a day, he could have stayed in New York."

After hundreds of thousands of dollars and a few short weeks, the project was nearing completion. Each room and villa was completely unique with its own charm and such personal amenities as a jacuzzi and steam bath in each bath salon. The grounds were properly manicured, backgammon boards ready in the old Birge library, staff hired, chaise lounges positioned so occupants could comfortably watch the sun drop behind the San Jacinto Mountains and the hills slowly fade to purple.

The restaurant, once so darkly European, was elegantly upbeat California with some resemblance to New York's once-famous Stork Club and Rick's, the American cafe of "Casablanca" fame. The showplace, among the wicker and antiques and waiters in white linen jackets, was a restored 1895 carved oak and mahogany bar that Haber brought across the country from Pete's Saloon in Philadelphia.

With some reluctance at the apparent show of egotism,

Haber changed the name of "Orville's" to "Melvyn's", justifying his decision by pointing out that no one ever calls him Melvyn.

Insisting then as well as now that he didn't have the vaguest idea what he was doing, Haber realized that his own judgment was excellent.

"I have enough difficulty figuring out what I like; I have no chance figuring out what strangers think. I finally decided to use my own taste and judgment, and hope there's enough people who like what I like to make my place successful."

In 1975, Palm Springs' color spectrum had two hues, green and yellow. Haber liked brown and beige so he decorated his restaurant in brown and beige. He jokes now that within two years, everything is Palm Springs turned brown and beige.

Opening night finally arrived the last Friday in September 1975. Haber played it low key.

"I chose to open quietly so that I could iron out any kinks that existed. I placed a small ad in the local newspaper announcing that Melvyn's was now serving dinner. As I walked through the doors that evening I was totally amazed to find the bar and the dining room full. To say I was nervous was an understatement. The Maitre d' informed me we were sold out. Wow! As I looked around the completely unfamiliar crowd, it seemed that all the women were beautiful and all the men were great looking."

Haber fell into his role of host as he had learned it — in the movies. He strolled around greeting guests, although in a bit of a fog, he confesses. Always poor at recognizing faces, he recalls agonizingly, he didn't realize he was hosting the equivalent of a Hollywood premiere, complete with Hollywood irony.

"At about ten o'clock I walked outside to get some air and just at that moment, a motorcycle pulled up with a guy dressed in dungarees, a tee-shirt and a beard, certainly not the Ingleside type. Seated behind him was a pretty girl. The guy said he had come to see the new place. I begged him, "Please, some other time. This is a special night." He smiled at me and simply drove off. I was pleased with myself for handling the situation so adeptly. Later on I learned I turned away Steve McQueen and Ali McGraw."

When the story spread, the faux pas actually enhanced Haber's reputation as a host. Celebrities beget celebrities, just as Rolls Royces beget Rolls Royces. (Haber parks his out front.) Frank Sinatra and Barbara Marx held their pre-wedding dinner at Melvyn's. June Allyson married Dr. David Ashrow in the garden. Debbie Reynolds hosted her fiftieth birthday party at the Inn. A sweaty Marlon Brando in cowboy get-up was almost refused a room, a la Steve McQueen. Bob Hope. President and Mrs. Ford. Lucille Ball. Hoagy Carmichael. John Forsythe. From the next generation of stars: Cher. Cyndi Lauper. Cindy Williams. Barry Manilow. Richard Pryor. Goldie Hawn. Brooke Shields. And on and on.

Haber caters to all his guests with equal attentiveness. The Ingleside Inn was the first to provide guests in its rooms and villas with amenities that have become standard at first-class inns: steambaths in all the rooms, complimentary continental breakfasts, free newspapers, fruit baskets at check-in, guest names on matchbooks, refrigerators in each room stocked with free snacks and drinks from the owner. Haber's operating credo is to provide the best for his guests and charge rates reflecting the value. A night at the Inn can cost from $75 for a room to $500 for a suite.

"I did things to my own taste and it has served me very well," Haber observes. "Everything I did in Palm Springs turned to gold, no matter what. Still, for me to be a success in the restaurant business was the biggest irony in the world."

Suddenly one day in 1979, Haber realized that he was making serious money! "This restaurant and hotel business is real business after all! Fortunately, I'm too busy working to take myself seriously," he thought.

Haber then tried out his alleged Midas Touch on new challenges. He opened Cecil's, Palm Springs' first high-class disco. Cecil's heated up so quickly that Haber instituted a new tradition in Palm Springs to control the traffic. He created the door charge. "That will be on my epitaph. I created an industry that generated millions of dollars," he laughs.

He opened other Palm Springs restaurants, all successful, all which he later sold. In 1983, there was Cecil's, ten blocks from Melvyn's; Saturday's, a hamburger place six blocks in the other direction; and Doubles, an elegant eatery built into a mountain and part of a tennis club, two blocks away. Four different concepts. All "from a guy who can't make a Bloody Mary to this day!"

Turning philosophical, Haber explains the reason for his good fortune. It's a concept that's not new to successful entrepreneurs.

"I never knew I didn't have a chance," he says with matter-of-fact directness. "Knowledgeable people said that a fifty-seat dining room and a hotel with twenty rooms would fail. I didn't know that. So I became very successful." He has told his story on "60 Minutes" and "Lifestyles of the Rich and Famous," in addition to numerous Los Angeles TV magazine hosts.

Today Mel Haber is living a quiet life, at least for Mel Haber.

In 1982 he married a wonderful and beautiful woman, Stephanie, and they are the proud parents of a little girl, Autumn Nicole, born in 1988.

Haber is toying with plans to follow his popular "Bedtime Stories" with a full-length edition of the Incredible Fortune of Mel Haber. The writing bug bit him hard in the summer of 1989. The story of Haber's career as a writer is a variation of a familiar and successful theme:

"I got a call from the Writers Guild of America to be the guest speaker at their June meeting. 'I said Okay, I'll be your guest speaker.' It was a fantastic experience. They have one hundred and twenty members and I was the guest speaker to sixty professional writers. And the requirements to be part of the Writers Guild is you have to be published. The idea that I am making a speech to published writers is — like everything else that has happened to me — incredible!"

Alan Rypinski
Armor All Products

-17-

ARMOR ALL PRODUCTS

This is a love story.

Very few business stories are love stories too, and very few entrepreneurs are romantic heroes, particularly not when they have started and operated one of the most successful consumer-products companies in history.

Certainly no one would look on Alan Rypinski as a romantic hero.

But what else would you call a man who at fifty-one years of age decides to walk away from three companies, from a new product in which he has invested $5 million, for the woman he loves, the woman he has loved for more than thirty years?

There's more to the story, of course. Rypinski, who carved for himself a mythic niche in entrepreneurial history by taking a single product — Armor All Protectant — from an anonymous inventor's buckets to $100 million-plus in sales, waxes philosophical about his decision to get out of the corporate rat race.

"I think it's a really unhealthy climate. That's why you're finding that more and more people are stepping away from it and trying to gather their lives around them. I know I was having a lot of trouble keeping my balance. I was either completely absorbed in the business, or I was wanting to sell it so I wouldn't have the worry of absentee ownership.

"I felt I needed to take a breather or I was going to explode. There should be a bang that you get out of business. I wasn't getting any bang, and I was seeing the most important interest in my life drifting away because she couldn't understand where I was going."

Alan Rypinski's life is the stuff of which legends are made, but no legend of entrepreneurial success could compete with the story of how he converted a hobbyist's home-made polishing solution into one of the largest-selling consumer products in history, of how he sold his company and then immediately turned around and signed an agreement to stay on and run the business, and how, after reaching the pinnacle of his profession, he decided that after all love and life were more important.

Less well-known are his earlier achievements, first as a hustling teen-age entrepreneur and frequent bit player on *The Adventures of Ozzie and Harriet*, and later as a leading marketing innovator in the housing, motor-home and food-products industries.

Today he works hard at his leisure. In the midst of a lush, wooded glade in Rancho Santa Fe, surrounded by three inquisitive and self-indulgent Springer spaniels, he lounges in comfortable blue shorts and a paisley-print shirt. Behind him workmen add a new patio to the house, which was built in the 1920s for an architect from Pasadena. He resembles a country squire rather than the self-described "street-fighter" who made Armor All a household name in less than a decade.

"I really think I am going to be very happy," he says. "We had five houses, and we decided to keep just this one and buy a new house in Aspen. We're very excited about that. And we bought a motor home; it's being outfitted right now. We're going to spend a lot of time cruising around the country." The next day he would leave for Hawaii, to supervise the closing of the house he had sold there.

Even in withdrawal from the business world however, he has not abandoned it entirely. "My new life plan is to spend no more than fifty percent of my time involved in the range of companies that I will be affiliated with," he says. "I've got a five percent interest in three companies right now for my expertise, and there are a couple of very interesting deals that I've recently been invited to join that sound pretty exciting.

"Now, understand, I said fifty percent of my time is going to be consumed with other deals, other involvements. I will not have another company, per se. I have no interest in that. I won't buy a company. I won't build a company. I've done that and I don't need to do it any more."

There is little that Alan Rypinski has not done. Before his involvement with Armor All, he says, he was serving his apprenticeship with other companies. Every incident of his early life, in fact, seems to have been preparation for the gargantuan task of introducing an unknown product into the hostile environs of modern retailing, and walking away a winner.

Rypinski's career began as a youthful hustler in Newport Beach, where his family had moved from Pasadena, California. "I always felt my friends were really lucky because they knew exactly what they wanted to do. They wanted to become lawyers or accountants, and I admired that because in my life — growing up through high school — there were so many things that appealed to me, that I wanted to try.

"I loved advertising, for example. I loved marketing. I loved selling. I loved retailing, and I did a lot of that. I was interested in show business at one time; I did that for a while, and I really enjoyed it. So I had a tremendous amount of interest in a lot of fields, and I wasn't sure what I wanted to do."

The more jobs young Alan attempted, the more interests he found. "When I was eleven years old I was making doughnuts on the side of a market....a little doughnut shop that I wanted to put on the side of every supermarket in the country, with the man who hired me.

"I begged the people in a clothing store to let me go to work for them because I wanted to own my own clothing store at one time. So I was doing that. I was detailing cars. This was when I was eleven years old. I was a very industrious person.

"I held at least two jobs all through the time I was going to school, all of which were giving me training and giving me an insight into how those businesses worked, and I was trying to decide....which ones appealed to me and which ones had limitations I didn't like. It was getting more and more confusing."

Alan Rypinski's fling in show business resulted from his mother's early association with Harriet Nelson, wife of band leader and "50s" television personality Ozzie Nelson. Ozzie and Harriet and their sons, David and Ricky, were featured in a weekly situation comedy, an early precursor of programs like *The Cosby Show*.

"My mother was a Juliet Prowse-type dancer. Harriet and Mother lived together when they were sixteen years old, in New York, and were in show business together. So we were kind of raised with the Nelson family and when I was in high school I was doing shows with them. I did about thirty-eight shows."

The budding actor used his mother's maiden name, Forman (his middle name), and was being considered for a continuing part on the *Maverick* series when his marching orders came from the U.S. Army, for which he had volunteered. He spent two years in Germany, putting on safety shows for troops stationed there, and when he returned to the United States he found that business had more appeal than television, so he headed back into retail sales.

"My first real career-type job out of school was with Bullock's. I was in their management training program, and I wanted to open a men's clothing store at the time. I won the all-store award for top merchandiser and all-around best employee in the company in a particular store branch.

"They rewarded me at the annual meeting with a $25 noncashable gift certificate, which I tore up in little pieces and flipped up in the air, and then I walked out. I felt insulted by that, and I wasn't prepared to stay and wait the time out to grow with a company like that."

Despite his rather melodramatic and unorthodox exit from retailing, Rypinski managed to land on his feet with little delay.

"I was hired as director of marketing and sales manager of a new building company. This was an extraordinary opportunity. The man who hired me really had no business hiring me for that job, but he was convinced that I could make a special contribution to his company — and he was right.

"It was called Vanguard Construction Company. I was the fourth individual to be hired. Building companies use subcontractors for everything, so management of the company consists of overseeing lots and lots of people.

"The company was very successful, and finally we had 120 employees. We were building in all different price ranges in Riverside, San Bernardino, Redlands."

Notwithstanding the company's successes, storm clouds soon loomed on the horizon. The nation was in the throes of the early civil rights movement, and California had passed the Rumford Fair Housing Act, one of the most sweeping such laws in the country. It permitted anyone to buy a home anywhere in the state, regardless of racial origin.

"Our company was very strongly in favor of selling to all nationalities. Way before the Rumford law, we had a couple of black families move into two of our subdivisions — we had about twelve subdivisions going at the same time, at all price ranges.

"My wife and I lived on one of the subdivisions, and we took unbelievable verbal abuse. We had our cars painted; we had stakes burned in our lawn....the most incredible experiences. I really had a chance to see how wicked our society can be.

"At that time, we were using the land-contract form of sale where people bought in for $595 down, which gave them the right to convert to a trust-deed purchase at a later date. That was what everybody was doing; the land contract was a very popular deal. And we had the most incredible damage done to some of our subdivisions where we were selling to military people. They were very biased and very prejudiced. They would do unbelievable damage to their homes and then just walk away from them in the middle of the night — because they had no real cash investment in them.

"I watched all that and I lived all that. I loved the company so much for doing what it did for me when I was so young — this was when I was in my mid-twenties — that I stayed with it. I was fourth from the last to leave before bankruptcy.

"It really hurt me to see that company die. I just didn't want to have it happen, and I did everything in my power to keep it surviving. I did some pretty amazing things in the sales that I was able to execute personally before the end.

"That was an interesting, thrilling experience.

"After that I decided to get out of the development business and go back into retailing and see what was going on there — and take a rest after the tremendous emotional experience I had gone through."

Although he didn't know it at the time, Rypinski's career from then on would hinge on whatever creative and innovative skills he could bring to his new ventures. He joined Hickory Farms of Ohio, a specialty food retailer that had just entered the California market, and quickly created a niche that the company had not expected.

"I designed the industrial division of Hickory Farms. In those days, a business person could 'over-capacitize' that store if he or she ordered more than a dozen gifts. They had these little back rooms that could only handle two or three packages for your family. But if a customer said, 'I need to give sixty gifts and I want thirty of them to be $5 gifts, and thirty of them to be $10 gifts,' they really weren't prepared to cope with that.

"So I created the industrial division for them, and developed that into a company called Tasteful Gifts Inc. I brought together not only Hickory Farms food products, but Harry and David food products, and I went to Twenty-One in New York City and got their soup line.

"I had all these food products from the best companies in America and then I got containers to pack them in that were exclusive to Tasteful Gifts Inc. I went on to sell the Diners Club on the most incredible gift package you've ever seen.

"I sold that company to Harry and David for a million dollars, which was my goal at the time." In the late 1960s, a million dollars represented a great deal of money, especially to a young entrepreneur still finding his role in the business world.

But before he could bask too long in the glow of that cash, Rypinski received a rude shock: the contract he had negotiated with Diners Club was repudiated.

"I had dealt with the office of Diners Club president Alfred Bloomingdale Sr., feeling that the president's office was the place to negotiate the deal. The president of Harry and David wanted to have Jim Bond, his executive vice-president, and me go to their Chicago office to meet the vice-president of Diners Club and review our new business with him.

"He did meet with us, and he stated that he knew nothing about this contract. Of course we had a copy with us and we presented it, and he asked us to come back in the afternoon, which we did.

"We found ourselves in front of a battery of attorneys for Diners, and they announced that they had no intention of fulfilling this contract. It was really a shock. That was when I first learned that a contract is a piece of paper that doesn't necessarily require anybody to do anything unless they want to."

Rypinski sued Diners Club and won, receiving what he describes as a judgement that "paid off my debts and gave us a few bucks." More intriguing, however, were the non-judicial results of the case, which brought Rypinski into contact with still another stratum of society. "I had people offering to buy my lawsuit against Diners. I'm a very ethical person and I would never consider such a proposition, but I was amazed at the whole experience," he comments.

In spite of the failure of his Diners Club project Rypinski stayed with Harry and David for a time, and assisted in the development of a program called 'Dial-A-Gift' for their clients. But he recognized his limitations in that particular corporate structure — Harry and David was family-owned and operated, and he was not a member of the family — so he decided to move on.

"Jim Bond had left Harry and David to form a conglomerate in the recreational-vehicle business, and had bought a motor-home company, and an all-terrain vehicle company. At that time — this is in the late sixties, about 1969 —

lawnmower motors were being put into everything, little jet boats and everything. Jim invited me to come to work.

"I was made director of marketing for Trans Industries assigned to the motor-home division, and I quickly oversold our production for the year. In researching this new industry I noticed the Subaru 360....this little Subaru vehicle — the van particularly.

"At that time we were selling a generator for the motor home for $1,295. I bought one of the little Subaru vans for $590. I knew Bruce Meyers, the guy who took the Volkwagon chassis, put a fiberglass body on it and created the dune buggy industry. I went to Bruce and said, 'Can we make this little motor become a generator?'

"My idea was to use it as a dinghy, and hook it on the back of the motor home, and have it be the auxiliary car when you get to your campsite; and if the little car could become a generator that was detached instead of vibrating the motor home, what a plus that would be!

"So we found a guy who is very clever to create an alternator system that fitted on the shelf over this little air-cooled motor, and by God, it worked! Then I put curtains on it and designed this little Subaru for kids to sleep in, you know, so that they could have their own motor home, and give their parents some privacy."

The Subaru dinghy brought Rypinski to the attention of automotive genius Malcolm Bricklin, who was the United States importer for Subarus at the time.

"When Malcolm saw that he went crazy," Rypinski recalls. "He said, 'Who did this?' And he came out here, I guess because he wanted to meet me. He said 'How much money did you make last year?' Just like that. And I said, 'Well, that's very personal but I'll answer it.' And I did. And he said, 'I'll triple it.' And I was making some damn good money."

Rypinski was earning around $35,000, which by 1969

standards was very good money. Adjusted for inflation, it would amount to more than $114,000 in today's dollars. Bricklin's offer to triple it was unprecedented in Alan's experience, but his response, while reasonable, showed no lack of self-confidence.

"I said, 'Malcolm, you don't know me. You happen to have the right guy, but it's ridiculous to offer that in the first meeting that we have. You don't even know who I am.' So we talked for about a month, and I finally agreed to go to work for him."

In the Bricklin organization, Rypinski learned more about business than he could have anticipated. But, more important, he learned about business people. Bricklin had people he was involved with who were some of the most important and famous executives in America. For Alan, it was an eye-opener. He still recalls the excitement of seeing some of the leading corporate executives — men who later went on to become the founders and chief executive officers of companies like Holiday Inns — powerful people.

"I had always thought that people at the top of major companies had to have extraordinary talents....because my father had sort of drilled that into me. My father is an MIT graduate, and always drilled into me the belief that in order to run a major company I had to be competent in legal affairs; I had to be competent in accounting, and in marketing, and in all these areas.

"So I had this god-like conception of these people at the top. And all of sudden I was with them, and able to get to know them and to see that, my God, these guys are wild, crazy people! They're all fun and full of energy.

"And I could measure myself and my talent against theirs. What that did was ring a bell that said to me that I was ready. All my experiences, plus the understanding of what these guys were made of, told me that I was ready to do my thing.

"So I left Malcolm after a couple of years. I had just a wild, wild time with him, though — a very exciting time. And it was so rewarding to me to meet all these people and to watch how things at the top get done."

Rypinski returned to California from Bricklin's New Jersey headquarters and began a search for a product he could invest in or a company he could build. He wanted to avoid the automobile industry, partly because he had a slight distaste for it from his earlier experiences, and partly because he was looking for new challenges. In the meantime he had enough money to buy one old car.

"I wound up buying an old Jaguar Mark IX that had been in storage for a long time, and I took it to the Briggs Cunningham Automobile Museum in Costa Mesa. I asked the curator, John Burgess, what products I ought to use to rejuvenate the leather and the wood and the rubber parts, and all the parts that had just withered up — not withered up, exactly, but just grayed away in storage.

"He brought out a jar full of a milky white substance and said this was what they used. I splashed it around the car and just went crazy over what it did. I had always been a car nut."

The "milky white substance," of course, was the mysterious liquid that later came to be known as "Armor All Protectant."

It seems the inventor of this fluid used to mix gallons of it every few months, and he would give some of it to the museum, because he always made more than he needed for himself.

Realizing he had found the product he had been seeking, Rypinski got in touch with the inventor, and the inventor and some associates formed a partnership to produce Armor All, giving Rypinski exclusive rights to distribute the product world-wide.

According to Rypinski the inventor of Armor All chose to remain anonymous. "He had a position with another company at the time and he always chose to remain in the background. But he's still a dear friend of mine, and we have a great deal of respect for each other.

"And then, shortly after, I became concerned about their ability to produce the goods fast enough for me. So I made a deal to take over the manufacturing myself and pay them a royalty income.

"About a year after that, two of the partners came to see if I would buy them out, because they had another company they wanted to start, so we made an agreement that I would buy all of them out and keep the chemist on a retainer fee.

"At that point I owned the whole enchilada. This was about two and a half years from the start in 1972. It was very exciting, very challenging, very thrilling."

Rypinski realized early on that Armor All would have imitators, so he chose to keep his initial marketing efforts quiet at first, concentrating on small auto-parts outlets and related businesses. Then, finally, he decided to make his move....

"When we were approaching $10 million in sales, I decided to go public with it and release some stories, and go on the offensive with what we were doing.

"Now we were starting to penetrate Sears, and Penny's, and Wards, and K-Mart....We were at that level. Ten million in sales, to me, was convertible to twenty million at retail. Now we were starting to be something."

With success, of course, came the suitors — and the pressures. Not all the potential buyers were willing to play a gentleman's game with Rypinski.

"Some very high representatives of one major auto-parts company came to me one time and said, 'Young man, we're very interested in your product and we want to buy your company. We want you to join us.' And I just sat there and listened. They got really hostile at one point and said, 'If you don't sell to us, we're going to have you for dinner.'

"I began to feel pressure from potential competition that I hadn't even seen yet. That was bothersome, because I didn't have any capital and I had full disclosure of my position all the time with Dun and Bradstreet. Anybody could find out that I owned the whole company and that although I had a few bucks in the bank, I couldn't mount a five- or ten-million dollar advertising war with anybody. So I was starting to get pretty nervous.

"At one point, I was offered a million dollars for the company. I'll never forget that day, because it was a legitimate offer. And then it was five million and then it was ten million, and then twenty million.....It tends to make you pucker up and lean forward when you're looking at twenty million plus.

"I decided I didn't need to own the company anymore, that what I needed to do was to merge with a major, major company — a powerhouse company — because I knew we were going to expand this thing to a hundred million plus."

With a choice of buyers, Rypinski was able to choose the deal that made the most sense for him, and for Armor All. He settled on McKesson Corporation, a broad-based consumer-products service company with a fabulous network of wholesale distribution.

"By that time the street value of the company was thirty-five million. So I went to McKesson and I said, 'Look. I'll make it happen. I don't need the money now. I don't really want to sell out. I love all the people that are in this company, and I want you to get to know them, and I don't want to abandon them. And I don't want thirty-five million, I want fifty. And I'll make it happen.' And so I structured an earn-out for five years.

"At the end of the earn-out five years later, I had earned $49.6 million and I had lived through Jimmy Carter's presidency and the wildest economic period. From 1972 to the early eighties, it was a roller-coaster economy, with twenty-two percent interest rates and craziness....craziness!

"So that was very successful. And then McKesson didn't want me to go away at the end of the earn-out. They offered me a wonderful program, a fifty-days-a-year consulting contract for a substantial retainer fee....and a piece of the annual Armor All business increases for my continued expertise."

For their money, McKesson Corporation got more than just Rypinski's expertise; they got a zealous and aggressive promoter, who believed passionately in his product — and still does, even today after retiring from the Armor All business.

"I've always maintained that it is a billion-dollar brand, and I'll still bet you it is going to be a billion-dollar brand. We're at $150 million right now. That's at our sales to our customers, which converts to $250 million at retail. Pretty exciting when you consider that we haven't penetrated household uses yet.

"There's a great number of potential uses—in the house and on patio furniture and on all kinds of things—that we haven't started to market yet. Soon you will see advertising coaxing customers to use Armor All indoors on sports equipment, furniture, patent-leather shoes, and so on."

Rypinski completed his second five years with McKesson in early 1989 and decided it was time to move on. In the meantime, taking advantage of his reduced schedule of work during the last years of his earn-out, he had begun looking at other business ventures.

His hobby, boating, rather than his entrepreneurial sense, led to his first move.

"There's a yacht from Italy called Riva. The production company produces the most exquisite boats. I owned two of them at this point and I thought 'Hell, somebody needs to represent this company on the west coast.' So, I became the importer of Rivas for western United States.

"Then I decided to open a consumer-products company, because for years people have contacted me with wonderful ideas. I decided to start a company and market two products: Wrinkle Free, a fabric-smoothing spray, and Blindbright, a process for cleaning Venetian blinds."

He also decided it was time to let his wife, Pat, a talented person in her own right, discover the kick he got from business. "The risk is very exciting, and it's a thrill to achieve national distribution after starting from scratch. I was so thrilled by it that I wanted Pat to have the same opportunity. And that was the reason we launched Lasting Endearments, a manufacturer and marketer of teddy bears and Christmas fantasy items. It was Pat's company, and she has been successful, having sold dealers across the United States; including Neiman Marcus, Saks, Bloomingdales, to name a few."

....Because Pat is the most special part of Alan Forman Rypinski's world, and because Pat in herself is so special, Alan Forman Rypinski, at the age of fifty, decided that he had had enough of the business world. In short, he wanted less of the business world, and more of Pat.

He had met Pat when he was in high school. "She was dating a very good friend of mine. We ran around with the same gang, and after a while we began to date. The rest of the romance we just built together for six and a half years before we got married; I wanted to get some perspective on what I wanted to do in life before we got married. Since then we've had a fantastic time together.

"Our first apartment was as big as that bar out there," he

recalls, pointing to a living-room-size bar. "The shower was so small I couldn't turn around in it. We've experienced about everything, really. We haven't experienced divorce, but we've experienced just about everything else."

It was the threat to their twenty-seven-year marriage, posed by the demands of four companies, that caused the Rypinskis to call a halt suddenly.

"About two and a half years ago we were attempting to coordinate our calendars, to determine when we were going to be able to spend a weekend together. Pat had been very busy for a couple of years developing the company I had talked her into, and I was in the midst of three start-ups myself. And in fact, on the particular day in November that we did this, we found it was going to be ninety-seven days before we could spend a weekend together. We looked at each other and said "This is absolute insanity!" So we decided then to liquidate some of our companies and normalize our lives a bit."

When the smoke cleared, all that was left of the nascent empire was Wrinkle Free.

"My Wrinkle Free business wound up taking more than half of my time, for travel in the promotion of the company.....I was very successful in getting tremendous billing and publicity on that company, as well as a terrific advertising effort that we did. But we spent almost five months apart last year and that's not good. I have built everything for the two of us together; we don't have children, and Pat's everything to me.

"She was thinking that I was going to be a business fanatic for the rest of my life, and we hadn't really faced up to the fact that we were as good as separated, that we were really going in two different directions.

"So I decided I would sell Wrinkle Free, and step away from the business world for a while....take a sabbatical and put my life back together — our lives back together — and that's what we did."

In addition to recapturing the essence of his life — his love for Pat — Rypinski has used his sabbatical to find new interests and discover new pleasures.

"I went through a period where, if I couldn't eat it, I'd buy it. I'm an avid collector; I collect tin toys, I collect all kinds of stuff. I've enjoyed collecting art. That's fun for me.

"Skiing is another of my passions. In the past I've only been able to ski perhaps seven days a year because of my crazy life, and this last year Pat and I went to Aspen in December and we got sixty days of skiing in, which is unprecedented. We've decided we're going to spend four months a year in Aspen."

He also has found a renewed perspective on humanity.

"I went to the funeral of one of my favorite uncles about eight months ago, and saw people there that I love very much — who are part of my family from the Seattle area that I used to know when I was a child. We used to go up to visit them every summer, and I realized how much I had been missing not spending any time with these people for the last twenty-five years.

"I was thinking, they're 'have-nots' this family, but they have everything! They have so much love and affection for each other, have so much fun together. We talked for three days straight, and not once did anyone ask me about my business affairs. It was such a fabulous experience!

"So I want to spend time with family and friends — developing friendships, which I had no time for when I was absorbed in my hustling, bustling business career."

Whether or not Rypinski will stay in his self-imposed exile remains to be seen. At fifty, he feels he has crossed most of the major bridges in the business world, and he is content with his present lifestyle now, enjoying the flowers, participating in charity activities in Rancho Sante Fe and speaking to budding entrepreneurs in colleges and other professional organizations that want to hear his story.

He has become philosophical — and comfortable. "When I drop, I'll be able to say that there's not one damn thing I wanted to do that I didn't do. In my opinion, that's the proof of a really full and fulfilling life."

Stuart Silver
Avon Rent-A-Car

-18-

AVON RENT-A-CAR

The $8 billion rent-a-car industry has a long history of being a business that thrives on understatement and compromise. In one of the advertising world's classic campaigns, a giant competitor proclaimed to a national audience that it was "Number Two", unabashedly playing on the public's sympathy for the underdog. On the local level independent companies sprang up around the country in the late 1960's, brazenly offering customers the opportunity to rent wrecks and junkers. And at every auto-rental company between the two extremes, customers could be the temporary custodians of low and mid-priced foreign and American cars designed with all the charm of a brick on top of a brick. The prime selling point of those competitors was that their cars were available and were guaranteed to run.

Then Stuart N. Silver came along and changed the rules.

In posh Beverly Hills, California, Silver recognized when he was just a teenager that car-renting customers were weary of lowering their expectations. He saw that people wanted as much class when they were behind the wheel of a rented car as they did when they drove their own cars; often they wanted more.

Silver founded Avon Rent-a-Car and Truck Corporation when he was barely into his twenties, thereby bringing the missing elements of class, imagination, and pride to the dull and dreary auto-rental industry.

The young entrepreneur offers the car-rental customers choices to make and opportunities to seize. The Avon customer can, if he wants, drive the standard compact or mid-sized car that is the meat-and-potatoes fare of every rental company in the country — but at Avon he pays less than he would at most other companies. Or, if he's willing to pay a little more, he can slip into luxury in a Lincoln, a Porsche 944, or a Mercedes Benz. Or, for an even higher price, he can ascend into the exotica of a Clenet, a Ferrari 328, a Rolls Royce convertible, or perfection on wheels — a hand-made Lamborghini Countach from Italy.

"This is really a brand new market, an undeveloped, untouched market and there's a real need and desire for it," Silver says of his approach to the car-rental business.

These luxury and exotic cars are not available at merely a handful of Avon outlets, as is the case in some large companies. High-end cars are ready for customers at every Avon location. The concept of offering customers more than many dare hope for is stunningly simple, yet with it Silver is challenging the leaders of his industry.

"I want to be up there with Hertz and Avis. And I tell you, there's no reason why I shouldn't be able to do it," he says.

President, Chairman and Chief Executive Officer Silver exudes youthful energy and ambition. Hollywood handsome, he runs Avon from a large office that has an atmosphere of controlled chaos. He has two telephones on his desk in the crowded room and, as often as not, he uses both of them at the same time — barking orders to buy dozens of cars at a crack, cajoling the service department to meet an important deadline, passing birthday greetings to a valued customer, chatting with his wife, Marilyn, or with their small children about a forthcoming family adventure. He also works from two desks in the office. One is a rich mahogany desk with a slab of green marble that serves as a no-nonsense work surface; the other is an old-fashioned roll-top that holds the miscellany essential to the head of a fast-moving enterprise.

From the office decor, one would deduce immediately that Silver is in the automobile business, and in the exotic end of it at that. Tiny scale models of beautiful cars are on display throughout the room — haphazardly parked on the top shelf of the roll-top desk, neatly arranged on shelves in a glass bookcase, and at random everywhere else. In the bookshelf sits the coffee-table tome, "The Great Book of Sports Cars: Over 200 of the World's Greatest Automobiles." Elsewhere in the office is to be found a paperback copy of billionaire Donald Trump's "The Art of the Deal."

The car that's the clear favorite of the office occupant is a sleek beauty, the Lamborghini Countach. Its distinctive profile is on striking display in a poster hanging on the wall, and a large scale model sits among several smaller replicas on one of his desks.

Silver's ambition is also on display, although with more subtlety and a hint of humor. In a far corner of the office sits a large vertical fish-tank. A dozen or so small fish, many of them goldfish, flit about the water. They share the tank with George and Albert, two oversized inhabitants that surely rank among the ugliest denizens that ever emerged from the deep.

George and Albert, big-mouthed, saw-toothed fish with the unblinking stare of true intimidators, are the president's pet piranhas. Silver acquired them in 1979 when his rent-a-car business was barely a year old and he was only twenty-one years old.

"No, those fish are just fish. There's absolutely nothing symbolic about them," he insists.

And then he smiles...

Stuart Silver got into the automobile business as much because of his love of hard work, and of the art of selling, as he did for his appreciation of cars. A native New Yorker, born 11 September 1957, and the first of two sons of Canadian parents, Silver became a Californian at the age of nine when his father's company transferred the family to Los Angeles. Silver was not one of those Southern California boys who spent his adolescence and teen years with a can of car wax in his hand. In fact, he's fuzzy on the details of the first car he ever bought.

"I think it was a seven-year-old Dodge Charger, something like that, just to get to and from work," he says matter-of-factly. Today, the head of the publicly-held company drives an automobile that is entirely in the style he has become accustomed to living. It's a Rolls Royce.

Silver changes gears and revs up when he talks about his first jobs and the early history of Avon.

Only sixteen years old but already anxious to be his own man, Silver heard about a used-car company near his home in West Los Angeles that was looking for sales people. The family pooh-poohed the idea.

"My father, who was a salesman himself, didn't think much of the used-car business, but he gave me good advice. He told me it's not how hard you work, it's how smart you work," Silver says. The teenager was also able to see the job for what it really was; it was a chance for him to get started.

A dedicated worker, he hawked cars after school and on weekends, often sneaking in homework time between customers. The teenager did indeed work as smart as he did hard. Within a year his reputation as a salesman who hustled to make his customers happy reached the owner of a new-car dealership. The man offered Silver a job, and the young car salesman moved on to the next phase of his development as a businessman.

"I was seventeen," he recalls. "I lied about my age and said I was eighteen."

After six months of watching, learning, and perfecting his sales style, Silver changed jobs again, this time in Beverly Hills, to sell cars at Beverly Porsche/Audi. By his second month on the job the eighteen-year-old had earned the title of Salesman of the Month. More honors followed. Soon afterward he won recognition on a grander scale, as the Number Two salesperson in the United States for Porsche/Audi dealerships.

"I was the type who would stay and work on a Friday night, when all the rest of the salesmen had dates," Silver says. "It was an ego trip for me — not necessarily to make the most money but to be Salesman of the Month or to sell the most cars. That seemed very important to me at the time."

Silver credits his father, Morris, and the owner of Beverly Porsche/Audi, Nick DeCourville, for their advice and for helping him develop his sales ethic.

"If a person comes in to buy, he should drive out in a new car. I always felt that way. As the salesman, my job is to accommodate the customer instead of accommodating the store. If someone wants a Delco-Bose stereo, for example, and the car has an Alpine stereo, I'll grind the sales manager to make the change rather than grind the customer to take something he doesn't want. If I can give people what they ask for and at the best price, then my customers will drive out in new cars," he explains.

"Too many people sell deals instead of satisfying needs. That's a big mistake."

At age nineteen, Silver was earning more than $50,000 a year as a saleman. The Dodge Charger was long gone, replaced by a Porsche 924 the dealership thought more suitable for its Saleman of the Month. Also long gone were any thoughts of getting an education the traditional way. Silver had enrolled as a freshman at the University of California, Los Angeles, but he quickly discovered that college took a back seat to real-life experience. The showroom had far more to offer than the classroom.

While the future business owner was honing his sales skills at the Porsche/Audi dealership, which is now the well-known Zipper Porsche, he made some interesting observations while hanging around the service department. Originally he took up a post there in the mornings hoping to put people behind the wheel of a new car when the old car was out of commission and they needed transportation. It wasn't that difficult a sales job, because Porsche had just introduced sixty-month financing. For the ridiculously low payment of $250, a customer could actually drive to work in a new Porsche.

But what really intrigued Silver was the number of people who asked the service department the same question: "Is there any way you could rent me a Porsche or a Mercedes?"

An idea was beginning to form.

Silver says he was taken with the concept of renting cars. "I was fascinated that people would pay money for something they would not own, that they would pay to use something and never establish an equity position in it. Thinking about it in terms of the car-rental business, particularly the exotic-car-rental business, I decided that was really kind of neat," he says.

The young salesman did not believe in renting for himself. When he began working full time, he decided to move out of his parents' house. Unable to afford a condominium, he chose instead to buy a 26-foot houseboat in Marina del Rey, paying $14,700 for it.

By the age of twenty Silver was in the clutch of another

ambition — he wanted to be in business for himself. "In my opinion, the American Dream is being able to have your own business and work for yourself," he says.

In reality that ambition pre-dated the selling of cars for Silver. He recalls thinking about his future when he was a young boy. Contemplating the professions, at the urging of his parents, Silver rejected them on the practical grounds that lawyers and doctors only earn money when they are actually plying their skills; they are paid for their invested time only, albeit very well. Silver was more interested in building a business with tangible assets that would continue to work even when he wasn't there. He also wanted a business entity that he could pass along to his children.

Stuart Silver's dreams came together when he was twenty-one years old, on a small lot at 1516 S. La Cienega Boulevard in Los Angeles. He sold his houseboat to finance the purchase of a Mercedes, a Corvette, and two Fords. He was finally in business for himself. It was the rental business and it was cars!

"I named the company 'Avon' because I wanted to be close to the top of the business listings for car rental companies in the telephone book and I wanted to be right next to Avis," Silver explains.

"Everyone told me I was crazy to leave a good job that paid extremely well to do something like this, but I remember my father saying 'You're young. If you don't make it, you can always do something else. It's no big deal.'"

Success was a big deal to Silver and he worked harder than he had ever worked in his life for it. He opened his office at 7 o'clock every morning of the week and stayed open until 7 o'clock in the evening. Often Avon's day lasted until 9 o'clock at night. Silver worked all alone at first. That meant if someone without a car needed a ride to Avon, the owner of the company locked the office and picked up his customer. Later, even after he had hired additional help, he still insisted on opening and closing the shop seven days of the week.

"That was my life for three years. There wasn't really time for anything else, so when the shop was closed I'd go home and collapse on the couch," he says.

On the personal side of his life, Silver changed his routine drastically after friends persuaded him to go on a blind date. "Why not?" they challenged, since he didn't seem to be able to spare the time to meet anyone on his own. Within a year of his meeting Marilyn, the couple married. Shawn, their son, was born in 1985, Laura followed two years later, and Ashley came along in December 1988. Pictures of the family, especially of the children, are on prominent display in Silver's office.

Silver's past efforts for Beverly Porsche/Audi now paid off for his fledgling company. His friends in the service department sent clients in need of transportation to Avon.

"When I left the dealership, I still wanted to cater to its customers, only this time I was trying to furnish people with rental cars, and eventually Avon got other dealer accounts," he says.

In Avon's first year revenues were $55,000, a modest amount, but enough for Silver to buy more cars and to move to larger quarters — a 25,000-square-foot lot closer to Los Angeles International Airport.

"Ever since then we've been growing, and we never looked back," Silver says, and he adds a quick summary of his company's development:

"From $55,000 the first year to over $20 million in revenues the tenth year; from four cars to almost 1,900 cars; from one worker on a single 2,000-square-foot lot to over two hundred workers employed in corporate headquarters near the Los Angeles International Airport, and in six company-owned locations throughout Southern California and one in San Francisco. We have California coverage in cities from San Diego to Sacramento and franchise-operated out-of-state locations in Las Vegas, Phoenix, and into Canada."

Silver knew early on that he had indeed struck gold with his strategy of serving every segment of the car-rental market, with a product line ranging from the utilitarian to the unique. His customers run the gamut from the high-school senior who wants a Dodge Colt for a day, to the visiting Fortune 500 CEO who fancies a Ferrari 400i for his stay in Los Angeles, to television and movie production companies that need beautiful cars for their beautiful people.

Silver certainly capitalized on Southern California's love affair with the automobile. Through it Avon has been able to do brisk business at the two extremes of its spectrum of customers. Luxury and exotic cars account for forty-five percent of Avon's business, and more standard cars account for the rest. Customers choose from a menu of automobiles and daily prices such as the following:

Standard
Yugo - manual transmission: $19.95
Colt, Escort - standard transmission: $21.95
Colt, Escort - automatic transmission, air conditioning: $24.95
Tredia, Aries: $36.95
Luxury
Cadillac, Lincoln: $55.95
Mustang 5.0 Convertible: $64.95
Porsche 944, BMW, Corvette Coupe, Mercedes (all models): $89.95
Stretch Mercedes Benz Limousine: $119.95

Exotic
Porsche 911, Clenet: $149.95
Ferrari 328, Rolls Royce: $259.95
Rolls Royce Convertible, Ferrari: $350.95
Lamborghini Countach: $795.95

The Lamborghinis on hand are consistently booked, Silver notes. "They go out every weekend for two days. The big thing for a Los Angeles customer is to take the car to Palm Springs for the weekend."

Cars are status symbols. Silver acquired this knowledge first-hand during his years selling Porsches in Beverly Hills. "A car says everything we can't verbalize. A fancy car commands respect and identifies the owner as a powerful person, with sex appeal," he observes.

Not surprisingly — at least to Silver — Avon's major market for exotic cars is quite mundane. It includes teachers, bankers, computer programmers, aerospace engineers, sales representatives — people who rent their fantasy cars to impress family members or lovers, to go to weddings or black-tie dinners, to add that extra touch to romantic weekend getaways.

Just about anyone can rent one of the best cars ever made, providing he or she meets Avon's specifications. Company officials verify customer credit cards for a minimum level; sometimes they even check employment statements on rental applications.

Avon happily accommodates the Southern California "weekend warrior," as Silver categorizes some of his favorite customers. That could be a thirty-year-old man who works an eight-hour day in an office and wants to drive a Mustang convertible, a Mercedes or a Porsche for the weekend. It could also be a man of menopausal age whose gold chains and unbuttoned-to-the-navel shirt strive to draw attention from his receding hairline; a Ferrari 328 would achieve the same goal.

Weekday customers are equally aware of the power of their cars. "When a person rents a Mercedes to close an important deal, it's the best ninety dollars he ever spent," Silver says. "L.A. phoney baloney? No, this is what Los Angeles is all about, including L.A. business."

In Los Angeles "the business" is, of course, the entertainment industry. Film-makers in need of glitz are naturally drawn to Avon as a supplier of such a commodity. Silver estimates that production companies regularly spend an average of $150,000 a month on Avon-supplied vehicles. Characters in the top-rated "Dynasty" television show drive Avon exotic cars and Richard Dreyfuss put an $8,000 dent in one of Silver's white Rolls Royce Corniches in the movie "Down and Out in Beverly Hills."

Silver observes that Avon has never been shy about using its status as car renter to the stars as a powerful marketing tool.

"We don't hide the fact that our cars have been driven by celebrities such as Burt Reynolds, Clint Eastwood and many others. On the contrary, word of mouth is one of our most effective forms of advertising. People in Fargo, North Dakota, know the name "Avon" because a visiting shoe salesman told his buddies back home that he drove the same car as Burt Reynolds."

Customers in "the business" have been known to pull some off-stage stunts that are as startling as the action on screen. Silver still winces when he recalls the day he picked up the telephone to hear the news that Aaron Spelling Productions had sent an Avon Jaguar over a cliff during a shoot. But, "not to worry. No one was hurt. It was part of the script."

"My heart skipped a beat. That was a $52,000 car," he

says.

All in a day's work...

Silver billed Spelling for the car and turned to the next order of business on his desk.

For the customer at the opposite end of the spectrum, Avon offers reliable cars at some of the lowest prices in the industry. In fact, Avon rents its entire fleet of cars for between thirty percent and fifty percent less than rentals charged by the industry leaders.

Silver has a special fondness for one particular segment of the low- and mid-priced market, a segment of the population in fact that is virtually ignored by the major car-rental companies and most of those in the next tier. Avon, unlike its competitors, caters to young drivers under the age of twenty. "I know there are plenty of kids under twenty who have the money and the credit status to rent our cars," Silver says. "All they need is someone to trust them. I'm the last person in the world who would turn away anyone of voting age who comes knocking on my door."

Avon even selects fleet cars with the trend-conscious mobile younger customer in mind. Volkswagon Rabbit convertibles and sleek Corvettes are popular among the undergraduate set.

The company is able to maintain its rock bottom pricing structure because Silver insists on running with rock-bottom overhead. Aware that some potential customers might interpret low prices to mean low quality, Silver makes a personal pledge of top-notch service in advertisements featuring his photograph:

"When you rent one of my cars, you rent me.

"No, I'm not a chauffeur, I'm Stuart Silver, president of Avon Rent-A-Car, California's largest independent rental company. I personally stand behind every one of my 1,900 cars. If you ever have a problem with one of my vehicles I guarantee immediate twenty-four-hour road service any-where in the USA. If you come in for a particular kind of car and we don't have it, I'll make sure you drive away in a more expensive car — at no extra charge.

"If you can't make it down to one of my locations, I'll have one of my drivers pick you up."

Avon is able to undercut its larger rivals for a number of reasons.

First of all, the Big Four companies — Hertz, Avis, National, and Budget — were forced to raise their rental fees when Congress passed a new set of tax laws in 1986. The regulation called for the elimination of investment tax credits and lengthened depreciation schedules on capital equipment, such as automobiles. Hertz owns ninety-two percent of the 160,000 cars in its national fleet; the others own more than sixty percent of their fleets. With the loss of tax credits, the majors had to make up for financial losses with additional revenues. Since the start of 1986, prices for rental cars from the Big Four companies have gone up more than ten percent.

Avon, as a partially franchise-operated company, gets all the benefits of scale of the large company — cooperative advertising, volume purchasing, peak-load sharing of vehi-cles, drop-off arrangements and cross-reservation facilities, to name a few — without having to make the capital investment in all the cars in the Avon fleet. The company, like other smaller operators, barely felt the bite of the new tax law.

Secondly, as a low-cost operator Silver made the decision early in the life of his company to set up shop outside the property lines of airports rather than working from booths inside airports.

"'The Big Four companies' presence is conspicuous in airports because they're trying to lure the business traveller.

The corporate customer represents about two-thirds of the majors' annual billings. But they pay through the nose for providing a convenience to those customers," he says. "Airport authorities take about ten percent of the revenues of the in-terminal car-rental companies. The airport also charges rent on booth space and parking areas."

Avon, like the myriad of smaller car-rental companies, avoids the burden of such expenses by maintaining a fleet of vans to whisk customers from the terminal exits to the nearby off-site locations. There, customers complete rental contracts and select their cars.

Without teams of brightly-attired and spritely reservations clerks to draw the attention of airport travellers to their showy booths, Silver knew he had to take steps to catch his potential customers' interest before they got off their airplanes. He chose a three-pronged method of attack.

Advertising in magazines, particularly in-flight magazines, and in business journals and newspapers represents the major thrust of Avon's marketing program. The theme is always the same — "Avon has the car you want and you can rent it at the best price you'll find." The company backs up its targeted advertising with brochures placed in display racks at such traveller-oriented outlets as travel agencies, hotels, and restaurants.

"And then there's me," laughs Silver. "I'm the not-so-secretive secret weapon."

Avon successfully supports its advertising with a very effective public-relations program aimed at publications that have strong influence on potential customers. Publications that have run feature articles and news items about Silver and Avon include *Time, Los Angeles Times, Investor's Daily, Auto Club News, Hollywood Today,* and *Entrepreneur,* to name just a few. The writers seem captivated by the rise-to-riches story of young Stuart Silver, especially when the interviews move into the car lot and, sometimes, behind the wheel of a high-class automobile.

"No, I haven't let all those photo sessions for the magazines go to my head," Silver says with a laugh. "I know that the spotlight is shining on the Rolls Royce as much as on me. Probably more. After all, you can rent the Rolls."

The third part of the formula for luring customers comes through the system for making reservations. Studies show that travel agents place fifty percent of car-rental orders and they do it through their computers, which are linked to airline-reservations systems. Avon has signed agreements with the major airline companies that own the four largest international airline/car-rental computer systems to display Avon cars and prices on their reservation screens. These are American Airlines' Sabre system, United Airlines' Apollo, Eastern Airlines' System One and TWA's Paris network. This means that after the travel agent checks the screen for the preferred car-rental companies, such as those with partnership-for-mileage awards with the major airlines, he or she can then search succeeding screens of information for companies offering preferential prices, such as Avon.

To support this investment, fast-growing Avon upgraded its own centralized computerized reservation system. An operator at the Avon computer logs each incoming telephone order for rental cars then relays the call, via computer, to the appropriate office for recording and handling.

The operational and promotional strategy obviously works. In 1987, Avon bested its fifty-five independent competitors, to earn the Number One ranking at Los Angeles International Airport.

"We're not a Hertz or an Avis yet, but with today's computer technology and our marketing strategy, we can be just as professional and even more efficient," Silver maintains.

"And," he adds, "we can prove to our customers that we are really concerned about their safety in our cars and on the road. We're a company that's small enough to let our imagination run free and large enough to afford to take some risks on behalf of our customers."

Avon showed brilliant imagination - literally.

A few years ago when the Avon fleet was comparatively small, Silver read in a Department of Highway Safety report that bright red cars are involved in twelve percent fewer accidents than cars of less vibrant colors, such as black and white, gray, light blue, beige and brown.

Avon responded by acquiring red cars - and only red cars.

"I decided we'd go into the red," he smiles. "It was an easy decision to make because we also know that people associate the color red with speed, romance, and bold statements."

Unfortunately — or fortunately perhaps, from Silver's point of view — Avon has outgrown its ability to sustain a scarlet fleet.

"If we tried, we'd own all the red cars in California," he says.

On the more serious side, the Avon founder also learned that fewer than three of every ten car-rental customers use their seat belts, despite the passage of mandatory seat-belt laws in California and other states. If people weren't interested in protecting their own lives, Avon had to take responsibility for safeguarding its customers.

"We can't get into the car with them every time and belt them in, but air bags are one way of providing for their safety," Silver recalls as the basis for his decision.

The idea looked so good on paper that even Avon's money men liked it. Silver's plan was to finance the air bags as part of the cost of the cars, paying less than $10 per month per car. In return for the reduction of the chance of serious customer injury, Avon's insurance company would reduce the liability coverage on each car by $15 a month, or so Silver told himself. He spent $1,200 to install one airbag in one car as a test.

The insurance company reacted strongly to Avon's proposal, but not positively. Instead of praise, Silver got a warning: "If that car leaves your lot, your insurance coverage goes with it." The reason, the insurers said, is that coverage is only extended for airbags installed at the time of assembly. Retrofitting is prohibited.

Silver was stunned, but he took the news characteristically in stride.

"I decided to wait, and ask again later. After a couple of years, they came around and I got my discount."

Silver sees that incident as typical of the way successful entrepreneurs operate, and the way he built his company.

"In my opinion, people don't realize that if you want something done, all you have to do is ask. You figure out a plan for achieving it, and you just go get the job done. You have to be prepared to work for it, but that comes with achieving your goal," he explains. "That's what it's all about. It's really as simple as that."

Siver made sure his go-get-'em attitude extended to the Avon sales department, beginning when the entire sales staff consisted of one person, himself.

"I tell everyone we never take 'no' for an answer and I tell the same thing to the corporate accounts we pursue," Silver says. "For example, if there's a hotel we want, we'll tell the manager — in a nice way, of course — that Avon is going to sign up his hotel or he is going to have to change his phone number to get rid of us." He notes that most car-rental agencies are not promoters. They put their ads in telephone books and wait for the phone to ring. Like many of the showroom car salesmen Silver left behind, car-rental agencies are not agressive; they do not identify their customers, and they sell deals before they sell to customer needs.

The extraordinary Silver single-mindedness extends to the "people" side of the business. The owner of four rental cars could take care of the entire shop himself, but the head of a corporation cannot. Silver made a policy of seeking out the best minds in the business and putting them on his team.

"I hired the best in the rental business," he says of his top commanders with a great deal of pride. "When the other car-rental companies heard these people had come to work with us, they looked at us with new eyes."

Marvin Arnold, executive vice-president and head of Avon's franchising program, had worked for industry leaders. Under his leadership Avon outlets will spring up all across the United States and Canada, and in countries across the oceans.

Cindy Dale came halfway across the country to join Silver as head of the high-tech central reservation system. She said she left the Number Two company for a firm that tries even harder.

Joe H. Knight, vice-president and general manager, had been a consultant to nearly every major car-rental company, working in just about every avenue of the business. He watched Silver for nine years before agreeing to join him in his Avon venture.

"We all see great opportunity at Avon because this company is in its first generation of management and its first generation of growth. We're all here on the ground floor," Silver says.

It's the ground floor of a skyscraper in the making. After almost ten years of building Avon one brick at a time, Silver has embarked on a bold plan to increase Avon outlets on a scale of grand proportion. He'll accomplish this feat by gobbling smaller companies through acquisitions, by merging with other companies, and by franchising the Avon name and operation.

The price has been high; Silver went public with Avon in September 1988, not long after his thirtieth birthday.

Characteristically, Silver, the owner of a Scarab speedboat capable of 100-plus miles per hour, and the downhill-skiing racer whose action photos are part of the office decor, took the speedy and imaginative route.

Silver made a summertime deal to sell Avon to Win Corporation, Inc., a publicly-traded Los Angeles-area company created to use its financial resources to participate in business opportunities. As the sole owner of Avon, Silver sold all his stock to Win in exchange for Win stock. Win, in turn, created a new client class of stock and issued most of the shares to Silver, who later changed the name of the company to Avon Rent-a-Car. After a reverse stock split designed to multiply the number of outstanding shares, Avon went to the public in spring 1989 and marketed the stock.

But Avon sprang into action well before the stock sale campaign. The memory of the move brings a smile to Silver's face.

"The day after we went public, we put an ad in the *Wall Street Journal* and *Auto Rental News*. It read: 'Avon Rent-a Car is actively seeking daily car rental operations for acquisitions and mergers. Principals only. Contact Stuart Silver.' We were on our way."

Silver himself, of course, had been on his way from the day he put on a tie and took up station in a used car lot. Although his confidence swelled with each succeeding year, he always harbored a question about the outer limits of his capability. He remembers precisely how it disappeared.

"One day I was offered a lot of money for the company," he says, a touch of awe creeping into his voice.

"Millions of dollars. To me. Enough money for me to retire on for the rest of my life without problem. It was at that point, with people coming after me, I realized I could build this thing into a big empire.

"I repeat, I want to be up there with Hertz and Avis. And I tell you again, there's no reason, no reason at all, why I shouldn't be able to do it."

Jerry Colapinto
Design Gifts International

-19-

DESIGN GIFTS INTERNATIONAL, INC.

The doors to Jerry Colapinto's private office are flung wide. As he passes through them in greeting, arms outspread, a smile that plays off every feature, you get the feeling these doors are never closed. After five minutes with the man you wonder if maybe you are not a long-lost relative. By the time you get up to leave you realize that in some small way you have become part of the family.

Colapinto is owner and president of Design Gifts International, Inc. of Corona, California, a multi-million-dollar diversified company that is the nation's largest manufacturer of resin-based gifts and houseware products, and one of the largest suppliers of decorative plaster products for the home.

Colapinto and his wife, Eileen, started the company in 1974, on money scraped together by mortgaging their home, cashing out a retirement program, and selling the family car. It was a gamble. But the Colapintos knew they held a trump card, the same one Jerry had played many times before in his life and knew he could count on. It was his personality — expansive, winning, energetic — that set him apart, that was his leg up in the world.

"Entrepreneurs are a rare breed," he says. "They are gamblers, in the sense that they bet on what they believe in. They bet on themselves. I feel that my own limitations are only in my mind. If I want to accomplish something, I can."

Jerry waves you to a chair. He puts you at ease, takes you into his confidence. His talk is a refined backchat; jazz musician meets Dale Carnegie. His manner invites you to throw in your lot with this man who cannot fail.

In addition to DGI, Colapinto's holdings include ownership in Riverside Thrift and Loan, a six-office industrial loan company based in Riverside County. He holds stakes in a packaging-material plant, a restaurant, a franchise cleaning company, an orange grove and a variety of industrial properties. Jerry's success is a testament to the power of positive thinking.

From his Italian shoes to the rich golden tan of his face, Colapinto is the picture of success. He looks the part, he plays the part. He has homes away from home, takes lavish vacations, keeps a luxury sports car. But there are obligations that attend his financial station too. He serves on the Riverside County Board of Education, President's Roundtable for the University of California at Riverside, and he has been a Director of the Corona Chamber of Commerce and past president of Rotary. In short, he cares about the community.

Making certain you have everything you need, he offers to show you around. Design Gifts International is a multi-faceted enterprise, and the building that houses it all is large. His office is on the second floor — spacious, comfortable, cooled by the arbor of camphor and eucalyptus trees that grow outside, it is decorated with products that are manufactured downstairs.

As he rises to begin the tour, you are treated again to the charm and diplomacy that have served this man so well over the years. He is proud of what he's done, and he enjoys showing it off.

Born in 1943, Colapinto was raised in Plainville, Connecticut, a small industrial town near Hartford. It was a traditional household: one brother and one sister, an attentive mother who provided a loving home, and a father who worked as a tool and die maker. Both sets of grandparents were hard-working Italian immigrants who had come to the United States in search of opportunity.

Young Jerry inherited the tremendous will to work that ran in his family, and even as a boy he was anxious to prove he too could be a hard worker. While still in grade school he worked setting pins at the neigborhood bowling alley. In junior high school he caddied at the Farmington Country Club. In high school he drove an ice-cream truck. By the time he left for college, he was running the ice-cream company's public relations program for all of New England.

At Western Connecticut College, Jerry worked toward a degree in music education and graduated as president of the Student Government Association. But it was away from school that he learned the most. During breaks he hit the road, to play at clubs and concerts, USO tours, and even on Broadway. He explored every kind of music, from rock to jazz to classical. Then from a brief stint with the legendary Gene Krupa Band he learned about showmanship, a skill that would figure prominently in his future plans.

"Music was my life," Colapinto remembers. "I loved being on stage. It's a powerful feeling when the crowd soars with excitement in response to your music. It's the thrill of both giving and receiving at the same time. I'm still hooked on it."

Colapinto stepped to a different beat after he met his future wife Eileen and fell in love. As the two planned their lives together, the aspiring musician (now a certified music instructor) realized he cared more about marriage and fatherhood than he did about travelling the club and concert circuit. He wanted to provide the same loving home life for his children that his mom and dad had given him.

Freshly minted as teachers and newlyweds, the Colapintos were ready to start life anew. At the time, 1965, California was experiencing a population boom and had a desperate need for qualified teachers. The Corona Unified School District, like many others, sent representatives across the country to bring back new recruits. The Colapintos were enchanted by the prospect of moving west, seeing for themselves a rich and rewarding future.

"Those were heady days," Colapinto recalls of the move. "I saw opportunity out here that just wasn't available in Connecticut." California was Colapinto's kind of place — a boardwalk on the edge of the continent, exciting and innovative, an atmosphere that tantalized a young man's dreams and aspirations.

Colapinto's unorthodox style and need for achievement surfaced in his first job of teaching music. He recalls organizing his marching bands in the early morning hours and leading them through Corona's diverse neighborhoods of turn-of-the-century homes and tract housing. "We'd wake everybody up and let them know we were there. It was very fulfilling," he remembers wistfully. He doesn't address the question of whether or not the people aroused from slumber at that hour felt similarly fulfilled. "I'd still be doing it today if it weren't for...."

Teaching, for Colapinto, had its drawbacks. He found the classroom somewhat confining, and the pay inadequate although the teacher-student interaction was extremely rewarding. Needing an outlet for his bottled-up creativity and a way to earn some additional income, he looked outside the classroom and back to the bandstand.

"I formed a band known from Big Bear to Palm Springs." Then he adds, laughing, "'the King's Court Jesters'."

Colapinto was the leader of the band, and as its most personable and persuasive member he took responsibility for booking the gigs. Then, further leveraging his skills and personality, he became an agent for other local bands, booking their engagements too.

Dreams were becoming reality in the land of opportunity. Jerry's enthusiasm soared and became infectious, and before long the rest of his family — parents, brother, and sister — were persuaded to move west too.

He readily found a business for his retired father, Pete. "What does a fellow do when he's worked in a factory all his life and then moves to rural California?" Colapinto asks rhetorically. "Open a music store. What else?"

What the father didn't know about music, the son would provide. He would also help provide something else — customers. Many students from Jerry's classes supplemented their school-hour lessons with personal instruction at Colapinto's music store. They could also rent their instruments there; everyone benefitted by the arrangement.

Colapinto's business acumen was starting to emerge, and with his appetite now whetted he began seeking other investments. One of the earliest was California Aircraft Brokers.

What intrigued him about this venture was the challenge of meeting new people, learning a new business, and turning ideas into profit. "It seemed natural," he says. "People who wanted to buy used aircraft had no place to go, the way people who wanted to buy used cars could. With a partner I set up a brokerage business at Corona Airport, and then later on at Riverside Municipal Airport. Our purpose was to bring sellers and buyers together."

With the bands, the music lessons, and now the investments, teaching for Colapinto had slipped into secondary importance. He finally abandoned school altogether when the father of a student recognized his talent for business, and promised him handsome financial rewards if he could turn a craft-type gift company into a manufacturer of full-run home and office gift items. The challenge caught Colapinto's imagination. He saw it as a chance to use his appreciable people skills and enter into the world of business.

His parents were skeptical about the change. In the mid-1960's, when he and Eileen had earned their college degrees in education, teaching had been a career that commanded respect, particularly in an industrial community such as Plainville. Business was a shaky proposition, and they didn't want to see their son make a mistake he would regret.

Eileen too was hesitant.

"She is much more conservative than I am," Colapinto says, remembering his efforts to win family support. "She's more frugal, less daring. But she had faith in me, because she knew I always had the family in mind."

Jerry gave his family another jolt in 1970, this time with the announcement that he was going to start his own business. He was thirty, the father of two (the youngest, Tony, was still an infant) and he was hungry now for the kind of success that only entrepreneurs can achieve.

This time Eileen was enthusiastic. After years of marriage, and seeing how well Jerry worked with people, she was a believer.

Still, neither the emerging entrepreneur nor his wife really had any conception of what lay in store for them. Running a business and owning one were two different things. "My strength was — and still is — my ability to excite and motivate people. In the beginning, I relied wholly on that, because I didn't have any business knowledge to speak of."

Today, Jerry encourages young entrepreneurs to have a wide-eyed innocence about a venture. "If people really knew about every potential pitfall — EPA (Environmental Protection Agency) and OSHA (Occupational Safety and Health Act) regulations, fire department regulations, capital needs and so on, they might never start their business."

Jerry chose the gift industry for his first foray into business because experience had shown him that it was an enterprise where brand name is less important than running a smooth operation, one that meets commitments, produces imaginative items, and develops good relationships with vendors, artists, and buyers.

"It's an industry for all times," he explains, "because everyone likes to give and receive gifts. In slow economic times, our products are a good value. In good times, they're impulse items."

To get the ball rolling, family members pitched in with a dozen or so regular employees. Eileen helped with the office work; his brother, Frank, took charge of sales; even his parents lent a hand. Jerry took on responsibility for personnel, financing, manufacturing, and new-product development.

The manufacturing niche that Colapinto chose for Design Gifts International was in resin-based products. Resin is extremely versatile, and can be poured in liquid form into any mold or shape. It is easily colored and combines with other substances to simulate the look, weight and feel of original pieces of art, whether they are made of wood, marble, glass, or even gold or bronze.

DGI started simply and, along with brother Frank, the company developed accessories fashioned with embedments of flowers, seeds, dried vegetables and even butterflies. Trivets, night lights, paperweights, decorative boxes, plaques, napkin holders, spoon rests and coasters became the foundation of the business. "We weren't fancy," says Colapinto, "but we produced quality products."

A new division called San-Ton (named after Colapinto's

children, Sandi and Tony) expanded the company into corporate sales, with motivational/promotional specialty items. Customers now include many of the Fortune 500 companies.

When Colapinto named his fledgling company, he deliberately chose a name that reflected a combination of his own flair, style, and optimism — and a small amount of wishful thinking. It also reflected the lessons he had learned about showmanship from Gene Krupa.

"Design Gifts International sounds like a big company, which is exactly the impression I wanted to give. I wanted our customers to view us as large and stable, as an established corporation they could rely on. No buyer from a major account wants to deal with a company that has no track record."

Plotting their earliest sales strategy, Jerry and Frank realized that DGI needed a big-name client to bring in the mom-and-pop-sized gift stores that would become their major outlet for sales. They focussed on Disneyland, whose buyers Frank knew from a previous job. Still, the brothers had the jitters.

"We'd get an item out of the mold, take it to Disneyland, and hope they liked it. If they did, then we'd hope they didn't order too many at one time, since we were already working nights and pushing our production to the limits."

DGI grossed less than $50,000 its first year, hardly a poor beginning but not one that guaranteed success either. Colapinto kept working, always looking for new materials, innovative designs, and new markets into which they could expand.

Today, artists are sent around the world to select artefacts and art pieces that will lend themselves to mass reproduction. These artefacts are copied by DGI's craftsmen, molds are made, and exact replicas are turned out in volume. It is not unusual to see a $5,000 African vase or an ancient Chinese statue lying next to its copy in the casting room.

DGI produces respected lines of hand-painted collectibles: sports figurines, animals and water fowl, Indians, and characters out of the Old West, and even gnarly, wood-textured "Tree Spirits" with names reflecting the mountain-men of yesteryear.

Some collections, like the "Judi's Pastime" line of clown statues, bear the names of their creators rather than those of their manufacturers.

Since resin can encase practically anything, Colapinto has received some unusual requests over the years. One came from an Arab sheikh who wanted his gallstones preserved. Another came from NASA, which wanted to present mementos of fallen Skylab to its top brass. Drops of oil, salami, and even cow dung all have been suspended in the glass-like substance.

"We're in the business of selling perceived values versus actual value," he explains. "The trick is to make the copy look like the real thing. That means it has to have the proper weight, texture, color and feel. If it looks right but doesn't feel right, the customer is disappointed."

Creating this illusion is not easy. "Our gifts are made by hand, not by machine, so they need a lot of attention and care," says Colapinto. "That means the people at DGI must take pride in their work, and that attitude begins with me. When people see that I care about what we do, they care too. I check in almost every evening after I'm home. I know first names, and my doors are always open. It takes many different people to make our products — artists, mold-makers, finishers. Each job is important, and it's my responsibility to make sure they know this."

Treat them like family, and they'll treat you like family. For Colapinto, this rule applies to those who work for him as well as to those who work with him.

One of Colapinto's strengths as a business developer is a fine-tuned instinct for spotting future trends and capitalizing on them. His investment in Riverside Thrift and Loan is a case in point. He and his co-investors studied trends in the national banking industry and saw that deregulation was eroding the state barriers that have kept banks from expanding their territories. The strategy is to build a solid commercial and industrial lending institution, and then sell the thrift on the wave of deregulation to a major bank looking for a greater foothold in the California market.

Another example of Colapinto's knowledgeable investments is Cleanserv Industries, a computer-based office-cleaning service. The cleaning business is a diamond in the rough. It is more economical for businesses to bring in an outside cleaning service than it is to maintain one in-house. Even in the home, especially when both people work, it is becoming more common for couples to hire out the cleaning rather than do it themselves.

Always hungry for an audience, Colapinto takes his successes on the road. He's in the seminar business with patent attorney Herbert Schulze. Schulze speaks to would-be entrepreneurs about the legal aspects of setting up a business, and Colapinto addresses the nitty-gritty of owning one.

"We teamed up mostly for fun, although it has been financially rewarding too," Colapinto says. "I point out the risks and the realities. Are you willing to borrow against your home? To work Saturdays, Sundays and evenings, even twenty-four hours at a stretch?" He also points out the feeling of independence and personal power that comes with business success.

Though many of his ventures are limited partnerships, Colapinto is wary of such arrangements. "I'm not a big believer in partnerships. The chance for disagreement or misunderstandings is always there. No two people have the same vision, and at some point this can become a subject of contention."

Following his own maxim, where there is risk there is reward, Colapinto is maneuvering to take DGI public. He concedes that he'll lose some control and independence by sharing some decision-making with a Board of Directors, but the advantages are too overwhelming to ignore.

"We're at the stage now, with good locations at gift shows and an established sales base, where it's time to take the next step," he says. "We want to diversify by acquiring other gift-related companies. It takes cash to do that — millions of dollars."

When asked if his children, Sandi and Tony, will play a role in the business, Colapinto is quick to react. "Sandi is pursuing her degree at U.S.C. as a psychologist and Tony is at Cal State Fullerton aiming toward producing or directing.....They've both got their own minds and dad will assist when asked."

It's obvious that Colapinto has his eye on a new mountain to climb, and with a resolve that is exceeded only by his adroit diplomacy there is little doubt that he will scale it.

Summing up the entrepreneurial spirit, he says, "We each have our own thresholds for pain, frustration, or failure. Some of us have higher tolerances than others. We're willing to stick with an idea a little longer, work harder, and dig deeper until we make it go. We're the ones who believe that success is always within our reach. But — most important —we believe in ourselves."

Gary Brinderson
Brinderson Corporation

-20-

BRINDERSON CORPORATION

Brinderson I is a tribute to its creator, Gary L. Brinderson. The first of a pair of futuristic black glass and granite office buildings, it rises dramatically on the Southern California horizon, reminiscent of the obelisk in the motion picture "2001 A Space Odyssey." Gray containers brimming with burgundy flowers, line the gray-paved plaza between it and its sister tower, now in the first stages of construction. The color scheme is carried into the interior, which is accentuated by an expanse of black granite flooring, with a six-story glass cutaway chiselled from the corner of the building. The triangular bevel is startling in its effect.

Inside, the only sound is the movement of the escalator. Even the air filtering system is hushed, electronically controlled. Lights, like the building's temperature control, quietly flick on or off as people enter or leave their offices. The high speed elevators are also silent. Only the people, and the cars in the adjoining parking garage, suggest that the building is occupied. It is a "smart building", integrating leading edge technology to provide the latest in amenities for its occupants.

Brinderson Tower is the epitome of quality in the area's office market. Regional business publications have dubbed it a timeless building that will remain the hallmark of quality in upscale office buildings for decades.

Despite a glut of commercial properties on the market in Orange County, Tower I was leased at almost ninety percent within six months of its completion. Some eighteen months before completion, Tower II boasted a twenty percent lease rate. "There is a need for the superior kind of product we offer," Brinderson says. "It surpasses the standards in quality and amenities that the business community wants."

Brinderson reflects upon the qualities which make commercial property such as Tower I memorable. He compares the Tower to other vanguard buildings in New York, Boston and Chicago: "You come back to some real basics. You want to make the main entrance exceptionally striking. You want to build it so it offers a timeless look and feel by using materials which, twenty years from now, will not betray its age and maintenance through excellent property management."

Brinderson Corporation is considered one of the top ten heavy construction firms in the nation, with work under contract in excess of $1 billion. Among the projects which have given the firm its outstanding reputation are the $160 million Travis Hospital, the largest hard-dollar contract ever let by the Navy; a $100 million coal fired steam plant in Seattle, Washington, completed one year ahead of schedule; the $45 million Henrico Country Wastewater Treatment Facility near Richmond, Virginia; a $23.5 million completion contract for a Trident submarine training center, in Georgia; a $100 million desalting plant — the world's largest — in Yuma, Arizona; the $100 million U.S. Army Ammunition Plant in Radford, Virginia; and the $140 million heating plant conversion at two Air Force bases. Each project was completed on schedule, or in many cases, early. "Completing each job on time is one of the criteria for success as a builder," Brinderson explains. "Our watchwords are quality, schedule, and safety."

Gray L. Brinderson is founder, chairman and CEO of Brinderon Ltd. Its two companies, Brinderson Corporation (heavy contruction) and Brinderson Real Estate Group are leaders in the marketplace, but it wasn't always that way. Brinderson began his career as a lone craftsman. "I went to work for a local contractor whom my grandfather had helped to get started in business," he says, and then he adds with great sincerity, "I figured if I did everything opposite of him, I would be successful." In 1964, with $5,000 in his pocket (the equity he had saved for a house), Brinderson launched his firm, a one-man operation, with a pick-up truck, tools, and a modicum of experience in mechanical contracting. Initially based in Pomona, he moved the firm to Orange County in the early 1970's, and shortly thereafter founded its real estate division. Indicative of his decision-making ability at the time was Brinderson's dilemma over whether to take the plunge and hire his first employees. The payroll expenses for a qualified craftsman seemed then like a huge amount of money.

Gradually, however, he established his reputation as a subcontractor and began staffing up. Typically, he returned the annual profits into the business and began classes at a junior college. He was graduated from Harvard's Advanced Management Program and became an alumnus of the Harvard Graduate School. Later, he earned an M.B.A. from Pepperdine University, graduating *summa cum laude*.

"You need to supplement your skills with education," he philosophizes. "Education is available to everybody, so it's really a matter of understanding yourself well enough to know what you don't know but need to learn."

To enhance his management expertise further Brinderson joined the Orange County Young Presidents Organization, a group dedicated to information sharing in business, geopolitics and international culture exchange. He has since become chapter chairman and a board member.

By 1975, Brinderson's operations had expanded on a national scale. A decade after its inception his corporation counted one thousand employees in its operations, with peaks of twice that during busy construction periods. Most of these workers are craftsmen who sign on for projects of three to five years' duration.

Firms must be pre-qualified, to bid on a contract in the construction business. "It's a tough   process," Brinderson says, "one that may take a long time. You start small and move on to bid on something bigger with one objective in mind — building financial strength." One of Brinderson's first sizeable projects was replacing pipe in nine hundred barracks at Edwards Air Force Base in California.

Looking back on the start-up phase of his business, Brinderson remembers that there were major areas of concern: contract bidding, customer relations, and technology. At that time, Brinderson handled all customer relations himself. "We were extremely goal oriented," he remembers. "We were, by necessity, very quantitive. We needed to accumulate capital to survive, and our capital was all based upon our earnings, and we achieved our goals," he says.

Brinderson says there are simple answers to how he achieved those goals. However, he does attribute much of his success to his own philosophy. "There are usually no more than five variables that make the difference in everything you do. These variables are different for every project, but you must achieve all five of them; no one of them will do it. By studying the five variables in each project you eventually learn to spot situations and make sure they happen. Those add up to earnings," he says.

Today, Brinderon Corporation is forging its reputation for doing the impossible. In 1987, the company won a $23.5

million completion contract for a 550,000 square-foot Trident submarine training facility in Georgia. Brinderson Corporation prepared the proposal in just seven days, complete with an accurate construction schedule, a list of headquarters personnel to commit to the project, the scope of work and a realistic budget. When the contract was awarded, the firm had barely fifty days to complete the first third of the project, including readying it for occupancy.

The substantial refurbishment required twenty salaried employees, mobilizing a crew of four hundred. Within the month, the employee roster reached six hundred. He describes the scene, "We had to take out more than one hundred truckloads of trash just to figure out what we had. Our crews worked around the clock. There was not time to schedule them on a staggered basis. Everyone worked at once.

"The challenge was next to impossible. Everyone said it couldn't be done." But Brinderson did it and on schedule, winning rare public acknowledgement from the Navy. His eyes still shine when he recollects it.

He formed his second company, Brinderson Real Estate Group, in the early 1970's to provide assets for his construction company.

"Construction companies are only worth the cash they have in the bank," he explains. "Now real estate is an asset business. We needed some type of asset to balance our portfolio, and real estate fit. It was particularly appealing because it isn't as labor intensive as construction. The Brinderson Real Estate Group staff numbers about twenty people."

Brinderson began the real estate company by developing industrial and office products. "We only did one or two deals at a time at first, but to keep my interest, the real estate company had to keep growing.

"The construction company had reached such a significant size that there had to be a valid reason for me to be away from it. That's how the real estate company evolved into an entity capable of building and leasing developments of the size, quality and prestige of Brinderson Towers."

At the time he founded the real estate group, he discovered Orange County was one of the best places to invest hard dollars. "Opportunity was here. There were no 'No Growth' movements, no antagonism between cities and landowners and a lot of deals were made on handshakes. It was a great environment to work in."

The real estate company modified Brinderson's involvement in the construction company. The result, Brinderson says, is a tendency for him to question whether he must be personally involved in every detail of the real estate group. "The operating company has a lot more issues demanding of my time," he says. Consequently, his relationship to the real estate group is primarily strategic. "The president implements the strategy for the real estate group. The president of the operation group also is gaining more strategic responsibilities.

"The analytical side of real estate is not complex, but you need to stay on top of the details," he explains. "You must be sensitive to rent rates, vacancies, emerging market needs, job growth in an area, local statistics, and myriad details associated with individual contracts. You must understand the type of market, its needs, and the dynamics of that particular marketplace, as well as financial considerations that go with it."

Brinderson predicts that the time between conceptual beginning and one hundred percent occupancy of Brinderson Towers will be approximately ten years, primarily because the project was redesigned early in the process to better meet the higher standards of an increasingly sophisticated populace. "When we started the project, the typical high-end office site was a five- or six-story glass walk-up. We soon discovered an evolution was occurring among the needs of the high-end user. Businesses wanted a sophisticated urban feel to their offices.

"We decided to produce something at the highest end of the scale, and it had to be top quality, or we wouldn't do it," Brinderson continues.

Brinderson Tower has attracted, and continues to attract the sophisticated market, boasting tenants from top legal, accounting and other professional firms.

With a new understanding of tenant demands in commercial real estate, Brinderson ponders the hidden ingredients in success: "Marketing is very important. Even though you think you're meeting the tenants' needs, you don't know that unless you communicate with them. It's very important to be aware of details, and to make certain the brokerage company is aware of those details and has communicated them to the prospective tenants. The most successful path to full occupancy is through satisfied tenants. But," he warns, "no communication tool in the world will redeem a bad project. There's got to be a market out there for your product." He ruminates on a strategy. "You have to produce exactly what you have said you will produce. You can't say you're creating an environment and a quality product and then not do it. The user is very smart. High quality products yield satisfied users, and that's how you sell your product."

Brinderson grew up as part of a large, extended family in Chino, California. His aunts and uncles all lived close by, on two acres of land his grandparents had given them for their homes. Everyone was involved in the family business, a stainless steel fabricating operation, specializing in the construction of creameries and dairies, only a few acres away. After his mother died when he was four, Brinderson found that growing up in a close family environment gave him "a sense of tradition and values."

Brinderson credits his family with instilling in him "the gift of knowing how to work. From sixth grade on I earned all my own money to buy my clothes and to support myself. All along the way I was able to achieve excellent relationships with my bosses, who later became my mentors." He remembers one dairy farmer with whom he worked before and after school, laying out hay and mixing grain. "He gave me a lot. Every day I came to work, he asked how I was. He really cared about me as a person. He shared his personal values and his values in business. He made a tremendous impact on my life."

He also speaks fondly of one uncle, who edited farm journals, owned a small publishing company, and was insightful. Whenever there was conflict, this uncle was the one who brought the family back together. Another uncle set the pace for the family business, guiding and teaching Brinderson by example.

"I believe in balance," Brinderson says, "and that means working hard and playing hard." This axiom carries over to his love of physically invigorating activities. "I'm not a spectator," he reveals, "I need to participate." His passion is windsurfing, a hobby he shares with his family.

No one in Brinderson's immediate family, however, is involved in his business. "The possibility of a person developing professional self-esteem in a family business is extremely difficult," he theorizes. "Family members are never given the same credibility as a young person coming into a corporation from the outside." He recommends that a family member establish him or herself as a professional first, and then come into the family business.

He considers maintaining a balance between his professional and family life his greatest achievement, and works to ensure that he maintains it. A typical day begins at 5:30 a.m., and he exercises for an hour before leaving for the office at 7:00 a.m. A great believer in the benefits of exercise, Brinderson is quite disciplined. "No matter what is going on, I continue to exercise," he says, attributing to his regimen the fact that he feels so well — balanced physically, mentally, and spiritually.

Brinderson relies on his administrative assistant to keep him organized. "It sounds ridiculous but at the office my assistant, Linda Pezzin, hands me these blue notes and due to them I show up where I'm supposed to be." He laughs, but it's true. "She knows my priorities and keeps me on track. She runs my calendar," he adds.

His hectic schedule includes a great deal of travel. Over the past fifteen or sixteen years he calculates, he has spent two full years sitting on an airplane. He makes about sixty trips a year, including those for business and pleasure, and those due to his affiliations with professional associations such as the Presidents' Forum of the Construction Industry, a coalition of the top leaders in the industry.

Brinderson has earned a sterling reputation in his field. Dubbed a member of Orange County's business aristocracy, he has reached this point in his life doing what he does very well. When he makes mistakes, he learns from them. "If I don't get the result I want, I ask 'Is there something I personally could have done better?' About 99 percent of the time the answer is yes, so I don't waste time blaming somebody else. I like to learn. I like to reflect on the process and what the benefits are," he says.

"We all make mistakes, but I have a way of backing up and reflecting on what can be done right.

"There is no magic formula" he comments for those who might mistakenly assume amassing a great deal of wealth is easy. "You make money doing something well. You don't make money by trying to make money. The focus is on doing something well. That's where the focus is when you look at people who have a dream but never have fulfilled it. You've got to *enjoy* the process and do a good job. The real satisfaction is in doing the job."

While Brinderson follows that philosophy with great success, he isn't one to rest on his laurels.

"I believe I'll always work," he says. "When I was younger, I thought there would be a limit to it, but there isn't. When you're young, you think of $1 million or $5 million or $20 million as signalling 'I have arrived'. But the people who believe they have arrived are ready for the return trip. So, to stay ahead, you never arrive."

Brinderson describes himself as a risk taker. "I expect rewards to parallel the risk, but I also like events I can control."

In his mid-forties, the dapper, impeccably-dressed Brinderson cuts a crisp corporate image. In some ways this image minimizes some of the risks he faces. By maintaining sole ownership of Brinderson Ltd. he further minimizes his risks. He once considered going public, but came to the conclusion it was not for him. "The CEO ends up spending thirty to forty percent of his time with stock analysts who have an infatuation with the price of the stock instead of the long-term strategy of the company."

Brinderson says he never doubted that his venture would succeed. "The thought of not maintaining our position was never a consideration," he reveals. "The question for me was 'Where are we going?' How we got there was more important to me than being there, and in the end that's what got us there. It's the process again. It works."

Throughout the years, Brinderson has invested in other enterprises and has participated in joint ventures involving both his companies. "The entrepreneurial type of individual does not work well in a 'equal' role in partnerships," he reflects when asked about joint ventures. "I work well if I have total control, or when I don't have total control and I respect the other partner. When I'm in a partnership, we usually have a sponsor who has total control and a silent partner without control, so you don't get into the two-boss syndrome."

Since Brinderson formed his businesses the marketplace has become even more competitive, with even greater demands for quality. "The quality and value you give the user is a key component," he assures, and hypothesizes it is this environment which has given rise to a greater proportion of foreign investors — investors willing to take losses on property or projects for several years against the prospect of long term profits.

"Another major change in the industry is the public bureaucracy. All a public bureaucracy does is diminish the product and increase the paper process. In most instances, the paper process has become bigger than the project."

A recent experience has moved Brinderson Corporation away from the government projects. "We are refocussing the company toward corporate America," he says. "We'll continue public work in ecology, water works and desalinization and will begin working with industry and transportation, but for the immediate future, we won't be involved in defense work." At the close of this decade, Brinderson ranked in the Navy's top two construction firms. Leaving that hard-won segment of the business to concentrate on a less secure market may take some time. Brinderson predicts it will be ten years before the corporation is firmly established. But he's ready for the risk.

To work on the Brinderson team, either in construction or the real estate division, you must have solid ethics, good business values. "No matter how competent a guy is,"

Brinderson states with conviction, "if he doesn't have good character, we can't work with him. Two kinds of people get you in trouble," he adds, "those who are brilliant but lack good ethics, and those who are dumb but energetic." Brinderson makes certain his parent company recruits only those with unquestionable ethics, outstanding intelligence and solid leadership skills.

He prides himself on his current staff. Among his senior managers, most have been with the company at least ten years. Brinderson has spent time with them building his companies and while those in the real estate group have had less personal involvement with him, they all share similar philosophies. "Our staff relationships are good. Senior managers are encouraged to love what they do, be proud of it. They are challenged and feel they've got a stake in the company." He adds: "I make sure they are aligned with the corporate goals and encourage them to write their own, then we discuss how to best achieve them. Every five or six weeks senior management sit down with their goals and objectives and share them with me."

The Brinderson team is responsible for the company's accomplishments and, whatever the project, has always done what was required of it with quiet, consummate skill. This is the philosophy Brinderson acquired as a boy, mixing feed for dairy cattle. This is the philosophy that helped propel him and his team to national acclaim, in real estate and heavy construction.

For Brinderson there is no magic......just hard work.